Emily Davies
and the Liberation of Women
1830–1921

—Emily Davies—
and the Liberation of Women 1830–1921

DAPHNE BENNETT

ANDRE DEUTSCH

First published in Great Britain 1990
by André Deutsch Ltd
105–106 Great Russell Street
London WC1B 3LJ

Phototypeset by Falcon Graphic Art Ltd
Wallington, Surrey
Printed in Great Britain by
Billing & Sons Ltd, Worcester

To my daughters-in-law
TESSA and PHOEBE
who came into my all-male household
and took my side

Contents

Preface 1

Acknowledgements 5

1 'A difficult child' 1

2 'Self-help not charity' 20

3 'Shut away from the light' 35

4 A Mission Discovered 45

5 Spoiled Children of Fortune 61

6 For Friendship's Sake 70

7 A Refusal is Sometimes a Blessing 79

8 'The trumpet must be blown with no uncertain sound' 86

9 A Cat and Mouse Game 96

10 Life Will Never Be the Same Again 104

11 'Everyone needs a purpose in life' 110

12 No Second Chance 116

13 'The way to kindle faith is to show it by taking risks' 140

14 'A prey to all sorts of fears' 131

15 'The way to kindle faith is to show it by taking risks' 140

16 Endless Winter 149

17 'Men like this have done much harm' 155

18 A Family Composed of Women 161

19 A Traitor in the Camp 169

20 'No harm in a little fun' 176

21 Patience and Tact bring Results 183

22 'No better than a slave' 189

23 'There is no going back' 197

24 Not Rights but Justice 206

25 'We'll take care the world shall know it' 213

26 'A treasure not lightly to be thrown away' 216

27 A Touch of Heartbreak 219

28 Fear as a Deterrent 229

29 'A novel and ambitious sound' 238

30 The Spirit of her Age 246

Appendix 252

References 255

Bibliography 271

Index 275

Illustrations

1   Drawing of Emily by Annabella Mason, 1851
2   Painting of Emily by Rudolph Lehmann, presented to the College by past and present students, 1880
3   Photograph of Emily, about 1866
4   Photograph of Emily in academic robes, after honorary degree conferred by University of Glasgow in 1901
5   Reading a letter, 1901
6   First building, Girton College, 1873
7   Original entrance hall, about 1873
8   Original dining hall, about 1885
9   'The College Five', 1869: standing, L. to R., Woodhead, Lloyd, Lumsden; seated, Gibson, Townshend
10 Students with Professor Clark at Hitchin, 1870–71
11 College Fire Brigade, 1887
12 Henry Tomkinson
13 Painting of Barbara Bodichon by Emily Osborn
14 Elizabeth Garrett Anderson
15 Sedley Taylor
16 Memorial plaque, Girton College

(All these are reproduced by kind permission of the Mistress and Fellows, Girton College, Cambridge.)

Preface

'Who was Emily Davies?'

It is shameful that this question can still be asked today, when so much has been written lately about the struggle of women to emancipate themselves during the last hundred years. Outside the college she founded, she is more than half forgotten, yet her name deserves to be at least as well known as Florence Nightingale's.

Basing herself upon the principle that women could not earn the practical, legal and social equality they deserved and were claiming unless they first showed that they were as educable and as intelligent as men, she did more than any other Victorian woman – indeed, probably more than any single woman before or after her – to establish the cause of women on a sound foundation. Without her work, modern feminism would be a house built upon sand.

Born fifteen years after Waterloo, Emily Davies was – like Florence Nightingale – in effect imprisoned at home (after the nineteenth-century fashion) until the early 1860s as the daughter of a prominent cleric and the companion of his widow. Then, in the space of only five years, with no formal education behind her and only her good sense for guide, she imposed her will upon a male-dominated society. Courage, persistence and unanswerable logic enabled her to ensure that the new university-sponsored school examinations were open to girls as well as boys. In consequence, she was invited (the first woman to be accorded this distinction) to give evidence before a Royal Commission. By 1869 she had founded Girton College, Cambridge, the first institution devoted to the higher education of women. The college flourished at once, and was soon an accepted feature of Cambridge life, but the obstinacy of a masculine and still almost monastic society prevented her from attaining admission to full membership of the university and to its degrees – the objective she had pursued with invincible cheerfulness and determination through many a bitter battle with the university authorities. It is an ironical reflection that Cambridge only yielded these privileges forty years ago, although Oxford and all the other British universities had opened their doors to women long before.

Returning at the beginning of the twentieth century to her first mission, to secure parliamentary votes for women – a mission she had

1

abandoned in the 1860s when she realised that women would have to deserve the vote by demonstrating their intelligence before they could expect to be granted the franchise – she continued in old age the forcefully persistent moderation which always characterised her endeavours. This led her to oppose the militant suffragettes, whose violence was exciting the very opposition she had always sought to assuage and was clearly delaying, not promoting, the achievement of the franchise. At the end of the Great War, the Representation of the People Act of 1918 brought her the satisfaction of casting her vote at the age of nearly ninety, a year before she died.

Astonishingly little has been written about her, and that little has never done her justice or recognised her remarkable qualities. Thus Simone de Beauvoir – sometimes erroneously regarded as the founder of feminism – could write that 'Feminism was very timid in England until the Pankhursts', and gave education only the barest mention in her widely read *The Second Sex*, published in 1949. Outlining the state of the women's movement at the end of the nineteenth century in *Lady into Woman* (1953), Vera Brittain wrote that three pioneers were ageing in 1901, Florence Nightingale, Josephine Butler and Sophia Jex-Blake, but omitted Emily Davies and could even say that 'Girton had been founded', without naming the foundress. In *The Female Eunuch* (1970) Germaine Greer followed Simone de Beauvoir in counting the suffragettes as the first wave of feminism, and although herself an academic, gave no emphasis to education as a leading feature of feminism. Among more recent writers still, the verbose but compendious Dale Spender (*Women of Ideas*, 1982) is another who believes that the suffragettes founded feminism and thinks it necessary to use archaeological techniques to 'dig for relics' of anything earlier. Although she devotes a chapter to 'Women and Education' her predisposition to regard men as 'the enemy' inevitably leads her to misunderstand Emily completely.

Because twentieth-century feminism has been predominantly theoretical and has insisted on seeing men as hostile oppressors, it has been quite unable to do justice to Emily, whose lighter touch and more relaxed style was not only radically different but far more in accord with human instincts. Modern feminism has misread its own history and, by concentrating its attention on women's bodies rather than their brains, has dissipated its strengths to no good purpose. By contrast, Emily's more rational and more disciplined approach secured results which have been of lasting benefit to succeeding generations. Her type of activity, not empty slogans about sexual liberation, has given women the assured position in society which they hold today. It is time that she was seen in her true light as the pioneer who first began to beat the broad path that now leads women from school to university and onwards to positions of equal responsibility with men in the professions and (most recently) in finance, business and commerce.

Having been accorded the privilege of an invitation to use the mass of correspondence and other papers preserved at Girton College, which have never previously been fully exploited, I have been able to paint a more accurate and a more realistic picture of one of the most remarkable women of the nineteenth century.

Emily Davies's tremendous achievements can only be properly appreciated if they are set in the context of the world into which she was born. It was a man's world to a degree which it is now hard to credit, and a female's prospects in it were dark indeed. So long as she remained single she could not live outside her father's house without scandal, and she was totally dependent on him unless she was fortunate enough to have inherited money or land. Even when she married, a woman had no rights in law. She did not exist except as an appendage to her husband: 'My wife and I are one, and I am he'; 'with all thy worldly goods I me endow.' Emily was in deadly earnest when she said that to be married was to enter into the state of slavery, the wedding ring the sign that a woman had given up all claim even to the little independence she had as a spinster. Men, on the other hand, were eager for marriage, especially if the woman were rich in property or the expectation of future legacies, for on the wedding day everything his wife possessed became his by right. No papers need be signed, no deed of gift exchanged. Nothing but the legal fact of marriage was required to establish that the husband now owned his wife and all her possessions, and could dispose of them as he liked. Merely because he willed it, he could throw his wife out of the marital home without a penny to her name, and her children with her if he chose: a woman had no legal rights over the children she had borne. There are several well-documented cases (and doubtless many more of which no record survives) where a wife was banished to make way for a mistress and forced to hand over to her unfaithful husband the major part of what she thereafter earned in her efforts to keep body and soul together. Alimony was unheard of, divorce and legal separation impossibly expensive because they might require a private Act of Parliament.

Occasional attempts had been made to redress this state of affairs, but without practical result. A few women – Mary Wollstonecraft and Harriet Martineau, for instance – had urged the need for reform in print, but most women were too ignorant or too cowed to heed their advocacy. No one before Emily saw clearly and precisely that the prime remedy for women's ills was education, that if women were ever to be able to defend themselves, to bring about fundamental changes and secure acceptance as the equals of men, they must first be released from the bonds of ignorance. To accomplish this was the task she set before herself in her mid-thirties, and she pursued it with rare singlemindedness for the next sixty years. Despite many a rebuff on the way, she lived to see her triumph celebrated on all sides.

Daphne Bennett

Acknowledgements

First of all I must thank the Mistress and Fellows of Girton College for the honour they have done me in putting their archives at my disposal for the purpose of writing this book. Among the Fellows, I thank two in particular: Dr Betty Wood, who suggested that I should examine the Emily Davies papers and the new accessions to them; and Mrs Margaret Gaskell, the Librarian, for her friendly welcome and kindly guidance through the archives in her care.

I am particularly grateful to Mrs Kate Perry, Assistant Librarian, who worked tirelessly to answer all my questions. I thank also the library staff for cheerfully carrying so many boxes of papers to and fro for me. Miss Susan Cross of the Fawcett Library has kindly shown me the Emily Davies letters preserved there and supplied me with photocopies.

Dr Mary Owen, Cambridge University Archivist, helped me to find material which throws light on the university's attitude towards women. Dr Janet Sondheimer, Fellow of Westfield College, London, gave up her time to assist me in finding my way through the Maynard diaries in the Westfield College Library, thus saving me much labour and frustration. Mrs Hester Burton, the biographer of Barbara Bodichon, gave me many of her notes on Barbara's life, and the invaluable Nash letters. They all have my deep gratitude for advice, information and assistance.

Dr Ronald Hyam and my husband have given me the encouragement and constructive criticism which no author can do without. Now, as always, they have been my chief support. My agent, Mr Andrew Lownie, and my editor, Mr Anthony Thwaite, have given me invaluable help in their respective fields, and I thank them both warmly.

Mrs Jo Wallace-Hadrill has once again faultlessly typed and retyped successive versions of my difficult manuscript.

1

'A difficult child'

When Emily Davies was ten years old her mother gave her the Bible that her own godmother had given to her at the same age, together with the note that had accompanied this present so many years ago: 'I hope you will often read in this good book and always ask God's assistance before you begin that you may improve from it.'

The Bible, and perhaps the short message that accompanied it, was intended as a gentle hint that Emily was giving her mother much pain and grief through her tendency to self-will, a fault of which her elder sister Jane had never been guilty. Whether the hint was strong enough we are not told (everything we know suggests that it was not), for soon afterwards Emily was composing a mock advertisement for a governess, supposed to be inserted by her mother in the newspaper she and her brother William ran for their own amusement. The governess was for a young lady who 'phrenologically speaking has the organ of self-esteem rather largely developed and it will require the utmost care on the part of her governess to prevent this from being unduly developed'. In the very next line the child unconsciously gives the clue to her conduct: 'the lady who is to fill the situation must be a person well skilled in languages and science as Miss D is ambitious to excel all her contemporaries in these departments of knowledge.'

Emily was bored and longed to learn 'something or anything', and because no one would listen to her cries her discontent increased. Her longing and her passionate feelings were too strong for her to control, and they were made worse by lack of proper occupation. Only hard mental work could subdue them, and someone to direct them into proper channels was urgently needed. She had outgrown the teaching of her mother and sister Jane and wanted a more demanding diet than they could give her. This made her a very difficult pupil. She begged her father to allow her to share her brothers' tutors, young curates earning a little extra money by coming each day to the Gateshead rectory in order to prepare the Davies boys for their public school entrance. Her pleas to join them were brushed aside: the boys were going to school and university, Jane and Emily were going nowhere; they were to stay at home with Mamma. 'Our education answered to the description of clergymen's daughters,' Emily wrote in the 'Family

Chronicle'. 'Do they go to school? No. They have lessons and get on as well as they can.' There was no help anywhere.

Many years later Emily wrote a letter to a close friend revealing her anger and despair with a candour that was not often usual with her: 'Probably only women who have laboured under it can understand the weight of discouragement produced by being perpetually told that as a woman nothing much is ever expected of them and it is not worth their while to exert themselves . . . that anything like original research and profound learning is not for them to think of – that whatever they do they must not interest themselves except in a second-hand and shallow way in the pursuits of men, for in such pursuits they must always expect to fail. Women who have lived in the atmosphere produced by such teaching know how it stifles and chills.' One good result did come from Emily's persistent pleadings to her father; he consented to correct one essay a week written by his clever active-minded daughter. Dr John Davies faithfully kept his promise, and it was because of his excellent teaching that Emily learned to write clear and pointed letters to the Cambridge dons and others with whom she had later to contend; the letters amazed and confounded them, and this went a long way to win her battles. At the tender age of ten, Emily learned a lesson she never forgot: that everything worthwhile in life has to be fought for and that nothing that one really wants comes easily.

Sarah Emily Davies was born in Southampton on 22 April 1830, the second daughter and fourth child of the Rev. John Davies, a scholarly divine of Welsh descent, and his wife Mary Hopkinson, the daughter of a well-to-do business man. Mary Davies had hoped to return for the birth to her father's home in Derby where every comfort awaited her, but labour came on prematurely and she was obliged to stay in a draughty old rectory in an alien parish, where her husband had consented to officiate for a few weeks while a fellow cleric took the cure for gout at Droitwich.

Dr Davies was delicate and suffered from what was then called 'nervous prostration', an ailment for which neither treatment nor cure was known. Three of his children had inherited his delicate constitution and tuberculosis carried away two sons and a daughter in early maturity, leaving only the eldest, Llewelyn, and Emily to live on into old age.

Because of Dr Davies's ill-health the family was forced to live a nomadic life for some years in a vain search for a climate that suited his frail constitution. In their early married life the Davies parents lived in Chichester where, like many clergymen, Dr Davies ran a school as well as managing a parish. The work proved too hard, the large rectory too damp and the air too relaxing, so a move to Southampton was achieved and there Emily and the last Davies child, Henry, were born.

With young children to look after, this was a terrible burden for

Mrs Davies, but she was an uncomplaining wife and it was doubtful if her husband even guessed how much she hated never having a settled home. Ironically it does not seem to have occurred to her that without her father's generous allowance they would never have been able to move whenever Dr Davies thought a place did not agree with him. Mr Hopkinson had made his only daughter co-heiress with his son, an enlightened and certainly an unusual act which enabled John Davies to indulge his whims and the family to live simply but in comfort.

In 1836 John Davies gave up school and parish in order to concentrate on his writing. By that time the whole family had moved to Avranches in Normandy, where the clear air was supposed to be good for nervous trouble. By the time Emily was eight they had returned to England and settled in the village of Ashley near Chichester, where life for such a lively child without the discipline of school or companions of her own age was very tedious. Emily may have been thinking of this rather dreary period in her life, without friends, books or pets to occupy her time, when she later wrote 'dullness is not healthy . . . [men] think dullness is calm. If they had ever known what it is to be a young lady they would know better . . .'

Emily's father never found life dull, and would have been astonished had he known of his young daughter's dissatisfaction. Writing took up much of his time, and his health was his hobby. The life of an evangelical clergyman, comfortably off because of his wife's fortune, suited him well. The vehemence of his nature found satisfaction in his sermons, in which he displayed all the fire and eloquence of a man confident that his opinions were right. Although not tall, his spare frame looked very fine in the high collar, white shirt-front and cut-away tail-coat of the evangelical cleric of that period. Severe in ecclesiastical matters, Dr Davies was at home a mild man, but so absorbed in his own affairs that he was hardly aware of what went on around him.

When it came to wrongdoers it was a different matter. Dr Manning, the future cardinal, came into this category. He had once been a frequent visitor, a very dear friend in whose erudition Dr Davies delighted. But when Manning defected from the Anglican Church and went over to Rome Dr Davies disowned him; he was 'a wolf in sheep's clothing', 'a traitor to his cloth', never again should he set foot in the Davies household, never again should his name be mentioned. Unfortunately Dr Davies was unwise enough not to leave matters there; he denounced Manning in pamphlets, in articles, and from the pulpit. Manning ignored him.

In 1828 Davies had published an elaborate philosophical treatise which established his reputation as a scholar, and two years later wrote a small book entitled *Splendid Sins*, all about the breaking of the sabbath by people of high rank and the fate they would suffer in the after-life; it 'sold widely'. On the strength of these two books he was offered the chair of moral and political economy at the newly founded London University. His sponsors could not have been more distinguished: Lord Macaulay the historian, Dr Thomas Chambers of Chambers' Dictionary and Michael Maurice, father of the famous Frederick Denison Maurice. On reflection, however, he declined, since the stipend of £300 a year 'could not be guaranteed'.

Mary Davies had to struggle long and hard to get over the disappointment at her husband's decision – which of course he took without consulting her – but she never questioned his right to take it. 'My carnal heart would certainly have preferred London,' she wrote honestly but without self-pity in her diary. She hid her disappointment and continued to tread the path of duty without a single complaint. But John Davies was already unwell and from then on the entries in her diary start with the phrase 'my beloved husband's health has begun to fail again'. It was a prelude to yet another move, this time one that was to last twenty years.

Much of the first part of Emily's 'Family Chronicle' – an account of her early life written when she was seventy-five to please a young nephew – is taken up with her father's health, for it very much affected the lives of the Davies children. Fortunately when they did finally settle in Gateshead, the rectory was roomy, the gardens large with a huge paddock far enough away from the house for the children to make as much noise as they liked.

When she could be spared from her duties in the house, Emily enjoyed vigorous games in the fresh air with her brothers – cricket, rounders, croquet, even football – and not one of them was better than she at climbing trees. Indoors all had to be quiet and orderly for Papa was writing, resting, or had a headache and must not be disturbed. Fortunately the rectory was big enough for the children to keep out of his way.

Emily sensed how much her mother welcomed a settled home at last; she had seen Mrs Davies, with tears in her eyes, thanking Dr Edward Maltby for his part in bringing them to Gateshead. However, her mother's worries were not over: she was afraid that it was too large a parish for an ailing man. The rector would have to take charge of three churches: the parish church of St Mary, Trinity Chapel and St Edmund's Chapel, all three some distance apart. In addition he had in his care twelve old bedesmen, occupants of almshouses, much as in Trollope's The Warden, and a small charity school, The Anchorage. The school, which held classes in a room above the belfry of St Mary's Church, had been founded as a mixed school, but Dr Davies restricted it to boys only – the presence of girls, he said, lowered the tone.

To help manage all this the new rector was allotted two curates who were allowed to take pupils to eke out their meagre stipend. Among these pupils were the three Davies boys, for whom their father had high ambitions.

There was a great deal about Emily's life that she would have liked to be different, but it never occurred to her to criticise her parents for her lack of education, though the longing to be well-taught never left her. There was so much she wanted to know. She had got it into her head that if she sat at a proper desk in a proper school with a real teacher to instruct her, the discontented feeling that so disturbed her would vanish. Instead she had to sit still while her mother tried in vain to produce something that would satisfy this 'difficult child'.

Mrs Davies was subservient, unselfish, obedient to her husband's wishes, a woman who accepted the fact that his mind was far superior to hers and that what he decreed must be right. She bowed to his decrees without a murmur, even (as in Emily's case) when it went against the children's interests. Emily remembered longing for her mother to assert herself, for even as a child such meekness gave her a feeling of humiliation. Without a word being said, Emily knew from an early age that she and Jane had been sacrificed to their brothers' needs without compunction and that their role in the scheme of life was worth nothing. Their parents believed that they had fulfilled their duty if they sheltered their daughters from everything that was impure, a form of over-protection that kept them 'children at thirty', as Madame Mohl, the English wife of a French diplomat, remarked contemptuously, thinking of their French counterparts. The average middle-class mother conveniently believed that if her daughter saw no evil she would think no evil, and but for her Gateshead wanderings Emily would have been thrown into the world very ignorant of life.

There were no books in her father's library that were not dry as dust for a young child, yet Emily was a natural reader. Novels and all light literature were forbidden. When she demanded to know why, she was told that they would tempt young people to look on the pleasurable side of life as a state to be coveted. Emily had never read a novel until 1857 when, staying with her friends the Crows at Unsworth Hall for Annie Crow's wedding, at which she was to be a bridesmaid, she picked up a book lying on the table. The book was *Pride and Prejudice* and Emily did not put it down again until she had finished it. 'I do so love a novel,' she would say to Girton students when advising a little light reading after a heavy period of work, astonishing them by her extensive knowledge as she carefully selected novels most likely to keep their minds off examinations. In the years since she had become responsible for herself, Emily had made up for lost time.

*

The Davieses were able to live much more comfortably than most clergymen's families, but they were hampered by the puritanical feeling that to live well was self-indulgent and therefore sinful. This went even as far as the rectory meals: the menus were economical to a fault, the boys filling up with plenty of plain bread and butter or bread and dripping. Milk (which Emily disliked) was drunk by the children, although they were allowed tea with dry toast at tea-time. This dismal diet was enriched at breakfast and dinner with meat (mostly mutton) and at night with vegetables and a simple pudding. No concession was ever made to greed. Conversation at meals was not encouraged, in case it led to the children arguing, which would be bad for their father's digestion. Instead, a curious artificial politeness prevailed, interspersed with stilted questions from the father of the family. The first meal Emily ever had when staying with the Crows at Unsworth Hall the relaxed atmosphere at table delighted and astonished her. There was argument galore, laughter and joking; for Mr Crow was a robust man much given to lively conversation and enjoyed teasing his pretty daughters.

After dinner Mr and Mrs Davies would retire to the library to drink port or claret and talk privately, a withdrawal from family life that the children were taught early to respect.

Even as a child Emily noticed how little resemblance there was between her father's private life and the personality he revealed in his sermons, and in the tracts and pamphlets which he loved to write. These were like the roar of a lion to strike terror into the hearts of sinners, whilst at home his voice was never raised and all rebukes and chastisement (if any) were left to his wife.

Emily spent much time in the company of the rectory gardener, Lister, a Scot who lived in a cottage next to the church: 'Lister and his wife were my constant companions.' 'Time should never be wasted,' was Lister's creed, and he was always finding jobs for them to do, for he abhorred idleness and saw very clearly what a bad effect it had on an active child. The weekly newspaper Emily and her brother William produced became an outlet for Lister's views and Emily often filled up an odd blank column with his sayings. A Tory, a staunch supporter of Sir Robert Peel, a bigoted anti-papist, he liked nothing better than to keep the children writing articles against the Oxford Movement worthy of the Rev. John Davies himself. One glance at the advertisement page written by Emily alone shows how much Lister influenced her. Several were for curates, who 'must be of sound evangelical faith'. A rigid Sabbatarian, Lister disapproved of the children going out to play in the garden on a Sunday, and if he caught them he would admonish them severely, telling them to go indoors and read the 'Good Book'. He had started life as a game-keeper and had endless stories of the dreadful doings of the wealthy on the sabbath that condemned them to eternal perdition. How nice it would be, Emily thought wistfully, to be the daughter of a rich landowner and enjoy Sundays.

The young Emily's desire for prominence brought scoldings from Lister, and he was really shocked when she confided in him one day that she was playing at being a member of Parliament. He rebuked her sternly and said that the only road to success was through humility and that she was to have 'civil and religious belief always on your tongue'. Since Emily had not the slightest idea what he meant, she continued to play very happily.

Her confidence was boundless. When Grandfather Hopkinson came on a visit, he took his grand-daughter on his knee and idly asked her 'Well, little girl and what can you do?' Back came the answer quick as lightning: 'I can do anything.'

Life in the rectory was full of prohibitions. Emily found the banning of all 'alcoholic beverages', except for medicinal purposes, very puzzling. Her father often drank a glass of port, her mother refreshed herself with claret, but evidently these were not drunk for pleasure, only for health reasons. Port was 'horrid tasting stuff', but it 'strengthened papa's blood'. One day when her father's back was turned Emily took a sip and found it delicious. When the pupils were asked at Sunday School to sign the pledge, she set her lips in a hard line and shook her head; the rector's daughter's signature was the only one that was missing. Cards were never allowed, hence her parents' dreadful shock when William confessed to gambling debts at Cambridge. The theatre (the delight of Emily's old age) and the circus were of course prohibited. Even when it was announced in the national papers that a travelling menagerie and a troupe of famous tumblers were camping in the courtyard at Windsor to amuse Queen Victoria and her children on the Princess Royal's birthday, such entertainments were forbidden the rectory children. Yet Dr Davies admired the Prince Consort and thought him a man of sense. But the duties that Emily had to perform were much harder than the pleasures she had to forego. On Sunday she lived on her knees in compulsory prayer, or listened to sermons she did not understand, played dreary hymns on the piano or walked at a snail's pace round the garden with Papa without running or skipping and certainly not bowling her hoop; small wonder that she came to associate Sunday with everything that was dreary. She vowed that when she was grown-up she would emulate that jolly foxhunting rector in the next parish where her friend Anne Richardson lived. He always looked happy and kind although he broke the sabbath in a hundred different ways.

To Mrs Davies was left the task of 'protecting' her young daughters from reading about vice and from hearing or seeing evil, and she did her best to keep them away from everything that was impure. Ignorance was indeed considered bliss. Yet the conscious double standard pitch-forked Emily from an early age into seeing and hearing the very things that her parents so painstakingly tried to keep from her. As long as her children were punctual for meals, were polite and did not quarrel in front of her, Mrs Davies never asked where they had been or what they had done. She did not have the slightest idea that once outside the rectory grounds Emily wandered all over Gateshead, a town with a population of 15,000, much of it very poor indeed. Here in this town with all its sharply marked divisions of rich and poor Emily's secret life began. Before she was twelve she knew every inch of the town, including the slums, very well indeed. She much preferred the slums. She walked in and out of the meanest hovels, getting to know the names of the people and learning how they lived. She soon noticed that while at the rectory they had a surfeit of such dull fare as bread and butter, in these slum dwellings the children were lucky if they had bread. Dirt, disease, drunkenness and its consequence – wife-beating and child-abuse – were common sights. She witnessed birth and death many times in thoroughly unsavoury surroundings. She got to know humanity at its worst and best. Sex, incest and dreadful depravities of every kind were familiar to her. She saw things about marriage she did not like: pregnancy, for example, did not bring extra care and attention from husband or older children. Even when far advanced with child, wives were forced to go out to work to earn the pitifully low wage that was supposed to help feed an extra mouth. The sight of a pale unkempt woman lighting a fire and trying to pacify crying children, while her husband sat slumped in a chair, was a sight Emily never forgot.

As she sat in a house with one of these she called her friends, the seeds of her future work were sown. Her father talked of the lessons to be learned in the 'school of life' in his sermons; Emily learned everything that there was to know in a rougher school than he had ever known. She was thinking of Gateshead when in 1862 she spoke at the Social Science Congress of how 'poor women were worn down by physical toil for which their frames were never intended. Their minds being utterly uncultivated while their earnings are so small it is impossible for them to maintain themselves in decency and comfort. Those who have come into immediate contact as I have with the female workers in glass houses, paper mills, brickyards etc. will confess that this is no exaggerated statement.' The baptism of fire that she received when still a child made nonsense of the claim so often advanced, that Emily was easily shocked because she was conventional and strait-laced. Nothing that came after this early experience could shock her half as much as life in the Gateshead slums as she saw it when still very young.

Growing up was a painful business for many girls in the nineteenth century. As early as she could remember Emily noticed that she and Jane were always given the most menial tasks and that girls were expected to undertake the most boring duties without complaint. At the rectory they were always served last at meals and if anything ran short it always turned out that she and Jane got the smallest slice – 'you do not need it as much as your brothers'. Emily came to believe that it was an unfair world. As she began to grow into womanhood she longed for independence. She received a small allowance in order to teach her how to use money properly, but she was not allowed to spend it as she liked. Everything had to be accounted for, seen and checked, and her mother was not slow to scold extravagance.She was made to understand that as she got older all physical exercise must cease – it was bad and unladylike. Apparently all her pent-up energies must be put into woman's work, which she detested and did badly. No amount of instruction could make her efficient at ironing muslin collars or goffering the frills on her mother's pillowcases. The maidservant did it much better.

From an early age she was puzzled by the contradictory teachings of the Established Church. The rantings of Dr Davies against Roman Catholics were difficult to reconcile with his preaching of brotherly love and forgiveness. The Church did not explain inequality between rich and poor, so glaringly evident in Gateshead, and this troubled her increasingly. Such a division was not natural, and since she was told that religion must be her solace, then religion must also explain why it was that girls were inferior to boys.

In 1851 Dr Davies took the three women of his family for a few months' holiday to Geneva. Emily had high hopes of this trip. She was just twenty-one years old, eager, inquisitive, full of enthusiasm and energy. She had always longed for more experience of the world, and now it was to come at last. She had been told that Geneva was a cultivated town, the inhabitants hospitable and interesting, and that she would find plenty of young people of her own age. New faces, new sights, a different language; she could hardly wait to start, and she filled in time by brushing up her French. But the trip was a great disappointment. The new society that she had so longed to meet turned out to consist entirely of Swiss pastors, full of Calvinistic fervour, and their dull families. It seemed hard that the many letters of introduction that the Davies parents took with them should lead only to such boredom. Some sightseeing was thrown in, but it tired Dr Davies, and since fatigue brought on a bout of nervous prostration, it could not be undertaken too often.

Not long after returning from Geneva, Emily met a young schoolmistress named Isabella Fadden. They became friendly, and Isabella took Emily to see her school just outside Gateshead. She thought Emily the right material for a teaching career, and she persuaded her to try her hand with the juniors 'as a start'. At that time the teaching

15

in girls' schools was of a lamentably low standard and it often happened that those early formative years in a girl's life were totally wasted. While she worked in the school Emily took notes on everything (including her own frustrations) and these were to prove invaluable later on: the poor state of the classrooms, desks often broken and worn and much too close together, poor writing materials and out-of-date school-books, not enough fresh air in the classrooms and too many pupils to a class. She noted the boredom, the wasted intelligence, the useless information learned by rote. Arithmetic was so badly taught that not one pupil could work a simple sum. Even feminine skills like sewing and embroidery or piano-playing, in which schools prided themselves, were also badly taught, and many of the children read very slowly and with hesitation. Emily hated teaching in such an atmosphere, and after one term she gave it up.

The experience deeply disturbed her. She wondered, not for the first time, whether to a properly educated person she too appeared just as ignorant. It was so much on her mind that she begged another friend, Anna Richardson, who was older and had learned a little Latin and Greek, to teach her what she knew. It was not that she was very interested in these subjects but she felt lost and aimless, not knowing where she was going or what use she was in the world; and it made her happy to learn anything, no matter what. Even this brave effort was broken into when Anna's mother was taken ill; as the eldest of a large family, Anna was expected to take over the running of the household, so the Latin and Greek were dropped.

Among Emily's close friends were the two Crow sisters, Annie and Jane, the delightful, well-read daughters of a prosperous business man; they had moved into the neighbourhood in 1841, thereby greatly enriching Emily's life. Both sisters had been pupils at Miss Browning's famous school at Blackheath, but they had not liked it there and so had been removed early by an indulgent father. To go to such a school had been Emily's secret ambition; so great had been her longing that her imagination had turned the life of a schoolgirl into a Utopian dream, a dream that had not been broken by her own unhappy experience of teaching because she was sure that an establishment like Miss Browning's must be totally different. Annie and Jane quickly shattered that illusion: school is hateful, they said; they had learned nothing and had been glad to leave; Emily was lucky to have escaped its horrors.

When Elizabeth Garrett, daughter of Newsom Garrett of Aldeburgh, stayed with the Crows at Unsworth Hall and Emily was invited over to meet her, Elizabeth confirmed everything that the Crow sisters had said about Miss Browning's, adding that she, too, had been so frustrated and bored that she had begged her father to take her away. Elizabeth was a perceptive, intelligent young girl and her immediate impression of Emily

16

is worth quoting: 'small and plain, her manner conventional, her face unrevealing between smooth bands of mouse-coloured hair.' She was introduced as Miss Emily Davies, daughter of the rector of Gateshead. As they talked – and with repeated meetings they talked a great deal – Elizabeth found that the first appearance was misleading. Emily Davies had a caustic wit and a clear and original mind.

Some years later one of the first Girton students formed an impression that was not so very different. 'Her dainty little figure and smiling face were most misleading: they concealed untiring energy, a will of iron and a very clear and definite set of opinions.'

The meeting at Unsworth of the two girls was the beginning of a life-long friendship between the foremost pioneer of the women's movement and the first woman doctor in England, both founders of institutions that were to be of permanent benefit to women.

Despite the differences in their ages – Emily was the elder by six years – she felt closer to Elizabeth Garrett than to her own sister Jane, who had separate friends and different interests. Emily and Elizabeth had much in common. Whenever Elizabeth stayed with the Crows the three girls would drive over to the rectory in their pony trap and carry Emily back with them to Unsworth Hall for a few days. Even more than Jane and Annie Crow, who often grumbled at the dullness of their lives despite being allowed to do much as they liked, Emily and Lizzie chafed at the restrictions which tied them to their homes and families. Both girls confessed that they were unhappy with nothing worthwhile to do and no prospects in the future to brighten their lives. If Emily felt hemmed in by the narrowness of her existence, Elizabeth was suffocated by too much affection and the demands of a mother who wanted to keep her at home despite the large size of her family. Both girls lacked a sense of direction and both craved useful occupation.

Elizabeth Garrett's openness about her feelings unleashed similar feelings in Emily which she had hitherto loyally suppressed. She confided to Elizabeth that little but duty kept her at home. Elizabeth has left a record of the depth of her own dissatisfaction: 'I was a young woman living at home in what authors call "comfortable circumstances", but I was wicked enough not to be comfortable. I was full of energy and vigour and the discontent that goes with unemployed activities . . . everything seemed wrong to me.'

Emily's realistic view of the world impressed Elizabeth, and she envied her the realism that showed her how life ought to be. She did not dream dreams as tenuous as cobwebs and as soon forgotten, nor did she weave the fantasies that held back the development of so many unoccupied Victorian girls. Elizabeth was convinced that here at last was a friend whose advice she could trust, a person of strong opinions who

17

would never allow herself to be hoodwinked by soft words and flattery.

In 1855 Emily's elder sister Jane, whose constitution had always been delicate, was found to be suffering from tuberculosis and was ordered to a warm climate. Torquay was chosen and Emily was told that she was to go with Jane as nurse and companion. No one thought it hard for a young girl of twenty-five to drop everything at a moment's notice, in order to accompany her sick sister into exile for an unknown period. After all Emily had nothing else to do; she was the daughter at home who could easily be spared. Her parents do not seem to have realised how much Emily would have to sacrifice. She was to be cut off from all friends of her own age and all reasonable pleasures for an indefinitely long time.

The Davieses had acquaintances in Torquay who were asked to keep an eye on the two girls, but they were old and connected with the church, and all that concerned them was that Emily should not miss Sunday service. Kindness of that sort, however well meant, could not make up for friends of her own age, and although Emily never grumbled, she was very lonely. But she was well and strong and when she looked at poor Jane she thought herself fortunate to be in such good health. Nevertheless it was hard for her to adjust the pace of her life to that of the dying girl. To walk at a snail's pace – all Jane could manage – to stay indoors in attendance on an invalid when the warmth of the sun made the small room that they shared unpleasantly stuffy, and when she longed to be taking exercise in the fresh air – these things bore hard upon her. She got used to getting up in the night to be with Jane when she was seized with a fit of coughing, or reading her to sleep again with a short story or a poem of Tennyson's. She was not a natural nurse, and illness made her impatient; she had become accustomed to nursing only through force of circumstances. Irritation with those who ailed, usual with her, became a problem when the invalid was Jane, but she fought to suppress all bad temper and won the daily battle because she knew that Jane was seriously ill and might die at any moment. She made every effort to nurse her sister tenderly, while Jane did not make her task any easier by submitting too readily to the will of God. It could not be God's will, thought Emily, that a dear sweet girl should die before her time. If only she would fight for a life that was so precious to all of them. But it was in vain. In the bitter chill of winter 1858 Jane died peacefully in her sleep and Emily had the sad task of bringing the body home.

While Emily was still in Torquay with Jane, alarming news of William arrived at their lodgings: he, too, had developed consumption and had been packed off to Algiers. Soon after Jane's funeral, Emily was sent to look after him. Again there was no one else to go, so it was impossible to refuse. Jane Crow showed her affection for Emily by immediately offering to go with her, a kindness that was gratefully accepted. Llewelyn took time off from his demanding parish to travel with the girls to Algiers and see them settled in. Emily was deeply touched, while the thought of a companion to share her burden lifted her spirits and gave her strength.

2

'Self-help, not charity'

Algiers was a revelation. Hitherto 'abroad' had meant nothing more exciting than Normandy and Geneva: both places had promised much but proved a disappointment, and both were cold. The blue skies, dark skins, colourful clothes, exotic atmosphere and glorious sun made Emily's pulse race with excitement. William was certainly sick, but not as ill as she had been led to believe (he was in a period of remission) and he took his terrible malady lightly, submitting cheerfully and showing an interest in the world outside that kept up his spirits. He was, in fact, as hopeful an invalid as Emily had ever met and her spirits rose as she wrote optimistically to her parents. A holiday mood seized her and she began to hope that some enjoyment could be squeezed out of this trip after all.

The feeling was strengthened when, taking a walk one morning with Jane Crow, she came across two young women busily sketching. Curiosity compelled them to stop and look. Because they were all English and abroad, they were soon engaged in animated conversation. The two painters were the newly married Barbara Bodichon and her sister Annie (always called Nannie) Leigh-Smith, daughters of Benjamin Leigh-Smith, Radical Member of Parliament for Norwich, an enlightened man who practised what he preached. He had astonished his constituents by treating his daughters with the same generosity as his sons, giving them all in turn an allowance of £300 a year at the age of twenty-one.

Barbara was the better painter and the more striking of the two. Tall, large-boned with thick red-gold hair, she attracted attention with her insistence on eschewing the fashions of the day: she wore loose flowing garments in imitation of the Pre-Raphaelite women, and this reminded Emily of a painting of Elizabeth Siddall (Rossetti's model and mistress) which she had admired. Emily thought she had never seen anyone so lovely, and Barbara, sensing her admiration immediately, warmed toward her new friend. As long as Emily and Jane remained in Algiers, the four girls met every day.

The real attraction that Barbara held for Emily did not lie only in her beauty but in her revolutionary views which fitted in so neatly with Emily's own secret thoughts. As a first cousin of Florence Nightingale

20

(but illegitimate and so brought up very differently) and niece of Julia Smith, a leader among the early feminists, Barbara might be expected to have opinions that were out of the ordinary, but she insisted that it was her Radical Unitarian background that had given her freedom to develop along lines of her own. Three years older than Emily, her daring talk (just touching on the *risqué*) and calm acceptance of the oddities of this world made her much more sophisticated. She lent Emily feminist literature, including two pamphlets of her own and one of her Aunt Julia's, an old member of Bedford College for Women (as Barbara was herself) and the person who had drawn Barbara into the movement. She told Emily of books she must read, including Mary Wollstonecraft's *The Vindication of the Rights of Women* and Harriet Martineau's works, all of which were new to Emily. 'Barbara was the first person I ever met who sympathised with my feeling of resentment at the subjection of women,' Emily wrote in the Family Chronicle.

It was a great surprise to learn that Barbara had been personally involved in the feminist movement, which Emily heard of now for the first time. Four years earlier she had been actively engaged in promoting a Bill in Parliament for Married Women's Property Rights, inspired by the terrible case of Mrs Norton who, twenty years earlier, had been forcibly divorced by her husband, deprived of her children and all that she earned by writing. Barbara had failed, but at least she had the satisfaction of knowing that she had made the public aware of a few of the many wrongs that women suffered, and she had every intention of trying again when the time was ripe. Thinking Emily exceedingly ill-informed, she illustrated her point by outlining the cruel injustices suffered by two hard-working friends of hers: Mrs Anna Jameson, the writer on art history, and the novelist Mrs Gaskell: although separated, both these women were forced by law to hand over their earnings to their husbands.

Her Bill had been supported by a number of well-known women, many of whom at some time in their lives had been trampled underfoot by the unfair privilege which the law allowed to men. Barbara talked of the attacks made on her by the press and of the rude drawings of her and her friends which *Punch* had published, far more devastating than any article; the influential *Saturday Review* had been bitter in its comments on 'Women's unwillingness to relinquish their money to their husbands. Such selfishness smacks of an independence which rather jars on the poetical notion of wedlock.'

At their first meeting Barbara, like others before her, misread Emily's character. Her judgement of people was never as sound as Elizabeth Garrett's. She decided on very small evidence that Emily was too conventional and prim, so she set out to shock her, but her tactics completely misfired. Learning that Emily was a clergyman's daughter,

21

she steered the conversation round to religion. Her own Unitarianism had gone stale on her, and she did not think she any longer believed in God, although she was not exactly an atheist. She would not allow religion to be taught in the Portman Hall School which her father had given her to run as an experiment. At this school, children of both sexes and all creeds and colours were welcomed, but no prayers were said nor was the National Anthem sung. Everything was aimed at making the pupils 'self-reliant, intelligent and thrifty future citizens'. She believed in free love, and told Emily that until she married she had had a lover, John Chapman, the bookseller and publisher, a married man with two children and many mistresses, one of whom lived under the same roof as his wife, masquerading as his daughters' governess. Chapman was a thorough libertine who had started life as a doctor, and the few letters that passed between him and Barbara are full of frank medical detail. Barbara showed them to Emily, who found them distasteful; but she was not shocked, rather she admired Barbara for giving Chapman up as soon as she fell in love with a French surgeon who lived in Algiers, Eugène Bodichon, seventeen years older than herself and an eccentric whose views on the independence of married women matched her own. Long ago she had decided never to marry an Englishman because of the injustice of British law towards married women. Eugène made no demands on Barbara and she made few on him; the marriage lasted, although the ties became tenuous towards the end. Unlike Barbara's other friends, Emily approved of what she knew of the marriage, thinking them two people well suited to each other; Barbara laughingly described herself as 'one of the cracked people of the world and I like to be with the cracked and am never happy in a genteel family home'.

When the time came to take William back to England Emily parted from her new friends with great regret, made more endurable by promises to meet again soon. She had a strong feeling that the chance encounter with the Leigh-Smiths marked a turning-point in her life. The sisters had drawn back a curtain that had shut her away from the light, so that she felt dazzled and confused, her head so full of new ideas that she hardly knew yet what was mere fancy and what practical common sense. What her own part was to be in what they called 'The Cause' she had as yet no idea, for she was still tied to her home; nevertheless she felt that she could contribute something.

Mistakenly she looked on Barbara as an original character (which she was) and a bold leader (which she was not). At this early stage 'The Cause' was symbolised by Barbara's dashing clothes (she went corsetless in the days of tight lacing), her outspoken comments, her carelessness towards convention and her outrageous religious beliefs about which she loved to joke: ('if anyone asks you what I am, say I am a sanitarian').

There were many facets to Barbara's personality, but in Algiers Emily saw her only as artist and friend, the child of nature, never in a hurry, shedding the light of her brightness on all around her. Unconsciously Barbara wanted very much to impress Emily. She sensed that there was something about her which she did not understand but which she might need, so she showed only her best and most generous side. The two young women were as different as possible, yet they became devoted friends. It was as though Emily had made up her mind about Barbara and had decided to ignore her faults and failings. Possibly the very fact of the two sisters being in Algiers at that time was more of a help to Emily than she ever admitted and for this she was grateful, although Barbara was not always loyal. Yet to most people she was one of life's golden girls, 'grandly innocent and simple', a woman who did not court popularity but expected it as her right. Emily always believed that 'Madame' (as she sometimes called her in public) had a special gift for handling people and difficult situations. What did her failings matter compared with a gift like that?

If a fortune-teller had predicted that she and not Barbara was to become the most prominent figure in the women's movement and that she would live long enough to see momentous changes which she alone had brought about, she would have laughed in his face.

In 1858 Emily innocently looked on Barbara as a woman of ideas whom she would gladly follow. Less than three years later the roles were reversed.

The year 1858 was a terrible year for the Davies family. William returned to England with Emily only to die a few weeks later. At about the same time news reached the rectory that the youngest child, Henry, a naval chaplain, had died in China, following wounds received in the Crimea. In one year, Jane, William and Henry had all been taken and the rectory was a house of mourning.

Emily longed to get away, but she knew that she could not desert her parents and leave them alone with their grief. For a time she thought of teaching in order to mix with cheerful people for part of the day at least, but the idea held little attraction. And she hated doing a job she would do badly. Anna Richardson begged her to attend Dr Hodgkin's lectures in physiology, while Annie Austin (the former Annie Crow) offered her a room in her home to hold classes for servants, many of whom could neither read nor write.

As she went about the business of consoling her stricken parents, Emily tried to divert herself by making extensive notes on the horrifying conditions in which women worked, taking Gateshead as her pattern. Nowhere in England was the exploitation of sweated labour greater than in Emily's home town. There was therefore no shortage of material for the pamphlet she had in mind. 'Working class women', she wrote, 'are undernourished, constantly sick, old before their time, worn out by child-bearing, ill-treatment and work that is far too heavy.' Her theme for the pamphlet was simple but unanswerable: 'Why does not somebody help direct them into better but lighter jobs with improved pay, teach them a skill which they could put to good use and thus release manpower for more important work?' With Samuel Smiles in mind she wrote: 'self-help not charity is what is needed.'

It occurred to her that she did not know what jobs, now done by men, could be performed as well or better by women. In order to find out, she sent letters to several middle-class housewives in Gateshead whom she had met at one time or another, enclosing a questionnaire she had compiled in order to discover what jobs were available for working women. Few replied, but those who did addressed their letters to the Rev. S.E. Davies, mistaking Emily for her father. Not one of them thought that a woman could have the audacity to ask such questions, which would not be resented from a man, especially a clergyman.

Emily had a fear that she shared with hundreds of other women, middle-class and working women alike; it is one that she mentions again and again in her writings – the fate of the untrained girl, thrown defenceless on the world when the father of the family dies. With this in mind Emily once tried to find out what security she and her mother would have were this to happen to them. She had never been encouraged to talk in an intimate way to her mother so, greatly embarrassed, she could only put the question in a very round-about fashion. What did her parents do with their money? Promptly she was given the answer: 'We are saving it for you children.'

In September 1859 Emily was invited for a long stay with Llewelyn and his wife Mary in the rectory at Blandford Square (Llewelyn was now Rector of Christ Church, Marylebone, in London). Mary was expecting her first child in October and said she longed so much in these dreary last weeks for Emily's cheerful company. The real reason went deeper. Llewelyn had recently spent a few days in Gateshead, preaching in his father's church, and had been shocked at Emily's appearance. She was pale, had lost weight and was more silent than he had ever known her. It was now a year and a half since she had returned from Algiers, and except for a few days with the Crows at Christmas and Easter she had had no proper holiday since then. It was no use speaking to his father, so he seized the chance when, finding his mother alone, he could tell her that Emily must be given a change of scene and that they would love to have her at the rectory; if she did not soon get some rest, she might meet with the same fate as the others.

Llewelyn had married a daughter of Sir Richard Crampton, a highly intelligent girl, and together they made the rectory a meeting place for intellectual London, for Llewelyn was a convivial man and attracted all sorts of people to him. Therefore the rectory was just the place for a girl who needed cheering up.

Llewelyn's parish was large and very poor, and he worked himself to the bone to improve the wretched conditions in which the bulk of his parishioners lived. At the time of Emily's visit he was trying to raise money for a medical clinic to serve chronically sick men and women who were too poor to travel a long distance to find free treatment. It was uphill work. Paradoxically he had at the same time become a fashionable preacher without in the least wishing it. Grand carriages drove to Christ Church every Sunday, and Llewelyn always preached to a vast congregation. Without begging or making a fuss about it, he let it be known that donations towards a medical clinic meant more to him than invitations to dine at great houses.

Llewelyn was Emily's link with the world outside Gateshead. She loved him devotedly and admired the strength of character which, a few years earlier, had helped him to decide to give up his comfortable life as a Fellow of Trinity College, Cambridge, to become an unpaid curate in Limehouse. He had gone from strength to strength, a symbol of life to the poor and needy and a friend to everyone in his parish. When in 1854 he became Rector of Christ Church, Marylebone, Emily paid him her first visit and was appalled to find how bare and cheerless his rectory was and how thin and overworked her brother looked. He was still overworked now, but marriage had brought many changes, as Emily noticed with pleasure that first evening.

The breadth of Llewelyn and Mary Davies's interests filled her with admiration and she chided herself for being (as she thought) dilatory in finding useful work in Gateshead. Unlike his father, Llewelyn showed no sign of evangelical narrowness and bigotry. He had friends of all denominations and none; Protestants and Roman Catholics mingled amicably in the rectory. It would not have surprised Emily if Dr Pusey, the Anglo-Catholic, had walked in and made himself at home. At last she was discovering an atmosphere in which she could breathe and expand mentally, in which she could discuss anything without giving offence. It says much for Emily's strength of character that the confining influence of her father's evangelicalism had not cramped her sympathies permanently. Only in one way had the unnatural, unsympathetic atmosphere of her home influenced her. She had taught herself the benefits of silence; she had schooled herself in restraint, and the discipline she imposed on herself was now almost second nature – but only at home.

Llewelyn was the sole member of her family (now, alas, grown very small) whom she could confide in, although it is doubtful if she told even him of her wanderings in the Gateshead slums. In return,

Llewelyn recognised that his sister was intelligent above the average and wished he could do something for her. In fact he did far more to help her in her future work than he knew, by introducing her to his friends, some of whom were among the most influential men in England. These men were to guide and advise her and often point the way to fresh fields. Her work would have been remarkable without them, but it would have taken much longer.

While Emily was still in the Christ Church rectory, Elizabeth Garrett heard that Dr Elizabeth Blackwell was in London and about to give a series of medical lectures which were open to the public. One of her ardent ambitions had long been to meet Dr Blackwell, the only Englishwoman to qualify as a doctor, although she had had to go to America to do it. Her life there had been tough but now she was universally respected and consulted everywhere – except in England.

With all speed Elizabeth left Aldeburgh for Manchester Square, where her sister Louisa Smith lived with her husband and children. Emily met her at the station and the girls flew into each other's arms. So much had happened since they last met: Lizzie had been exploring the possibilities of becoming a doctor, although she found the final decision very difficult to reach and could not do so until Dr Blackwell had told her a little more about its hardships and whether she was a suitable subject. Lizzie herself was convinced that she had enough stamina to shoulder the burdens that would be her lot, but she had yet to convince her father that she could do it.

It was fortunate that Dr Blackwell was a friend of Barbara Bodichon's and that Emily arranged for Barbara and Lizzie to meet. Lizzie had come to London with a letter of introduction from Valentine Smith, a business acquaintance of her father's (and also a cousin of Barbara's), which explained who she was and what she wanted to do. The two girls were invited to tea at Blandford Square, the Leigh-Smith town house, and Barbara, all kindness and sympathy, promised help.

The lecture was well attended and Dr Blackwell, clear and encouraging without diminishing the difficulties in any way, gave hope to them both. The hard life she had endured showed in her face; she was prematurely aged with a disfigured eye, the result of an infection, and her hair was almost white, although she was only in her late thirties. Both girls felt that there was something about her that marked her out as a woman who was fulfilled and regretted nothing. Afterwards, with the way prepared by Barbara and supported by Emily, but trembling a little all the same, Lizzie went on to the platform to present her letter of introduction to Dr Blackwell, who behaved as though Lizzie had already made up her mind to follow in her footsteps. Thus the die was cast without Lizzie lifting a finger.

'She assumed I had made up my mind to follow her,' Lizzie wrote to Emily after returning to Manchester Square. 'I remember feeling very much confounded as if I had been suddenly thrust into work that was too big for me, while talking and listening to her.'

Lizzie was right; Dr Blackwell had taken it for granted that the young girl who had listened so attentively to her lecture had already made up her mind before she spoke to her, as an extract from the following letter shows: 'The most important listener that night was the bright and intelligent young lady whose interest in the study of medicine was then aroused . . .'

At first Lizzie was beset by fears, wondering if she was equal to the task. But Emily promised not to desert her and was as good as her word. It was as difficult and thorny a course as two ignorant girls had ever taken, yet their hearts were light as they discussed the first steps. Before anything could be done, Lizzie should go home and tell her parents of her decision. Her father would back her, Emily was sure, for Lizzie had inherited his ability to withstand hardship and his determination to succeed. Only her mother might be difficult, afraid of what people would think of her daughter. If she was intractable and took some time to come round, Emily advised 'patience and firmness mixed with understanding and affection as well as absolute resolution'.

Two remarks in Dr Blackwell's lecture seemed to have a special significance for Emily and she kept them in the front of her mind all her life. The first: 'real and useful work for the betterment of mankind gives one the feeling of belonging to the world in fact, instead of living a crippled and isolated life.' The second was the force with which she cuttingly rejected 'the idea of some separate and inferior qualifications for women'.

During the long and exhausting battles Emily later fought for women in general, she would never compromise on this point. To accept second-best – which was what her opponents tried hard to make her do – would be to put women in a separate and inferior position for ever and to acknowledge that men were superior.

As soon as Lizzie had gone home to break the news to her parents that she had decided to become a doctor, Emily left for a few days' rest in Barbara's country home, Scalands, near Robertsbridge in Sussex, a cottage built to her own design. It was Barbara's retreat from the world – her 'castle of defiance', Rossetti called it – where only those close to her were invited, mostly literary and artistic people like the Rossettis, Elizabeth Siddall, William Allingham the poet, Elizabeth Barrett Browning and Bessie Parkes. To this holiday retreat John Chapman had been a visitor. Scalands was sufficiently shut away from the world for gossip

27

not to leak out and was so difficult to find that unannounced callers never came – not that Barbara cared in the least who knew of her liaison.

It was all the more strange, therefore, that she should invite Emily, whom she did not know very well and who on the surface looked a typically conventional young woman. Barbara was almost sure that there was a good deal of the rebel in Emily, but she wanted to be certain. The testing she had subjected her to in Algiers had almost proved that she was both unshakeable and tough, and Scalands was to be the scene of the final test.

Much to Barbara's satisfaction, Emily was delighted with Scalands, it was so different from anything she had ever seen before. There was scarcely any furniture but plenty of cushions strewn on the floor where guests were expected to sit. The walls were white with shelves on which blue and white Algerian pottery rested beneath a frieze of the Bayeux tapestry. By the open door a large round table was laid for supper and, since the autumn evening was chilly, a fire burned in the grate. To modern eyes it would have looked stark and uncomfortable but to that group of Victorians who wanted to be different it was remarkably restful after living in airless over-furnished rooms. There was no garden as such, only the green grass which was encouraged to grow right up to the front door. Here and there sheep grazed contentedly and there was no sound except the normal ones of rural England. Emily was to get to know this scene like the back of her hand and, town-dweller though she was, she never failed to delight in it.

The very first morning when Emily looked out of her window she saw Barbara with nothing on but her druid's robe, walking barefoot on the grass. She shouted to Emily to strip off her corset and do the same, it was splendid for 'reasons of health'. But Emily could admire without wishing to emulate.

Barbara was a late bird and encouraged Emily to sit up with her talking until long after midnight. They dissected Lizzie's career from end to end and Barbara, who knew nothing of the hardships involved, had her qualified in no time: difficulties were sloughed off with a wave of the hand, 'she will do it'.

The weather was so good that they decided to go on a walking expedition. Barbara half expected Emily to refuse, but she accepted with alacrity. They started off in brilliant autumn sunshine, Barbara wearing men's breeches and thick boots, her sketching equipment strapped to her back. The only concession Emily made to the walk was her thick tweed skirt and stout buttoned boots. Her stamina astonished Barbara: after several miles she showed no sign of fatigue and was cheerful and talkative. When they came to a stream Barbara removed her breeches and boots and plunged straight into the icy water, Emily removed her boots and stockings and lifting her skirt in one hand, leapt onto some stones and was quickly over, without once getting her skirt wet.

In October 1860 Emily became an aunt for the first time, when Llewelyn's wife Mary gave birth to a daughter, Margaret Caroline, at Blandford Square. Emily went to London to look after the rectory while Mary was laid up. Even while she was packing, she felt very uncertain about going. Her father's health had recently become even more precarious than usual. The death of his three children had hit him hard. Then suddenly he expressed a wish to see his new grand-daughter and seemed so much better in London that he and his wife decided to go to Harrogate on their return journey where the air was so healing and had done him so much good before. A curious restlessness seems to have seized both parents, for a few days later Emily heard that they had gone instead to Ilkley Wells to see what the water could do for the invalid's aches and pains. When they set out it was beautiful weather but on the way a storm arose. Dr Davies caught a chill which rapidly turned to bronchitis and in a few hours he was gone. Emily was sent for but she reached Yorkshire too late to see him alive.

Emily had thought her father failing for some time, his grip on life very tenuous indeed. When her parents reached Harrogate he had written to her in the gloomiest of terms. He did not think the advice given him by his specialist the right one, but believed that despite the man's high reputation he had not diagnosed the malady correctly. Their daughter-in-law Mary with whom they had stayed in London reassured Emily; she and her husband saw nothing wrong with him that had not been there before, and there was no cause for alarm. In a letter to Anna Richardson written while she was in London, Emily mentions her father only in passing and goes on to talk cheerfully of the books she had read, especially George Eliot's *Silas Marner*, which she had just finished: 'I think it a more healthy and helpful book than the "Mill on the Floss".'

When Emily reached Yorkshire she was surprised to find her mother calm and collected. 'I feel so much cause for thankfulness that he did not suffer' were her first words. She had no thought for herself, except that she wrote in her diary 'it will be a life-long loss'. They had hardly been apart for over forty years and Emily was worried that her mother's anguish might be all the worse for being suppressed.

She was amazed too at her mother's grasp of business affairs. She had not realised that all her married life Mary Davies had managed the accounts and that every item of business had gone through her hands. John Davies was a hopeless business man and had been content for his wife to give him a half sovereign a week, none of which he spent on himself. Never once had she weakened her husband's authority by giving the slightest sign that her money had been left in her own name in the bank, and never once had he assumed authority over it. By law

29

it became his on their wedding day and of course he had benefited from her fortune in so many different ways, but he would not take it from her just because the law said he could. Emily marvelled at the harmony that there had been between them and that she had seen real marital happiness without ever realising it. Waiting on her husband and ministering to his needs had been a labour of love for her mother, not a sacrifice.

Emily knew what she wanted to do now: to live in London where she was sure she would find work of some kind, for she did not yet know what money they would have to live on or what her mother herself wanted. Even after the funeral when they were alone together, the future was never mentioned, and also Emily was too embarrassed to bring the subject up herself; her mother's failure to open her mind made her apprehensive and shy.

This curious reticence was by no means unusual in large Victorian families, where the green baize door often shut the children away from the parents. Emily's life had not been like that, and yet there was a barrier; and the children were not consulted even when they were growing up. For instance, Emily was quite old before she knew that her mother had been bitterly disappointed that her husband had refused the professorship in London. It amazed her that her mother did not even tell her eldest son about it. By Mary Davies's standards that would have been disloyalty; one did not divulge anything private to one's children.

In the end Llewelyn decided for them. They must live in London, anywhere else would be too far away from him to keep an eye on them. In less than a month he had found a small house in St John's Wood, 17 Cunningham Place. By the spring mother and daughter, with a cook and a housemaid from Gateshead, had settled in this quiet part of London which Emily described as 'ideal'.

The move to London was to open the way to a career which was to make her one of the most influential figures of the Victorian age.

Number 17 Cunningham Place was small but cheerful. It had a minute garden in which Mrs Davies could potter about to her heart's content, leaving Emily free – for what? Emily knew what she must do at once – help Lizzie Garrett become a doctor.

Lizzie had been overjoyed to hear Emily was going to live in London. She took it as a sign that Divine Providence was on her side. 'It will be very nice to have you so near,' she wrote happily. 'I keep imagining all manner of ways of getting help out of your presence. I believe it is a great thing for me to have you near enough to speak to pretty constantly.'

Already Lizzie had tasted the bitterness of the prejudice against women in the medical profession and had drunk deep of the miseries of loneliness. Surrounded by rowdy male medical students, she felt isolated in the vastness of the Middlesex Hospital, ignored and unrecognised. She might have been a disembodied spirit for all the impact she made, had not one or two of the senior doctors shown flashes of kindness to the lonely girl.

Emily had guessed that Lizzie was unhappy. While she was still in Gateshead, frequent letters had come from Lizzie asking for advice on quite trivial matters, simply in order to keep in contact with someone who understood her difficulties: 'the loneliness is considerable and rather trying' spoke volumes to Emily.

In the mid-nineteenth century, society as a whole felt not just prejudice, but loathing amounting to hatred and fear of women pursuing the same studies as men. From Lizzie's letters Emily could see that the male medical students were not ashamed that their excuses were so lame: women messed things up, had no talent for the work, would faint at the sight of blood; let them stick to nursing, it was more in their line; to enter a man's world made women unwomanly, women competing with men would make very poor wives and mothers; so much learning would make them mad, would wholly unfit them for those quiet domestic offices for which providence intended them: they would lose their gentleness and grace, the sweet vivacity, which were their principal adornment and would become cold, calculating, masculine, fast, strong-minded and in a word generally unpleasing.

Medical students working alongside Lizzie tried to impede her whenever they could, and if possible to make her look ridiculous. Emily guessed that Lizzie's dexterity, swift reactions and quick mind caused jealousy and fear, but the men's animosity was hard to bear since she was defenceless and alone. Emily made a point of seeing Lizzie some part of every day whenever she was free; they went over Lizzie's work together, and Emily's cheerfulness and amusing imitations of students and doctors (although she had never seen them) sent depression out of the window and gave encouragement for another day.

New and artificially manufactured problems arose almost daily to tantalise Lizzie. There was a ridiculous fuss when she asked permission to use the dissecting room, for instance. Even Lizzie had to laugh when solemnly warned that the students might become 'larky' if she as much as dared to enter the room. Emily urged her to go ahead and march in, to be bold was the only reply to such nonsense.

One of the surgeons, Mr Nunn, tried to be helpful by telling Lizzie that her task would be easier if she was not the only woman medical student: a group could have a dissecting room all to themselves. Possibly this remark was not intended to be taken seriously, but it shows how desperate the girls had become that they were so ready to clutch at straws. The two young women concocted what they thought was a brilliant plan. They decided to take up the idea. They would seek out those women who wanted to become doctors wherever they might be, and without delay they put advertisements in every large newspaper in the country:

> Ladies who may be desirous of qualifying in the medical profession are respectfully informed that particulars concerning the prescribed form of study and the opportunities at present available may be obtained on application to Miss Davies, 17 Cunningham Place, St John's Wood.

Replies flowed in, so many that Emily had to ask her mother to help deal with them, but disappointingly none of the writers pursued their inquiries beyond the first stage. In April, Llewelyn told Emily that he had heard that London University was to be granted a new charter and that he thought this might open up possibilities for women. They must act quickly. Immediately Emily composed a short letter for Lizzie to copy, applying for admission to the matriculation examination. The letter was posted that very day. If only the bastion would fall, how much easier, richer, better life would become. Both knew that they might have done a foolhardy thing, for if the new charter excluded women there was little likelihood of amending it in time for Lizzie. Llewelyn tried to keep their spirits up. On looking over the list of members of the Senate, he told them cheerfully that their chances were good: 'these men are all advanced liberals'. Unfortunately, as it turned out, their liberality did not include women in its scope.

In May he gave them another piece of news that he hoped might lift their spirits. He had been told that Mr Grote, the Vice-Chancellor, had moved in the Senate that by the new charter women should be admitted to London University degrees though not to Convocation. Hopes ran high; therefore it was all the more devastating when they heard that they had lost and by only one vote. Lord Granville, whom Lizzie liked and trusted, had used his casting vote on the other side. It was hard to believe such perfidy.

Emily blamed herself for this failure: she had been too hasty, she had not prepared the ground thoroughly enough, nor had she read the terms of the original charter carefully enough, for now she saw that it stated clearly that the university was 'to provide a liberal education for all classes and denominations without any distinction whatsoever'.

Straightaway Emily put a new plan into operation: she began to canvass names for a petition. The wording was to be straightforward and simple, no mention was to be made of medicine, and the question was to be approached on the most general ground, simply asking that women should be allowed to matriculate in the same way as men. The names on the petition when it was ready to be sent off were very distinguished. There were 1500 in all and Emily had printed a number of favourable opinions which she circulated among those she thought might have influence. She was beginning to believe that half measures never paid.

The list on which Emily and Lizzie had spent so much time and energy contained so many distinguished names (it included Gladstone, Cobden and Lord Milner, for instance) that its validity was questioned. Mr Grote, the Vice-Chancellor, asked to see the signatures and scrutinised them under a magnifying-glass with the greatest care, looking for signs of forgery. He showed his insensitivity by doing this in front of Emily, who had been commanded to attend the shocking spectacle of which he was not in the least ashamed. 'Forgery is the sort of thing that women do,' he said insultingly. 'Women should only attempt things within their capacity.' Emily replied sharply that in this case there were special obstacles and that Elizabeth Garrett was doing all she could to prove her capacity in spite of her difficulties as a woman.

After treatment like this it came as no surprise that 'after long and careful discussion' the Senate threw out the petition by a large majority, and Lizzie was forced to give up her hope of matriculating. Even so Emily was certain that more had been gained than lost. The list of names on the petition alone would make the authorities wonder if they had acted wisely. Later it occurred to her that what she should have done was to ask some of those who had signed to help her form a powerful committee to agitate; if she had done this the result might have been very different. Jo Manton, in her excellent biography of Elizabeth Garrett, says that after these initial mistakes there were clear signs of Emily's generalship. She quickly learned her lesson and was now to put it to good use.

Elizabeth was cast down. Friends (hoping this would comfort her) would tell her of those they knew who had failed as she had, and this discouraged her. That Jessie Meriton-White's father had written to fourteen hospitals for leave to enter his daughter as a medical student and all had refused, was not quite the kindest thing to say to a depressed girl who felt her way blocked for good.

There were even signs that Lizzie was ready to give up the struggle but, using a mixture of tact and persuasion, Emily encouraged her to continue the fight: to give up now would show that they did not deserve victory.

Nevertheless she could see that Lizzie was becoming worn down by the struggle to open doors so securely locked against her. Snubs and discouragement were her lot and in June 1862 matters came to a head when in a viva voce examination at the hospital Lizzie came out top. This infuriated the male students who organised a vendetta against her in order to get her out. Next, the College of Surgeons refused to allow her to compete for the special diploma in midwifery and the *Lancet* took a strong line against women attempting to enter the medical profession at all. Verbal skirmishes now became almost a daily occurrence until Lizzie was quite drained. 'It is distressing, nervous work,' she wrote sadly to Emily who had gone to Oxford for a few days, 'standing about with nothing to do amid the consciousness of a line of criticising eyes'.

Tired and dejected though they both were, there was still a ray of hope. In June 1862 they discovered that the Society of Apothecaries was willing to examine Lizzie; they jumped at the sudden opportunity. Emily was not surprised when she heard that Lizzie had obtained very high marks and that on the strength of them she could gain admission to St Andrew's University. Scotland would be a change of scene and the Middlesex Hospital had become hateful to them both.

Emily saw Lizzie off in cold October weather, a forlorn little figure, lonely and apprehensive. For the first time for many months, the general had to direct operations far from the battlefield. A month later a sad letter reached Emily and touched her so deeply that she made up her mind to go at once to St Andrew's. Despatching her mother to her sister-in-law's care, Emily made the long cold journey to Scotland to be with her friend. As always, Emily's cheerful optimism and amusing stories acted like a tonic. A great deal of Lizzie's misery was caused by the vicious tales put about by the town gossips. Living alone in lodgings and doing something unusual had set tongues wagging. The ringleader was one particular woman with some influence in the town. It so happened that Lizzie took Emily to a university dinner, and the chief gossip was present. Emily asked to be introduced, 'and after one encounter with Miss Davies she became very civil all the rest of the evening'.

Moved only by love for Lizzie, Emily had plunged unreflectingly into a struggle with officialdom in the shape of institutions staffed entirely by men. No woman had dared to do anything of the kind before. Emily made mistakes, when her heart ruled her head. But from the experience she learned lessons which stood her in good stead later on. With Lizzie happily established at St Andrews, she had won her first victory and had emerged from her apprenticeship.

3

'Shut away from the light'

A society with the clumsy title of 'The National Association for the Promotion of Social Science' had been founded in 1857 by Emily's brother Llewelyn and a group of his friends. Membership was open to women on equal terms with men: this meant on the one hand that the association could serve as a platform from which women could air their sense of injustice, but on the other that it at once became an object of scorn and derision to the newspapers and the general public. *Punch*, for instance, never referred to it by any other name than 'The Universal Palaver Society'. Mockery, however, did not deter the early members, many of whom bore distinguished names, and the Association was an instant success.

Emily was soon elected a member, and her first paper was written with Lizzie in mind: 'Medicine as a Profession for Women'. She used it to hit at the Royal College of Surgeons for refusing to allow Lizzie to compete for the Diploma in Midwifery, at the *Lancet* for following the college's lead, at the Middlesex Hospital for trampling her finer feelings underfoot, and at the University of London for refusing to let her matriculate merely because she was a woman. Emily took great pains over the paper: for instance, in order to avoid mistakes she asked Llewelyn to let her see the minutes of past meetings, and was gratified to find that the only woman before her who had spoken up for women doctors was Florence Nightingale. In accordance with custom, however, her paper was read for her by a man, Russell Gurney, the Recorder of London. But she found the experience so undignified that next time she was invited to speak she boldly mounted the rostrum and delivered her speech herself. This one gesture formed a precedent which was soon followed outside the Association as well, and before long women were speaking in public on the same footing as men. Within the Association, the principle of equality was observed when the first secretary appointed a woman, Isa Craig, as his assistant; within a few months, Emily herself had succeeded to the office of secretary.

It was at a social science meeting that Emily first met the Rev. Frederick Denison Maurice, the Christian Socialist. She had heard such contrary opinions about him that she was curious to find out what he was really like. Men of action always appealed to Emily, and to find one in the Church was unusual. She soon discovered that Maurice had been active in trying to improve the education of women: in 1846 he had been among the founders of Bedford College, a combination of school and place of adult education for women, and shortly also of Queen's College, Harley Street, which aimed to raise the status of governesses by improving the standard of education. This made her ready to like him, but her immediate reaction was not favourable. His hollow cheeks, piercing black eyes and stiff manner made her feel awkward. When she got to know him better and realised that he was shy, she was able to appreciate his real kindness, and her admiration returned. Soon she was writing to Lizzie 'Mr Maurice's face is the most beautiful I ever saw'. Nevertheless, she failed to understand why such a kind-hearted man did not condemn the ignorance and servile state of women as degrading, or their lowly position in the social hierarchy as intolerable. It was an unpleasant surprise to discover that Maurice disapproved of women entering the medical profession and would have opposed Lizzie as fiercely as the doctors and students at the Middlesex Hospital had done. Prudently, she decided not to argue with him, nor did she tell Lizzie, whose ideal Maurice had recently become, and who wrote: 'One feels as if everything could be aided by studying with Mr Maurice.'

Maurice knew the slums as well as Emily, but saw their problems quite differently. 'The matter with the working class,' he told Emily, 'is the lack of places in which to worship. Does not Miss Davies think that is the cause of so much unrest?' To which Miss Davies promptly replied 'No, I do not. We need more schools, not churches.'

One Sunday, Lizzie persuaded Emily to go with her to St Peter's, Vere Street, to hear Maurice preach. Emily did not find the experience enjoyable. Maurice's sermon was too mystical for her to follow, and she could not understand what he was driving at although she gave him all her attention. Lizzie, however, took copious notes. When Lizzie urged Emily to go with her to Maurice's Bible class, she refused point-blank, saying that she had had enough of Bible classes, Sunday school – even of church itself – after those twenty years in Gateshead.

It puzzled Emily that so few women members attended Association meetings, and she asked Llewelyn what he thought was the reason. He shrugged his shoulders and suggested several, all trivial, it seemed to his sister. The truth was, she felt sure, that women were lazy and most felt that politics – which came up at every meeting in some form or other – was men's business and not for them, since they did not have the vote, nor were many of them aware of what the Women's Movement stood for. So when it was suggested that she become secretary of the Association, she accepted with alacrity in spite of her lack of experience, in the belief that it would give her the chance to attract more women to meetings.

Lately she had been collecting material for a small book or pamphlet which she had it in mind to write, about the various myths which men believe about women. She listed some:

1. Men were afraid that if women had anything else to do they would be unwilling to marry ('This speaks volumes against marriage,' she commented).

2. Public life was injurious to women, because women were specially created for the domestic circle ('How can men possibly know this? There have been no women in public life since Florence Nightingale, and she flourished.')

3. One must not interfere with the laws of nature. ('What laws of nature? The only laws women know are those made by men.')

4. Indolence is feminine and refined. ('Let the standard of men's creature comforts drop, then men would soon see a change.')

5. Large courses of study would be overworking the feminine brain. ('What man can possibly know this? Women have never yet undertaken any heavy mental work.')

To put women on their guard against what acceptance of these views carried with it, Emily drew up a separate list of warnings. They included illustrations of women with natural force of character who, when denied a healthy outlet, had indulged in unhealthy extravagances simply because it was a necessity of their nature to be active in some way or other. 'Frivolity is not harmless,' Emily wrote. 'The absence of any definite occupation is, in itself, calculated to encourage a trifling habit of mind.'

Since coming to London Emily's life had not been all work and no play. She was the most gregarious of women, and her early years had been exceedingly lonely; now she could indulge her love of meeting people without the slightest twinge of conscience. Everything was new and fascinating, and her enjoyment was all the keener for tasting these pleasures for the first time as a mature woman. She had just passed her thirty-second birthday, but felt and looked younger than her years. Her sister-in-law, Mary, found her a joy to take about, she was so unspoilt and so delighted with everything: theatres, concerts, receptions, were all equally exciting to her, the fashions a wonder to behold. With such a response, it was not surprising that Mary enjoyed arranging treats for her ageing (as she privately thought) sister-in-law; she must be allowed a little fun before becoming too old to enjoy it. Just as Barbara Bodichon had been, she was taken aback by Emily's stamina. She would turn up for a party, neat as a pin, calm and collected, and prettily dressed, after a gruelling day spent on social science affairs, two hours' research for her latest pamphlet or speech and all the time she could spare testing Lizzie on her medical notes, yet excitedly looking forward to the evening's entertainment, whatever it might be. Her letters to her Gateshead friends at this period are full of descriptions of all she had seen and heard: Jenny Lind in the 'Messiah' had held her spellbound, Robert Browning reading his own poems gave 'a new beauty to his words'. He seemed to change before her very eyes and to become 'less astonishingly ugly, as literary men generally are'.

Emily never missed a rectory party if she could help it, because of the variety of people invited: Dr Jowett, Master of Balliol College, Oxford ('ugly, but one forgets about that when he speaks'), Dean Stanley, until recently the Queen's chaplain and now Dean of Westminster ('so calm and reasonable and happy to be outshone by his beautiful wife, Lady Augusta'), the Bakers of Africa ('so simple and kind, you would never dream from their appearance of all the important things they had done'), Lady Amberley ('I like her very much. She seems very simple, good and alive'). Names and places tumbled out of her, making her incoherent with pleasure, but her strict evangelical training soon began to make itself felt. 'It is rather nice seeing the people, but I don't think I have any raison d'etre for being among them.'

Lady Amberley was much taken with Emily and invited her to tea to meet her mother, Lady Stanley, who was to become one of Emily's staunchest allies. She also invited Emily to one of her breakfast parties that were then all the rage, but Emily hesitated to accept and would have refused had not her friend Charlotte Manning urged her to go, saying that 'it would not be too grand'. Emily went, but was not completely at her ease: 'The talk ran on people and things I did not know and were quite out of my way, like picnics at Brocket' (Lord Melbourne's country house). But some things much-looked-forward-to turned out disappointments. Tea with John Stuart Mill, the political scientist, and his step-daughter, Helen Taylor, was not an enjoyable experience. With Lizzie, Emily had travelled all the way to Blackheath, but Mill was in a silent mood and Helen Taylor not at her best, Lizzie too frightened to relax, and Emily unnaturally awed. They were happy to return to the easier atmosphere of the rectory where they never knew whom they would meet – Anthony Trollope, Louis Blanc, R.H. Hutton of the *Spectator*, all of them cheerful and friendly, discussing politics or books, conversations in which Emily and Lizzie were encouraged to take part. 'How London spoils one,' Emily wrote to Jane Crow. 'I feel quite injured now if I don't see everything that is going on, the moment it comes out. As regards parties, business is very dull just now, Lizzie and I remarked with a sigh that there were no engagements in view. The love of dissipation grows upon me as I get more at home in society. But it is always a risk and a really dull party is a dreadful sell.'

In December 1862 Barbara Bodichon invited Emily to work part-time on the *English Woman's Journal*, a feminist magazine run by women for women. Its conception had been the fulfillment of a romantic dream of Bessie Parkes, only daughter of the business man Joseph Parkes and his American wife, the former Elizabeth Priestley.

For some years Bessie had longed to do something to awaken women to the many degradations they were suffering, with the idea that if women united under proper leadership they might be able to remedy the many injustices under which they now laboured. The purpose of the Journal was to be a clarion call to the women of England to rise up and demand their rights. Full of courage, she began with a few friends, all untried, all unpractical but eager, their hearts aflame with zeal to push forward the 'woman question'. Not one of these enthusiastic amateurs had the least idea of the fierce competition they were up against from other magazines. They did not realise that the magazine industry was a thoroughly commercial business which flourished because the new railways and W.H. Smith's bookstalls had created and supplied a new market among women travellers who wanted to be amused. Magazines appealed to a woman's vanity, inviting her to be indolent, filling her head with romantic stories, the latest fashions, and hints on gentle gardening. *The Ladies' Boudoir, The Ladies' Cabinet, The Woman's Companion* and many more were all bought and relished.

The *English Woman's Journal* was meant to be a serious magazine like *Fraser's* or *Macmillan's*, but for women only. However, it turned out to be so serious that from the beginning it attracted only those already devoted to the cause and failed to make new converts to it. Hence it lost money from the start and something drastic had to be done. While in Algiers, Barbara had come to the conclusion that Emily was the right person to save the magazine. She was intelligent, industrious and not afraid of responsibility, and now an eager exponent of the cause; most important of all, she seemed to have organising ability. In 1861, when Emily was staying at her brother's rectory in Blandford Square, Barbara took her to the office in Langham Place where the group who worked on the *Journal* operated. Emily was impressed. The young women were good-looking, fashionably dressed and friendly, so that Emily immediately felt at ease. She was much taken with Bessie Parkes, the owner and joint editor, tall and a little grave now with the weight of her responsibilities, but pretty and looking younger than her thirty-seven years. Emily found her easy to talk to, and had heard that she was highly talented. Among the others she was particularly struck by Emily Faithfull, an individual young woman clever enough to run her own female-operated press on which the *Journal* was printed; Jessie Boucheret, who ran the only women's employment agency in London and whose shyness hid a very determined character; and Adelaide Proctor, who wrote the 'Lost Chord' and gave general help in the *Journal* office. They were all industrious, working harmoniously together; and Emily thought how happy she would be to join them. But until her father retired she would have to remain at home.

With her father's unexpected death and the move to London all obstacles were suddenly removed. In the New Year, 1863, Emily joined the group as part-editor with Bessie Parkes, who was feeling the strain after five hard years. No one warned Emily that Bessie was going through an emotional crisis which made her difficult to work with. In recent months she had found that she could no longer accept the Unitarian faith in which she had been brought up, particularly its denial of the Trinity. For the past two years she had been drifting steadily towards Rome and already had met and discussed her problems with Cardinal Manning. This left Bessie more sure than ever that his Church would suit her temperament far better than her own. She did not tell Manning that she was also dabbling in spiritualism and seeking guidance from those who believed in the occult, nor admit even to herself that in consequence of all this she was thoroughly confused.

Emily had hardly been a week at Langham Place before Bessie casually left a book about spiritualism on her desk – *The Night Life of Nature* by Mrs Katherine Crow, which had been a best-seller in 1848 when it was first published. Emily had no time for spiritualism, and without a word she returned the book unopened. It was a tactless thing to do, but she was taken by surprise and disgusted that someone as intelligent as Bessie could take such ignorant rubbish seriously. In consequence, Bessie changed her mind about Emily overnight and decided that Emily was hard-hearted, lacking in sympathy and friendly feeling, a woman she could never like. She wrote acidly to Barbara, 'I can work with people of all religions except Anglicans. They are impossible.' Of course Emily knew nothing of the effect of this unfortunate incident and went blithely on with her work. And she felt sorry for Bessie, who always seemed to be in an emotional state, either questioning her faith or worrying about her abilities and wondering whether she was making the most of the opportunities the *Journal* offered.

From the beginning Emily had been struck by the strange coincidence that the editor herself was just the sort of person the *Journal* set out to help. Born into a wealthy family, Bessie knew nothing of finance. She had never in her life written a cheque – when she needed money, her father gave it to her – but she longed for the independence which a proper allowance would give her. Despite her lack of financial training, Bessie had had the confidence to think that she could run a magazine and make a success of it.

Emily's position as joint editor was fraught with difficulties. Barbara's childish deception in not telling her the truth that the *Journal* was failing fast was not the main cause of the trouble, but it was an added irritant. It did not take her long to discover that the large orders which the group talked of were mainly artificial: at the start, friends who wanted to help had placed orders for one or two years, but became bored with a highbrow magazine and had let their subscriptions lapse. New subscribers had not taken their place. She did not think that the group understood that they were competing with experienced professional editors who knew their job. The articles in the journal were of excellent quality, but well above the heads of all but a few of its readers. The middle-class women at whom the *Journal* aimed were not interested in the Reformation of the sixteenth century or the life of a German housewife at the same period, nor did they care much about the latest changes in the divorce laws, for most were content with things as they were or totally convinced that their lot could never be changed. Moreover, there was a general feeling among the group that an article sent in by a distinguished author must never be touched, however long it was. Matthew Arnold was a bad offender here. On her own initiative, Emily shortened a thirty-page article of his, and improved it by so doing. Immediately Bessie demanded to know why Emily had taken such a liberty, for even more than the others she laboured under the misapprehension that Matthew Arnold's name alone helped to sell the *Journal*.

Emily was not timid, but she saw no sense in quarrelling, so she gave in and promised not to cut or alter in future. She liked Bessie and sympathised with her, and was sorry to see her five years' hard work collapsing at her feet, but she was so occupied in trying to save the *Journal* that she attributed Bessie's antagonism to anxiety rather than to sheer dislike of herself. Her own thoughts and feelings towards Bessie were kindly; she sympathised with her religious dilemma and supposed that she had forbidden all mention of religion in the magazine simply because she did not know where she herself stood. She felt certain that she was right about this when Bessie refused to print a short article Emily had written on the priesthood in Ireland, which criticised the Catholic priests for not showing enough concern for the poor and oppressed. 'I would never have written it,' she told Lizzie contritely, 'had I known that Bessie was trying to make up her mind to go over to Rome.' Lizzie had little sympathy for Bessie on the ground that 'such an omission in any worth-while magazine makes it appear atheistic'.

The attitudes of Emily and Bessie to each other could not have been more different. Neither had any idea what the other felt, and neither understood why they were so often at cross-purposes. Emily really believed that Bessie's bursts of temper, her irritability and contradictory orders, were the result of her mixed-up feelings about religion; it never occurred to her that she herself was the cause. So they went blindly and unhappily on together, Emily doing her best not to notice Bessie's recurrent bad moods. Things came to a head when Emily countermanded an order of Barbara's 'because it is not in the Journal's interests'. Bessie then accused her of 'steamrolling' them all, and wrote to Barbara, who had seen them arguing, 'as to Emily Davies, I am glad you saw her as a sick porpoise crossed in love because, if she could be so to you, whom she admires, what can she be like to those for whom she has a deep-seated contempt which crops up in many ways, of which I really believe she is half unconscious.'

Emily's letters to her friends show how careful of Bessie's feelings she tried to be: 'It is her journal, and she also no doubt feels that she has a right to do as she likes,' she wrote to Nannie Leigh-Smith. 'I should think it very hard on Bessie if taking up her work I pay no attention to her wishes.'

How could Emily know that Bessie had always been touchy where the *Journal* was concerned? Although highly intelligent and a poetess of some distinction as well as an ardent feminist, Bessie refused to co-operate with Emily and use her skills to save the *Journal*. When Emily made a good suggestion, Bessie put obstacles in her way, a form of blatant self-destruction which puzzled everyone. Here again Emily could not know that Bessie found it difficult to take advice even from old and valued friends whom she trusted. Mrs Anna Jameson had audaciously offered some advice when Bessie was setting up the *Journal*: 'Get the help and sympathy of good, intelligent men, and do not feminise your magazine too much. If you do, it will break down.' A feminist to her fingertips, Mrs Jameson had worked hard for some years to improve the lot of women, and the *Journal* was dear to her heart, but unwittingly she criticised an anonymous article in an early number which had in fact been written by Bessie, thereby treading on Bessie's sensitive feelings. She objected to the article on the ground that there was 'a touch of vulgarity about referring to "gentlemen" and "ladies" instead of "men" and "women".' It was a trivial matter, but Bessie had been hurt. In similar vein another correspondent wrote, 'If you unwisely provoke the opposition of the more popular journals you will speedily smash yourself.' But this, too, Bessie ignored.

By the summer of 1863 money was rapidly running out, and winding up could not be far away. When this point was reached Bessie ordered that all the remaining funds should be divided among the contributors, but Emily objected that this was unfair to the staff. She wanted no payment for herself (indeed, she offered to help pay for the *Journal*'s demise), but the others had worked hard, and if women worked they should be properly rewarded. She was so forceful about this that Bessie had to give way. That women should work and be paid for what they did was a new and revolutionary idea. While still at home Emily had written three articles for the Gateshead *Herald* warning husbands and fathers that they must get used to the idea of their daughters wanting paid work: 'It is certainly not easy to see,' she wrote, 'why it should be unfeminine for a girl to sit in her father's office, as one of his paid clerks under his immediate eye, gaining experience so that she could eventually take his place and relieve anxiety for provision for the family'.

By the autumn the end of the *Journal* was in sight, but Bessie wanted to delay final closure for a year, until Barbara and Nannie should return from Algiers. Emily said this was impossible. In exasperation Emily wrote to Lizzie Garrett, 'Bessie is evidently in a state of delusion about it altogether.'

To work with someone like Bessie who could not delegate, could not inspire and could not give a lead was wearing in the extreme, and Emily longed to put the experience behind her. Yet she had learned something about herself in the process which was to be valuable to her in the future: that she was not at her best unless she was in complete charge. Responsibility was what she liked and desired, and it brought out the best in her. She felt no animosity towards Bessie; she saw that she was suffering because of her failure, and her heart was touched. 'It makes me sorry to think of poor Bessie's disappointment,' she wrote to Barbara, 'but one blow is better than constant worry.'

Why was Bessie so antagonistic towards Emily? In the beginning she had been eager to have Emily's help, and was pleased that she was willing to join the group. Worry about money could not have been the whole answer, otherwise she would not have hindered Emily's efforts to make the *Journal* pay. The reason was deeper and more insidious than Emily guessed. Over the weeks that Emily worked at Langham Place Bessie developed the fear that Emily had supplanted her in Barbara's affections. To someone as well-balanced as Emily, who liked her own sex (her tireless work on their behalf proves this) but who never nurtured passions for other women, such a reason would have seemed absurd.

Before Emily appeared on the scene Barbara discussed everything with Bessie, not only the affairs of the magazine but her own love-life, her reasons for marrying Eugène Bodichon and her disappointment that he did not want to live in England. All these confidences were poured into Bessie's sympathetic ears, and this gave Bessie the happy feeling that she was indispensable and that Barbara could not get on without her. Emily's coming seemed to have changed all that, and in her unhappiness Bessie imagined that Emily had said something to turn Barbara against her. Early in their friendship Bessie had written to Barbara: 'I do not think that I could ever quarrel with anybody I love as much as I do you . . . I have had the deepest and most explicit confidence in you from the day I knew you.' Now that confidence was shaken and Bessie was miserable.

The language of affection, even sometimes of passion, which women commonly used towards each other a hundred years ago may easily suggest lesbianism to a modern mind. But this was far from the truth in the vast majority of cases, and most certainly in Bessie's: her five-year marriage to Louis Belloc was as idyllic as a marriage can ever be, and his early death blighted her life. Language of this kind usually had no sexual connotation whatever. George Eliot and Barbara Bodichon wrote passionate letters to each other, yet neither could live without men. In those days women were thrown so much together with their own sex that warm and lasting friendships sprang up spontaneously, whether the women were married or single. Women were a class apart, an inferior class, downtrodden and frequently ill from causes which they were too ignorant to understand, lonely, depressed and often unloved, their talents uncultivated. It was other women that they depended on for companionship, and it is not surprising that affection developed, as well as trust and loyalty. Therefore it would be wrong to read twentieth-century meanings into nineteenth-century words.

4

A Mission Discovered

In the summer of 1862 a special meeting of the Social Science Association had been held in the Guildhall to discuss the education of girls. At this meeting Frances Power Cobbe, an ardent but not always prudent feminist, read a paper on 'University Degrees for Women', a subject which at that time excited such universal merriment that she was made to look ridiculous. 'Next day every newspaper laughed at my demands,' she wrote in her autobiography. The very idea that women would ever be in a position to attend a university was absurd.

Emily was seriously perturbed. She had thought the paper level-headed and sensible, its only mistake being to demand too much too quickly, thereby making women the butt for endless jokes. Emily wondered whether they would ever live it down.

The arguments against university degrees for women were well known and simple: girls were not taught well enough at school to gain admission to a university because those who taught them were not properly qualified. Perhaps, if given the same chances as boys at the same age, they would do just as well, but at present there was no hope of that. Nevertheless Frances Cobbe's paper gave Emily food for thought. After pondering on it for some time she began to ask herself if the dream was really quite so impossible as it seemed. Unless a miracle happened, there would be years of prejudice to live down, and generations of women might come and go before it could be realised. Meanwhile, untapped sources of intellect would run to waste.

Ever since the inception of the Social Science Association countless papers had been read on the education of women, and all the male speakers (the women cravenly following their lead) had been against what they referred to as 'book-learning for females'. It seemed, they said, to go against nature. Learning could not make women better wives and mothers, the purposes for which nature had created them. It was views like this which made Barbara Bodichon say in all seriousness 'there is still slavery in England' and Emily to talk of marriage as 'entering into a state no better than that of a slave'. Emily rebuked her brother for not vetting the papers before they were read, to prevent such extreme views from being broadcast. Members should not be allowed to make a serious subject appear trivial. Ignorance was a terrible barrier to everything worthwhile.

For months Emily had had long and fruitful talks with Lord Lyttelton, a man deeply committed to education. They agreed well: education for middle-class girls must be drastically improved. Once established, a better system would have effects which would seep downwards, and schools for working-class children of both sexes would benefit. This was the way progress always came in England. She talked also to F.D. Maurice, but his ideas were too mixed up with church control of schools and the welfare of the poor to be of much use to her; it was hopeless, she realised, to expect sound practical advice from a clergyman.

A conversation with Lizzie Garrett suddenly showed her the way forward, though at first her new idea did not seem so momentous as it turned out to be. If it worked, it would affect generations of women and turn the tables once and for all in their favour. To begin with, she purposely played it down in case it proved incapable of realisation. She wrote laconically to Anna Richardson, 'I cast about as to what we could reasonably ask for from the older universities which, through age and custom, have established a precedent. Local examinations, as involving nothing in the way of residence, seem to meet the case.' Local examinations! Why had she not thought of them before? These examinations had only been established a few years earlier, and were of course only open to boys. They were the creation of Dr Frederick Temple, Headmaster of Rugby and later Archbishop of Canterbury, and aimed at giving all middle-class schools the same standard of teaching. No one before Emily had had the effrontery to suggest that girls might profit from sitting them too, and when she began to canvass opinions among her friends she found that many of them felt very uncomfortable with such a droll idea. But those close to her thought it excellent and backed her for all they were worth. Lizzie was delighted, and told Emily that 'It could lead to great things'. Barbara was wildly enthusiastic: all innovations appealed to her, and she would do anything to stop authority from becoming complacent. Emily wrote to Anna Richardson from Scalands, where she was staying: 'We are going to make a try for them'. (The 'we' was a compliment to Barbara, who had generously offered money for the campaign but was not, of course, expected to lift a finger. Her role was moral support only.) 'It occurred to me that a memorial from ladies actually in tuition would have considerable weight. If you think this a good idea, will you give me the names of any heads of schools, or governesses, who you think it likely might be interested.'

The correspondence between Emily and Anna upon this subject went on for the whole summer of 1863 and makes it possible for us to follow every stage until Emily became weary of letter-writing at the end of August: 'The amount of mechanical labour I see before me is something stupendous, but I enjoy that kind of work.' She explained her purpose clearly: to secure permission for girls to sit the

Local Examinations, fully aware that the consequence of their doing so would be twofold: those who did well would want to go on to the next stage – which would then have to be constructed to meet their demands – while those who did badly would, by their failure, draw attention to the deplorable state of girls' education. The germ of her overriding concern for higher education is discernible here, and even more plainly in another letter: 'The examinations would be worth having, though I do not care for them very much in themselves, because I think the encouragement to learning is most wanted after the age of eighteen. It seems likely, however, that if we could get these examinations it would be a great lift towards the University of London . . . The agitation is hateful work, but it becomes clearer every day that incessant and unremitting talking and pushing is the only way of gaining our ends . . . We are fighting for those who cannot fight for themselves.'

With the moral support of four women – her mother, Anna Richardson, Barbara Bodichon and Elizabeth Garrett – all as different as could be, but all united on this one subject – Emily was emboldened to write to the secretaries of the Oxford and the Cambridge Local Examination Boards, politely asking whether there was any possibility of admitting girls to their examinations on the same terms as boys. Replies came by return of post, and Emily sensed before she opened the envelopes that the answer was 'No'. John Griffiths of Oxford was coldly definite: 'The examination of young girls is altogether beyond my sphere of duty.' Dr John Liveing of Cambridge was no better: 'The regulations would never bear such an interpretation as to admit girls.' Nevertheless he had been so struck by the nerve of an unknown young woman with no letter of introduction and no sponsor daring to make such a request that he added a kindly postscript: 'I will gather the opinions of the Local Examinations Syndicate on the subject with a view to the presentation of a petition.' Emily interpreted this as encouragement to press on, and from that moment directed all her efforts towards getting the door opened at Cambridge, hoping that if she succeeded Oxford might follow suit. With even greater boldness she organised a committee of women anxious to promote the cause: Barbara Bodichon, Miss Bostock (one of the founders of Bedford College), the redoubtable Lady Goldsmid, very influential and with advanced views on women's rights, and Isa Craig, a former member of the Langham Place group and the first woman to hold office in the Social Science Association. These were industrious, quick-witted women, but even so Emily did not think that they made a powerful enough committee. She therefore asked three distinguished men to join them, men who would be strong in adversity and whom she could trust to back her up in a fight: Russell Gurney, the Recorder of London, George Hastings of the Law Amendment Society and soon to be MP for Southampton, and George Heywood, FRS, a wealthy philanthropist sympathetic to the women's cause and a friend of Llewelyn Davies.

It was time to let her three schoolmistress friends know what was afoot; their support, though not essential, would be helpful. Frances Buss, Headmistress of the North London Collegiate School, was an old friend: there would be encouragement there, Emily was sure. Dorothea Beale of Cheltenham Ladies' College was unpredictable, but Hannah Pipe of Laleham School, Clapham Park, would follow Frances Buss. Their replies startled Emily. All three were too timid to allow their names to be attached to such a controversial project. Their letters were so alike that Emily guessed that they had conferred together and that Dorothea Beale had vetoed their co-operation. Later, she learned that this was indeed the case. Frances Buss had every intention of supporting Emily until Dorothea Beale forbade her: 'If she wants to do this thing,' Dorothea had said, 'let her, but she must leave us out of it.'

Activity brought the best out in Emily. When she contemplated her committee she could not help feeling a certain inner satisfaction. Their first meeting passed off smoothly, and it resolved to ask the Cambridge Local Examinations Syndicate to join them in getting up a petition to the university. The invitation was refused rather rudely – it was not in their interests to give themselves more work, they said. Next day there came an unexpected piece of good news, a letter from the same John Griffiths of Oxford who had snubbed her before. His tone had quite changed as, unasked, he offered to introduce her to the 'instigator of the Local Examinations, Dr Temple himself'. What had caused this change of heart? Emily wondered. She soon knew. Dr Frederick Temple had been impressed by what he had heard of Emily through friends at Oxford, and had written favourably of her scheme to Griffiths: 'With her ability and perseverance, she is bound to succeed.'

Dr Dyke Acland, who had helped Temple to bring the Local Examinations into being, now entered the fray. An Oxford man, he was himself connected with the Local Examinations centre in Exeter, and felt it his duty to warn Emily that she was playing with fire. He followed his first short letter with a longer one: 'If publicity and freedom be by the general consent of educated men necessary to the full development of boys' nature, a certain degree of privacy and clinging for protection is equally indispensable for the full ripening of the precious qualities of womanhood. I confess therefore a shrinking to throw the girls of England into competition with the boys. . . . I rather doubt whether university examiners who are, as a general rule, unmarried men, possess the experience of the ways of young people which many a country clergyman in frequent contact with his village school possesses. It requires considerable experience of family life and of the actual working of the school-room to judge a girl's knowledge and mental training.'

The stupidities of educated men never failed to amaze Emily. 'The precious qualities of womanhood', indeed! How she would like to take Thomas Dyke Acland on a tour of the Gateshead slums and show him a large number of women who had no one to cling to for protection. The whole point of wider education was eventually to lift all women out of their hideous environments and give their 'precious qualities' a chance to bloom.

How much easier her fight would be if she could dismiss the Dyke-Aclands of this world as insufferable and then forget all about them. Instead, she had learned already, men like him had to be answered courteously, since otherwise his adverse influence would do her campaign much harm. His third letter had ended up in the waste-paper basket as not worth an answer: 'In conversation with friends, ladies and gentlemen,' he wrote, 'I find great repugnance to your plans, especially the competition between the sexes.' Unhappily this 'great repugnance' to her plans really was widespread. Every day there came letters from complete strangers opposing her demands as though they were quite outrageous, instead of a simple and logical scheme to lift women out of the rut in which they seemed happy to remain. 'Girls are different from boys', 'their brains are too light, their foreheads too small, their reasoning powers too defective, their emotions too easily worked upon to make good students', 'women are mentally and physically unfit for what Miss Davies suggests', were among the more extreme remarks her correspondents made.

Emily was not easily discouraged, but the opposition of her own sex seemed little short of treason. A timely invitation from Lady Brodie to spend a few days in Oxford prevented serious loss of temper. The Brodies were a delightful couple, with grown-up children. Sir Benjamin had been Professor of Chemistry, his wife energetic in public works, and both were already among Emily's strongest supporters. For three days she was petted and pampered and made much of. Lady Brodie was not sanguine about the chance of Oxford surrendering: 'The university is an imitator, not an instigator. They will do nothing now, but later, when you have got your wish – which of course you will – Oxford will quickly change its mind and follow Cambridge.' It was disappointing, but not unexpected. How few there were around her to encourage and praise – even the schoolmistresses were against her. If only she knew someone in whom she could confide regularly, someone who would advise her and tell her whether her tactics were sound or not. She was of course thinking of an imaginary man whom she could lean on. She did not mean a husband, for like many others in the feminist movement she had deliberately eschewed marriage long ago, but a friend to whom she could turn in time of trouble.

Quite suddenly, such a man materialised.

We are never told exactly how or when Emily met the delightfully amusing and clever Henry Tomkinson. Emily tried to keep her private life separate from her public actions, and all we know is that he crossed her path at just the right moment. Tomkinson was a Cambridge graduate, and Cambridge dons were among his friends; this at once gave Emily an advantage in dealing with them which she had hitherto lacked. A little younger than Emily, he was a bachelor and had been a Wrangler and a rowing blue, and thus had access to two quite different worlds. He was now Managing Director of the Sun Insurance Company, and to Emily's delight he had recently become, through his interest in education, secretary of the London Local Examinations Board. What could be better?

Two days after they met Emily overcame her shyness enough to write him a short letter asking for his help; an enthusiastic acceptance lifted her spirits. She invited him to dine at 17 Cunningham Place, where he fascinated Emily and her mother with his reminiscences of Cambridge life. She gave him the Dyke Acland and all the other letters to read, and his laughter sealed their friendship.

John Potts had recently succeeded Liveing as Secretary of the Cambridge Syndicate, and he was more kindly disposed towards Emily than his predecessor. He made himself plain at once: there would be no change of policy, but since he felt it only fair to look into the matter a little further, he had discussed it with several friends (all male, of course) – 'most had laughed, some thought they ought to think about it, but all ended by looking grave'. He evidently hoped that this warning would be enough to put her off altogether. Emily took the letter to Henry Tomkinson, who reassured her. He knew John Potts well, for they had been at Trinity together: 'There is no harm in him. He simply gets scared at the slightest sign of innovation. Conciliate him if you can.'

Henry Tomkinson's advice was always practical. The following week he turned up at Cunningham Place to show Emily a short cut through her difficulties. Had she thought of sending out circulars to as many people as possible, explaining exactly what she was trying to do? If not, he would draft one for her. He would also talk personally to every one of twenty-eight members of the London committee, asking for their support.

Dyke Acland had written again suggesting an experimental examination for girls, for a single year only. Henry Tomkinson advised her 'to take it', and Emily at once did so. How good it was to be shown exactly what to do in a straightforward way! She told Henry Tomkinson in a grateful letter: 'there is nothing so provoking as being told vaguely that things will do.'

The months rolled by without Emily noticing them. By the end of October, to her great joy she received a favourable answer from the Cambridge syndicate: they would allow the experimental examination for girls, but the committee would have to make their own arrangements 'as to place, collection of papers and examiners' by 14 December.

Cool on most occasions, Emily was thrown into dreadful agitation by this news. Only six weeks to find candidates, where there had never been candidates before! She wrote in despair to Lizzie Garrett that 'this has been going on for weeks, and they only tell me now! Can I do it?' And to Anna Richardson, 'Our breath was quite taken away on Saturday by receiving quite unexpectedly a favourable reply from the Cambridge syndicate . . . I fully expected they would politely get rid of us by saying it was beyond their powers . . . We have only six weeks to work up our candidates, and who can expect them to come up on so short a notice? . . . We shall look unspeakably foolish if we have no candidates after all, and people won't understand the reason.'

By some miracle, 91 girls entered, 25 of them from Miss Buss's school. It seemed that at last headmistresses were seeing the advantages this examination would bring to their schools; whereas before they had turned their backs on the idea, they now seemed to be falling over themselves to get their pupils entered.

All Emily's friends rallied round. Lady Goldsmid and Mr Heywood offered to pay all the girls' expenses, while Mrs Gurney was prepared to provide meals and chaperonage and showed her good heart by putting up five of Miss Buss's pupils in her house. The choice of examiners proved difficult. The dons whom she approached with Llewelyn's help demurred at taking on so much work for £3, which was all Emily could afford to offer, but after a little persuasion agreed to do it for £5, the extra money coming out of Henry Tomkinson's pocket. Nevertheless they demanded unlimited time for correcting the papers.

Another problem was posed by the schoolmistresses, some of whom developed second thoughts and had to be reassured. They feared that the examination would foster the spirit of confidence and independence 'which is so common among girls of the present day', but Emily guessed that this was only an excuse and that they really feared that the examination would be the beginning of a new and better-educated type of girl who would take their jobs from them.

Now that they had been given the go-ahead, with the help of Isa Craig Emily set about making the necessary arrangements, for time was beginning to run out. They must first find a room large and comfortable enough to accommodate so many girls. They tramped all over London, but such a room appeared not to exist. In the end, they hired a small and rather expensive room in Suffolk Street, just off Pall Mall, which had the advantage that it was close to Willis's Rooms, where the boys were to be examined, so that it would be easy to hand over the papers quickly. 'After all, they are the lords and we the beggars,' Emily wrote to Mr Charles, the clerk in charge of making arrangements for the boys.

New problems arose hourly, and Emily was on her feet from dawn to dusk. Chairs had to be hired, pens, ink and paper bought and carried to the Suffolk Street rooms. One morning she was busy placing the chairs and looking dishevelled, when the door opened and in marched Henry Sidgwick, a Fellow of Trinity and a member of the Local Examinations Syndicate, whom Emily had only met once before. He had come, he said, to find out what arrangement she had made for dealing with 'faints and hysterics'. At first Emily thought that he was referring to her and replied coldly that she never suffered from either. Sidgwick assured her solemnly that on the rare occasions in the past when girls had been examined fainting had been quite a problem. He hoped that the Syndicate had saved her from this embarrassment by insisting on separate rooms for male and female candidates. In icy tones Emily replied that as long as the papers were the same it made no difference whether girls and boys sat the examination together or not. For weeks Emily had been trying to meet Henry Sidgwick, but he had avoided her. Now that a merciful Providence had sent him to her, she would not let him go until he had answered her question: were the girls' results to be published in the same list as the boys'? 'If anybody thinks that any possible advantage can be gained by separating the names I should be inclined to give up the point,' Emily had written to him some weeks earlier, but had received no reply. Taken by surprise by this young woman's anger, he now answered stiffly that he thought she knew that the results of the girls' examination were not to be published at all and haltingly tried to explain that if the results were as bad as everyone expected publication could have a most adverse effect on young girls. Emily suppressed a hot retort. Henry Tomkinson had warned her to be conciliatory, otherwise she would only gain a momentary self-satisfaction at the cost of perhaps losing all.

On the day of the examination no one was more nervous than Emily. But she hid her fears and presented a smiling face to the girls, greeting them all at the door and trying to make them feel at ease. When helping to seat them she became calmer, and had time to look round at their cheerful expressions and to note how composed they seemed.

In a moment of weakness (and against the advice of Henry Tomkinson) Emily had consented to the girls being tested for proficiency in reading and writing (the boys were not tested in this way, of course). But she now bitterly regretted her weakness as she saw her flock roughly handled by the examiner, who insisted on the girls standing up to read, calling them by their first names and generally treating them as though they were still at kindergarten. He added insult to injury by dictating at a snail's pace, showing that he knew nothing about female sensitivity. When the papers were opened, the girls remained calm, and very

52

soon the room settled into a breathless silence, broken only by the scraping of pens and an occasional cough. Emily took her seat by the fire, pad of paper on her knee headed 'Examination now going on'. She felt she must scribble a line to Lizzie on such a triumphant day, for she knew that this close friend would be thinking of her: 'We are enjoying ourselves here,' she wrote. 'The girls are very nice, and Mr Charlton, the conducting examiner, keeps coming up to me and testifying in whispers to their not looking jaded and to their seeming to enjoy it.'

Interruptions were becoming too frequent, and were most distracting. Dr Strasser (an enemy) came to see how the girls were getting on. Emily indicated that he was breaking their concentration as he walked slowly round the room, scrutinising the bent heads, a look of astonishment on his face: 'I gave him no encouragement to stay,' Emily wrote severely to Lizzie next day. 'Perhaps he was disappointed that there were no mishaps, no stretcher cases, no mass hysteria. Indeed, everything went well and happily, except the porter, who made it a principle to conceal himself whenever we wanted him.'

It was over. Emily stayed behind in the empty room after the papers had been safely dispatched.She felt as though she was dreaming. Now that they had all gone she could hardly believe that anything unusual had happened. How wonderfully ordered and calm the whole performance had been; the girls had behaved as if they had been doing this kind of thing every day.

She had been so full of admiration for them all that she had quite forgotten that the schoolmistresses had written a joint letter to her, asking – or rather demanding – that prizes be given when the results were announced. Emily replied that she much preferred certificates of proficiency, but she had to give way to what she called 'unseemly clamour'. They made such foolish suggestions! If there must be prizes, Emily said, let them be books, but the schoolmistresses wanted something more spectacular – laurel wreaths, or a sovereign struck specially to mark the occasion. Some wrote to ask whether it was true that the prizes were to be presented by the bishop of Oxford. 'How did these rumours get about?' Emily wrote to Henry Tomkinson. 'What ever happens, we should not want the bishop of Oxford. No one supposes that girls would want ear-rings, but the privilege of free choice is very dear to them, perhaps because they so seldom have the chance of exercising it!'

When the results came, they were better than Emily had dared hope. She confessed to her brother that after the first surprise she found the figures extremely gratifying; only six had failed out of 91 candidates.

The other 85 had all passed with varying degrees of credit; so much for the critics who had said that girls could not compete on equal terms with boys! But all had done badly in arithmetic.

Emily had always thought that too much fuss was made about arithmetic. Was it really as absolutely necessary as the authorities claimed? Recently she had met, and had a long talk with, a Miss Prescott, who had been teaching in Bombay, where Indian girls found difficulty in grasping even the rudiments of the subject: 'So I asked why should not Bombay girls learn Latin instead? It is much more useful than arithmetic to women who have no money to add up.' Yet despite the arithmetic the results were so good that congratulations poured in: Matthew Arnold, Harriet Martineau, Octavia Hill were among the many who wrote. Octavia Hill, who knew something of Emily's difficulties, wrote with delight of the good effect of the examination on the pupils at her own school: 'Some such plan as the Local Examinations must be adopted before the education of our girls will improve.' Well-wishers and friends were talking as if the battle was over and victory already won, but Emily had to remind them that the campaign had only just begun. This examination had been only an experiment, and the Cambridge syndicate would not want to repeat it unless she kept up the pressure.

She had persuaded the Social Science Association to hold a special meeting in April to discuss three points arising from the experimental examination: (1) that the girls who took part were unharmed by their efforts; (2) that schools had greatly benefited, since it showed up the weak spots in their teaching; (3) that it was desirable to make the examination regular and annual. Emily laid her plans for the meeting with great care. Lord Lyttelton promised to preside, and J.S. Mill said he would come if he could: 'We are going to invite Cambridge men, especially enemies, to give them a chance of being converted,' Emily wrote to Henry Tomkinson. She had already asked him to come and testify 'if you can conscientiously' that the candidates behaved perfectly and that nothing alarming or scandalous happened. She had given him a few instructions, since even the best-intentioned men sometimes put their foot in it: 'If you will state facts, that is just what is wanted. I only hope the speakers on our side won't go off, as our enemies always do, into theories – it is dreadfully unsafe!'

Emily had not lived in a male-dominated household for nothing, and she perfectly understood how a man's mind worked. She wanted to squash once and for all the stupid theory that 'learning will make women masculine'. With this in mind she invited to the meeting a handful of pretty, smiling, feminine girls, known to have academic aspirations, Lizzie Garrett (a strong-minded young woman if ever there was one) among them, in order to show the enemy that education left a woman's femininity untouched.

On the night of the meeting it looked at first as though everything was going to pass off perfectly. Henry Tomkinson assured his audience that all the rules had been followed to the letter: 'There is no ground whatever for supposing that girls are not fit to take part in these examinations.' Dr Plumtree of Queens' College, Cambridge, was amongst the first of the dons to speak, but all he did was to restate what could not be hidden – that the girls' arithmetic was deplorable. Dr Robey, a Fellow of St John's and author of a Latin grammar, spoke last, and revived the old argument that a lower standard should be set for girls, the very danger that Dr Blackwell had warned against in her lecture. Emily was furious: 'Dr Robey's speech was the most mischievous of the evening,' she wrote in high anger to Henry Tomkinson. 'My views on the subject are exceedingly strong.'

In order to combat the forces of conservatism and prejudice and to show the benefits of an equal education for boys and girls, Emily read a carefully prepared paper at the next social science meeting in the summer of 1864 in York. It was not well received. There was a lot of talk about women becoming strong-minded if needlework and music were neglected in favour of more academic subjects, because then they would no longer be 'good sisters, wives, mothers and nurses'. Women did not need to concern themselves with subjects unsuited to the female mind like arithmetic. Instead, 'let them understand all domestic questions and so much of the accomplishments of life as will tend to make the evenings delightful'. Several others added that the mere idea of girls sitting examinations in competition with boys took their breath away. University men were not the best judges of a young girl's ability, and the examiners ought to be married men of older standing and more knowledge of society.

The temper of the meeting was rising, and there were cheers when the Archbishop of York made an impassioned speech against girls sitting any examination whatsoever. 'The education of girls,' he said, striking one hand against the other as though he was in the pulpit, 'ought to be organised separately by a council of ladies and clergymen, and not by the universities, who can know nothing about it.' He sat down amid tremendous applause as Canon Norris got up to support his chairman. He opened his speech with what was now becoming a well-worn cliché: 'Unmarried men do not know how to examine girls; celibate Fellows of colleges, living in the semi-monastic atmosphere of the university, know only that girls are bought up in some private, mysterious way to be as unlike men as possible. Let men or women, if they wish it, study the same branches of knowledge with a most obdurate liberty, but let them do it, each in his own way, following their own nature freely and under nature's free unconscious guidance.'

Emily seethed with anger. Now she knew exactly what she was up against: ignorance, prejudice, stupidity and fear. To have to fight one would be enough, but all four was asking too much. And Canon Norris was a scholar of repute! Later Henry Tomkinson explained to her that Canon Norris had a clutch of unmarried daughters, all replicas of their mother and all living at home, whom he was dying to get off his hands. Emily's answer was short and sharp: 'Education has done little for men.'

These two meetings had shown her how profound was the ignorance and how intense the prejudice which opposed her, and how hard a task she had taken upon herself. The good results of the examination evidently counted for little or nothing, and in any case she now realised why Cambridge had given in so easily. They were prepared for a single experiment, but not for regular annual examinations. Her resolution tightened; nothing would make her give up the fight, however long and hard it might be.

She had already started to work on a report showing how beneficial this examination had been. For instance, ten of Frances Buss's pupils had failed in arithmetic, so she had set about raising the standard of mathematical teaching in her school immediately. Frederick Denison Maurice did the same at Queen's College. 'The benefits of an external standard could scarcely have been more conclusively shown,' Emily wrote in her report. Meanwhile, she herself set out to discover what actually went on in girls' schools. Nobody seemed to know, not even the parents who so trustingly sent their daughters to these schools. It seemed as though all they wanted was to get their daughters off their hands for a year or two. Mothers had a lot to answer for, she thought. It was they who dinned it into their daughters' heads that men did not respect clever women – worse, that they did not want to marry a clever woman, and certainly not women cleverer or better educated than they were themselves. Girls had to take this kind of talk seriously, for if they did not, how would they ever escape from home? It was only the exceptional ones who fought against such pernicious talk, and Emily felt that they deserved help.

'Women are not healthy,' Emily wrote. 'It is a rare thing to meet with a lady who does not suffer from headaches, langour, hysteria or some illness showing a want of stamina. Dullness is not healthy, and the lives of ladies, it must be confessed, are exceedingly dull. Men think dullness is calm. If they had ever tried what it is to be a young lady, they would know better . . . Of literature, women of the middle classes know next to nothing. Newspapers are scarcely supposed to be read by women at all. When the Times is offered to a lady, the sheet containing the advertisements and the births, deaths and marriages is considerately selected. Almost complete mental blankness being the ordinary condition of women, it is not to be wondered at that their opinions, when they happen to have any, are not much respected.'

Emily wrote this in a white-hot fury, when the mind discards everything except what is necessary. Her temper was not improved by the first sentence in a letter from Thomas Markby, a Fellow of Trinity Hall, who had temporarily taken over from John Potts as Secretary of the Cambridge Local Examinations Syndicate. With great solemnity he warned her that there were too many difficulties in the way of granting her request for an annual examination. Emily interpreted his words to mean that boys would not like to be beaten by girls. 'The scheme for boys,' he wrote, 'has now become so large that there are not enough examiners to go round, and if the university takes on extra work the local examinations might have to be stopped altogether.' ('Nonsense,' Emily wrote in the margin, 'plenty of idle young dons with nothing to do.') Then quite suddenly his tone changed, and as Emily read on she became more and more puzzled by his contradictory views as he added: 'I do not see at all why you should not get what you want without the official assistance of the University. If you can hold together a permanent committee in London and keep in correspondence with one or two resident members of the Universities . . . you would readily find a body of competent examiners to undertake the work.'

So there was hope after all! 'Oh what a lot of misery he caused me before he came to the point,' Emily wrote to Lizzie. Six months later he changed his mind again. He was now full of gloom and despondency, so that Emily suspected that he was a man too easily swayed by the last person he had talked to. She had written to ask that if the examinations were made permanent, the girls' class-lists should be printed alongside those of the boys. 'I object very much to bringing girls' names before the public,' he wrote. 'I should be sorry to encourage that furious competition which is the curse of our schools and universities.'

At heart, this strange man was kindly and helpful, and he had no idea of the effect of his pessimism on the recipient. That was one of the pernicious results of living a monastic life in college. Markby so mellowed that he soon invited Emily to lunch in his college rooms, and she accepted. She went to Cambridge well primed with facts and ready to argue her case, only to find him charming and conciliatory and ready to help her fight her battles.

*　　*　　*

Matters were coming to a head, and like a good general Emily scrutinised her troops for weaknesses.

The existing committee was too small to be effective, and was the weaker because it consisted mainly of women. It must be enlarged at once. Putting respectability before power, she wrote to Dr Alford, Dean of Canterbury, asking him to act as chairman. When in London, he always stayed with the Llewelyn Davieses, so Emily knew him, though not well. His views on women's education and the injustices of the laws against them were only moderately favourable, but she felt that with care and tact he could be won over. Public speaking was not his *forte*, for he had the fatal habit of repeating himself, and at the special Social Service meeting in June he had made Emily smile when he suggested that 'the unobtrusiveness which is the charm and strength of our Englishwomen would be quite sacrificed were women to become educated'. He had developed tentative scruples about degrees for women after attending Frances Power Cobbe's lecture in 1862, and Emily had to explain that she was certainly not yet agitating for degrees for women but for something much more elementary – to have Local Examinations made permanent for girls. After she had spelled this out most carefully, Dr Alford consented to act as chairman. A well-known economist, Dr Hodgson, and an old friend, Mrs Charlotte Manning, consented to work with Dr Alford. Long ago Henry Tomkinson had been co-opted on to the women's committee, and had always been the greatest help. She was a little dismayed to discover that she was leaning on him more and more, and hoped very much that people were not beginning to notice. How much wiser and more competent he was than other men!

A petition was the next step. When consulted, John Potts of Cambridge thought this a good idea as long as it contained distinguished names. 'One scarcely imagines that the mere fact of being a marchioness will count for much at Cambridge,' was her dry reply, yet she bowed to his judgement and wrote to as many well-known and titled people as possible. Nearly a thousand consented to let their names go forward, and the petition was well received by the Council of the Senate, the governing body of the university, although Dr Whewell, Vice-Chancellor and Master of Trinity, asked for 'time and quiet to study the question'. This was annoying, because he obviously intended to put it on one side and forget about it.

Little things could tip the scales. Dr Whewell had been annoyed by an article in the *Spectator* defending Emily and praising her tenacity and ingenuity. He took this personally, so persuaded the Vice-Master, Professor Thompson, to see that none of the Trinity dons voted for Emily's scheme. 'You would think,' Emily wrote to Henry Tomkinson, 'that two such highly-educated men would want all the women in the country to be educated too.'

*   *   *

The vote in the Senate about annual examinations was to take place on Thursday, 9 March, at noon. Emily had forgotten that every Cambridge MA was entitled to vote, whether resident or not, so Thomas Markby's note alarmed her: 'Bring up everyone you can,' he warned. 'It is possible, but I think not very likely, that the enemy may whip up the country clergy against it.' She found this very alarming, for she had not met a single clergyman, except her brother, who supported her. The worst that could happen was to lose by a vote or two, for then she would have to start the fight all over again in the face of an even greater handicap than at present. 'If one had only a personal interest in the matter it would be impossible to interfere,' she wrote to Anna Richardson.

The night before the vote was to be taken Mrs Russell Gurney gave a small dinner party for Emily at her London house in order to take her mind off her troubles. But she had left it rather late, and could not get the guests she wanted at short notice. Not unnaturally, Emily was not at her best, and she was not helped by the presence of Leslie Stephen, deaf as a post, and the formidable sister of an Oxford professor, whose glance could have stopped a wild boar in its tracks. Miss Smith was not slow to let Emily know her brother's views. 'Things are very serious,' she said, drawing her chair closer to her victim, so that they could talk confidentially. 'The country clergy are expected, and all are against. I should drop it, Miss Davies, if I were you.'

Mrs Russell Gurney begged Leslie Stephen to go to Cambridge to vote, but he shouted back that he could not do so since he had been writing against the idea for weeks in the *Saturday Review*. 'The suspense is acute,' Emily wrote to Henry Tomkinson that night. Next day, as she paced the floor of her tiny dining room in Cunningham Place (the room that doubled as her office), she was very low indeed, yet every time the tiny spark of hope died almost completely, she managed to fan it back into life.

It had not occurred to Thomas Markby to put Emily out of her misery by telegraphing the result to her; he forgot that any news is better than none. Then, as despair descended on her, there was a knock on the door. Emily rushed to open it. 'It was a note from Miss Buss. An undergraduate whom she knew had telegraphed to her. I was almost afraid to open the letter', Emily confessed, 'that gave me the wonderful news that we had won.'

There were no more details, but Emily was content. By evening she was in such good spirits that she went to a party given by Emily Faithfull, and on the way called at the rectory to give her brother the good news. Next day she learned that it had been a close-run contest, 55 votes to 51. As usual, Lizzie was the first to congratulate her: 'This will be the stepping-stone to much more. It is to you . . . that our success is mainly due.' Henry Tomkinson learned the news from *The Times*. A directors' meeting in London had prevented him from going to Cambridge to vote. If Emily had lost by a single vote, how guilty he would have felt! 'I know you would have gone if you could,' Emily wrote kindly. 'The scheme has prospered by a majority of four. I had so thoroughly made up my mind to defeat, never having counted on success even when things were promising, that now it has come I can only half believe it.'

Victory was only won at a cost. The Local Examination for girls was now permanent. But there were to be no class-lists and no names of female candidates were to be published. Emily knew that, small though the price seemed at the time, the prohibition held within itself the seeds of future trouble. Neither the Women's Movement as a whole, nor the girls themselves, would put up with enforced anonymity for long, for if no names were published there would be no outward sign of victory, and at this early stage outward signs mattered a great deal – almost as much as the victory itself.

The Vice-Chancellor sent Emily a cheque for £10, the fee for invigilating.

Emily thought of framing it, on the ground that 'I suppose it is the first payment ever made by the university to a woman not a menial'.

5

Spoiled Children of Fortune

In June 1865, when the fight to make local examinations a regular yearly event was at its height and Emily knee-deep in correspondence about it, she heard that a Royal Commission had been appointed to look into the condition of boys' schools. Immediately she saw her chance and without hesitating for a moment seized it with both hands. This was a heaven-sent opportunity and one she must not miss; but how to convince the Commissioners that to investigate girls' schools was just as important?

On the same day that she heard that she had won her point on local examinations, she put her triumph behind her and wrote to the three Commissioners whom she had the good fortune to know, asking them to include girls' schools in their inquiries. She did this with a certain amount of confidence after listening to a speech by Lord Brougham at a social science congress a few months before, in which he loudly condemned the current provision in education made for middle-class girls. He had wound up his speech by telling his audience that the teachers in the schools frequented by these children were subject to no higher authority than their fellow teachers: '. . . it has become a saying that when anyone has failed in all other ways to procure a livelihood, let him keep a school or let her become a school-mistress'.

She picked her three Commissioners with care before writing a carefully worded letter. George Grote, Vice-Chancellor of London University did not reply, Thomas Dyke Acland was evasive, and Matthew Arnold unhelpful: 'I hardly think,' he wrote, 'that the New Commission with all that it will have on its hands will be sitting to inquire into girls' schools'. These were old tricks but Emily was not to be put off. She travelled to Cambridge where the Commission had its headquarters, to talk to Dyke Acland, the most approachable of the three, but all that the hour-long conversation produced was a feeble 'nothing can be done in a hurry'. Determined not to be put off Emily organised one of her high-powered petitions which included among its signatories a number of schoolmistresses: Octavia Hill, Charlotte Manning, Fanny Metcalfe, Frances Buss and Hannah Pipe. Dorothea Beale, ungracious as ever, refused to allow her name to go forward. The appeal was sent to Henry Robey, Secretary to the Commission, a Cambridge don and a man in a highly influential position, who gave Emily her first ray of hope. He sent her a message to let her know that the commissioners had reported favourably on her request: 'although the Senate who have the final word in these matters may be of quite another opinion'. At this stage she could not hope for more, but anxious to get started she invited headmistresses to Cunningham Place in order to discover their grievances and the difficulties under which they laboured daily: '. . . I expect it will be useful as a propaganda instrument,' she told Barbara, 'the most intelligent enlightening the dark and ignorant'. Laughingly she told Anna Richardson, whose father was in the Church, that the meeting would be '. . . analogous to a clerical meeting' which was all fuss and bustle but produced nothing.

She needed some weapon, some concrete evidence with which to fight the Commissioners, inside information which would tell her why essential subjects like arithmetic, English and history were not adequately taught even at the lowest levels. The answer that was given was simple: there was no one properly qualified to teach more than simple sums and the mere rudiments (often wrong) of history and English when the schools were run for girls only.

Emily could not let matters rest there. While waiting for the Commissioners to make up their minds she decided to set up her own investigation into girls' schools; thus, well primed with facts which could not be disputed, she would be well armed to fight a refusal. It was too big a job to undertake alone – time would be against it – but the only women to help her would be those with leisure, perhaps the ladies of the Kensington Society, elderly voluntary workers for the Women's Movement, like Barbara's aunt, Julia Smith and her circle, highly intelligent and passionately dedicated. Could these women be persuaded to look into the state of schools each in her own area? When enough information had been collected she would prepare a paper for the Social Science Association on the state of girls' schools. With such evidence, the Commissioners could never refuse her a hearing. The only objection to this excellent plan was the evasiveness of the schoolmistresses. Emily herself had sometimes found them untruthful; at all costs they did not want their ignorance discovered. Therefore tact was essential. It would be important to remember that, shocking though girls' schools were, there was no law preventing an unqualified woman from setting up a school. Spinsters of slender means or destitute widows with a family to support did so frequently; their assistants mere ignorant pupil teachers, young drudges too frightened of losing their miserable jobs to demand a proper salary.

By the autumn the Society's findings were in Emily's hands. They were very different from what she had expected, but no less enlightening. The report on teaching was short and thin because there was so little evidence to discuss. History and geography were taught by rote, English grammar was found too confusing to be understood, while arithmetic seldom got beyond mere addition and subtraction. But if the Society could not report as fully as it could have wished on teaching, it did a splendid job on conditions in the schools and the pinch-penny way in which they were run. Julia Smith noticed that in sewing classes the pupils hemmed old sheets or darned worn blankets belonging to the school, for instance. Girls' boarding schools were housed in old-fashioned buildings with unhygienic sanitary arrangements; dormitories were overcrowded and dirty, beds too close together, blankets and sheets torn and unclean and too thin to give warmth; windows were closed by day to keep out the dust and at night 'to exclude dangerous air'. Washing facilities were few and far between, and since hot water was expensive, cleanliness was not encouraged. Food was of poor quality and there was too little of it, so that the girls were hungry and suffered from indigestion, acne and langour. Girls were talked into taking music lessons (an expensive extra) and forced to practise in unheated rooms early in the morning: 'the movements of their fingers would generate heat'!

These were hard facts that Emily could use, and exactly the kind of thing that a committee of men would never have discovered. Emily herself had not been idle: she had been investigating the way religion was handled in girls' schools, and was surprised to find that it was treated as a delicate subject; a lot of nonsense was talked and much of it simply wrong. Rigid old-fashioned religious ideas went down well with parents although badly with the pupils – a fact that did not count since the school was not run for them. Most of the schools had a convenient rule – that should a parent object strongly to something and ask for it to be changed, the headmistress 'graciously gave way'.

To sort her information on schools into a form suitable for a speech was a laborious job, for some of the Kensington ladies repeated themselves and others felt so ill at the sight of so much disorder and even squalor (and by the dreadful realisation that they had forced their daughters to endure it), that much that could have been useful passed them by. But no matter how many omissions, Emily was grateful.

By this time Emily had become a very able public speaker, partly because she enjoyed talking to a large audience, getting the attention and holding it, partly because she was working for a cause dear to her heart. Her voice, for such a small, fragile woman, was a surprise: it was clear and carried well and could be heard distinctly by those at the back of a hall. Nerves had long since vanished. This was not the only difference a few short years had made. Her attitude to the Association itself had undergone a chance. Once she had delighted in the thought that there was one society, at least, that looked on men and women as equals: this had been progress, but recently her expectations of that progress had become almost cynical. Members had become lazy, too pleased with themselves as symbols of an enlightened age, and prepared to sit back and let others do the work. It was a bad sign, too, that some of its most distinguished members had drifted away, too occupied with more important things to spare the time, leaving only the mediocre behind.

Emily had remained an active member for want of a better platform to air her views. From the very beginning Lizzie had warned her that she was expecting too much from such a motley crew. She called them 'reactionary and a lot of puppets'. Could Emily tell her how much good they had done women in general? Very little, except to allow women to read their own speeches. Emily had to admit that it had been a disappointment when Lord Brougham resigned and a great pity that Lord Salisbury and Lord Lyttleton hardly attended any more, unless some special person was speaking. For the past year Llewelyn Davies (one of the founders) had been far too busy in his large parish to spare an evening for the Association. Without the invigorating presence of the men who had kept the meetings on their toes, the society had begun to run downhill. Even Emily got the distinct impression that this once-useful body and all that it stood for had passed its prime; one night she made a passionate appeal to the audience for their support in her fight with the Royal Commissioners, but got little response. The atmosphere was cool, to say the least, and the clapping perfunctory. 'I got the feeling,' she told Anna, 'that I was beating my head against a brick wall and the group of faces looking at me from the front row was distinctly hostile. Afterwards only Lord Lyttleton shook my hand and praised my speech.'

Emily disliked wasting her time on second-rate performances by lethargic people. Perhaps the time had come to drop the Association altogether, or to try to stir the members to action. In the end she did neither, for she had more important things to think about: her energies had to go into provoking the Commissioners into action. She wrote to George Grote very politely: 'I hope you will not think it unpardonably troublesome when I again venture to ask your help in connection with female education. Hitherto we have not been able to discover what was intended, reports and opinions being contradictory.' But Grote was too weighed down with work to give any hope, nor would he enlighten her in any way. '. . . I have some doubt whether the Commission is likely to undertake the work'. It was all very frustrating.

Recently Emily had begun to wonder if her success was not doing her harm in some quarters. Her friends now looked on her as some kind of miracle worker ('You can do it, you always do'), who had only to clap her hands and whatever she wanted would come about. She had first noticed this over-confidence in her abilities when she asked the Kensington Society to help her. They had looked surprised and many of them showed a touching faith in her which she did not like. 'Of course they will not dare to refuse you now,' they said, but she knew only too well that they could do exactly that. At one time such encouragement would have braced her and added a new dimension to her courage, but now she feared it was merely an automatic response. Only Henry Tomkinson knew how low her morale had fallen, and he agreed when she said that it was not as if she was asking the Commissioners to do anything revolutionary. As she had discovered when researching for the paper on 'The Application of Funds to the Education of Girls' which she presented at the Social Science Congress in 1864, no distinction had usually been drawn between boys and girls in the statutes of the many charitable schools founded in the sixteenth century, but in a large number of cases girls had been progressively excluded from benefiting from them in later years. She was therefore not proposing a revolutionary innovation, but reverting to the practice of a more enlightened past.

It was vitally important that she should get her way, for if she failed the Women's Movement might be put back for several years. Despite Henry's sympathy she felt very alone. Her mother saw nothing amiss: Mrs Davies had relied on Emily for years to brace and encourage her, and take as many burdens off her shoulders as she could. With no invalid husband to care for, she was taken up with her own aches and pains and hardly looked beyond her own home. It was as though domesticity and ill-health had worn her out. Yet on the rare occasions when Emily confided in her mother she was surprised how much common sense she possessed. Emily could just vaguely remember that once she had been a pretty, lively girl, intelligent and optimistic. Where had it all gone? It was women like this whom Emily wanted to help. It was too late for her mother and all the thousands of women like her, but what of those yet unborn? Sometimes she wondered if she had done more than just scratch the surface.

The Commission had hung fire for over a year and Emily had quite failed to discover what was happening: everything was veiled in mystery, so it was not surprising that her troubles were much on her mind, driving out all festive feeling. By midday on Christmas Day Mrs Davies had developed a temperature and had to go to bed, and since the two maids had returned to Gateshead for a holiday, she was unable to join the family party at the rectory where there were children to entertain and cheer. But Emily did not mind; she was in no mood for jollity.

The New Year 1865 came and went. Emily tells us in her 'Family Chronicle' that she opened her bedroom window in order to hear the bells ring out the old year and usher in the new with a dreadfully depressed feeling that in the past twelve months she had achieved very little. New Year's Day was celebrated at Cunningham Place with Llewelyn and his family joining them as they always did. Mrs Davies came downstairs, there was turkey, plum pudding and a small tree with the children's

65

presents. Next day Emily went skating and returned in a much better mood: she was full of life and saw no reason why the Commissioners should refuse her. She made a late New Year's resolution that she would stay hopeful until she knew for certain one way or the other.

In March, Llewelyn went to Cambridge to preach in Trinity, his old college. He stayed three days and was just about to leave for Norfolk before returning home when Henry Robey, secretary to the Commission and a fellow of the college, came to see him. He brought a message for Emily: 'He asked me to tell you,' Llewelyn wrote, 'that the Commissioners have decided to grant your request to extend their inquiries into girls' schools and that he himself would be glad to aid the inquiry in any way he can'.

The news ('so hoped for, so long awaited') was like a flash of light in a dark tunnel. For months Emily had been praying that something like this would happen, but it had been so long delayed that she had come to believe that perhaps it never would. Happiness swept over her, she felt almost faint with joy and relief, and tears filled her eyes. Yet caution kept her silent until, ten days later, written confirmation reached her. Henry Robey wrote in a manner that suggested that the decision to include girls' schools had been settled weeks ago but no one had remembered to tell her.

It was a real triumph, though when she remembered her determination to keep cool whatever happened, Emily did not crow over it. But when in November 1866 (the Commissioners moved slowly) another astonishing letter came from the same source, she can be excused for purring a little: 'The Commissioners had decided to request some ladies to give evidence before Christmas on the subject of girls' schools. It is proposed to examine yourself and some other ladies on that day . . . will that be convenient to you, and whom shall I ask to follow you? I thought of the principal of Bedford College but should be quite ready to adopt any suggestion you will kindly give me . . . If you will draw up some lists of heads under which your evidence could best fall, it will contribute much to the good order of the examination. You will be able to form a better idea than I can, as to the points of most importance, but at any rate I shall be glad to do anything I can.'

The contents of the letter made Emily gasp. The Commissioners had gone further than she ever expected. Five years ago she was quite unknown, now here was a Royal Commission of distinguished men trusting her enough to call upon her expert knowledge. The change was staggering. It meant that the cause of female emancipation had taken a gigantic step forward; it had gained recognition in the highest quarters. Was it too much to believe that the ice was broken and that an immense thaw would follow?

*　　*　　*

During the long months when Emily was waiting to hear from the Commissioners, she had prepared a full and informative, not to say damning, dossier on girls' schools. Now that work was to prove invaluable. With a return of her customary briskness, she took the papers out of their drawer and began to go through them, setting herself imaginary questions and composing short crisp answers, so that she would be well prepared to tell the inquiry exactly what they needed to know. She suggested Miss Buss instead of Mrs Bostock of Bedford College to follow her – 'she has more experience of girls' schools'.

If she was to sing for her supper she would do so to some effect and make other suggestions. Boldly she mentioned the Rev. Mark Pattison, Rector of Lincoln College, Oxford, Professor Huxley and J.S. Mill as witnesses. They held divergent opinions, she knew, but their replies might be most enlightening, for all were experts in one way or another in the field of education. She wrote Henry Robey a letter which shows the authority that she was unconsciously assuming: 'I should like to have Huxley examined about the brain because the physiological argument is constantly used and people believe it. It seems to me the most rational plan to examine schoolmistresses who know the subject . . . but the evidence of distinguished people has more chance of being read. It might answer our purpose best to get someone like Mark Pattison and Lord Wrottesley to testify; I don't think they know anything, but they could be primed.'

In another letter she told Henry Robey 'What I have to say may be arranged under four headings:

1. Local examinations.
2. Education of girls after leaving school.
3. Uses of endowment.
4. Government of endowed schools.'

'Education, of course, means the absence of,' she told Robey, 'but I suppose that heading will be understood as including the want of examinations for women. If you think that these four headings would make a very long story, the uses of endowment might be left out. I should be very sorry to take up too much time so as to run Miss Buss short, as she can speak from long experience on school work and knows the subject thoroughly.'

Emily's great strength, as the Commissioners soon realised, was never to allow her arguments to become smothered in detail. Barbara Stephen tells a story that shows how perfectly Emily understood the necessity of not wandering from the point and thus confusing the issue. When asked to give an opinion on one of her Girton students who was applying for a job, she wrote: 'Miss X does not know what things are important and what are not. It is a bad fault.'

* * *

On 1 December 1866 two purposeful figures descended from a cab outside King's Cross station and made their way to the Cambridge train. Emily and Frances Buss were on their way to be interrogated by the Royal Commissioners. Emily walked with a firm step, confident that she was well prepared for her 'ordeal', for as such both women looked on it. But her spirits were high because she was proud and pleased that she was to be the first woman ever to give evidence before a Royal Commission. She was nervous too, how could she help it?

It was bitterly cold with an east wind blowing, but both women were well wrapped up in thick overcoats and scarves. Frances Buss carried a rug while Emily had had the foresight to bring a food hamper which among other things contained a small flask of brandy. Frances Buss was white with nervous tension. Taken out of her natural environment, that of a school, where as headmistress her word was law, she was ill at ease and fussed about the timetable, her hand luggage and whether she was wise to bring a rug or if it would have been better to bring an umbrella. Did Emily think that there would be time next day to refresh her memory with the notes Emily had given her, or should she do this on the train? She did not want to leave it too late. Emily refused to fuss and outwardly looked calm: her resolve to acquit herself properly kept her going.

Next day, seated at a table face to face with the Commissioners, all nerves fled and Emily was at her best, clear, concise and to the point: she neither hesitated for a word nor repeated herself. By all accounts she was so good that many eyes were opened and consciences stirred. Her evidence brought out the advantages of local examinations, the need for endowments for girls' schools as well as boys', the better training of schoolmistresses, and some provision for the education of girls after school age. Asked what she would recommend for this, she replied that some kind of examination for young women over the age of eighteen was the chief need, and the opening of university examinations would be the most useful direct means. More colleges were needed; 'there are two in London,' she said, 'Bedford and Queen's Colleges but they are kept down by the ignorance of the girls who attend them'.

Frances Buss did better than expected ('I thought your and Miss Buss's examination went off capitally,' Henry Robey wrote) but her voice was a mere whisper and several times the Commissioners had to ask her to speak up. She gained a little confidence when Emily was called back to support her. Nevertheless she talked good sense, stressing the need, as Emily had done, for some form of education after girls left school: 'they are not old enough or strong enough to think for themselves without help or encouragement'. Both women were thankful when the examination was over and they were taken away and refreshed with claret and biscuits.

68

Their 'perfect womanliness' made an impression. Dr Fearon (one of the Commissioners) told his wife that there were tears in Miss Buss's eyes. Miss Davies, he said, left him speechless; such a grasp of the subject and so composed throughout, but not in the least masculine. After her return home, Frances Buss gave in to her pent-up feeling in a letter to Emily, complaining bitterly of the 'terrible examiners' and the dreadful experiences of the day.

As she always did, Emily wrote a full account to Barbara while the facts were still fresh in her mind: '. . . I feel very hopeful about things in general. The schoolmistresses seem very anxious to join in any efforts at improvement and of course this is an immense point. It is quite startling and almost pathetic to see the eagerness with which they responded to any encouragement . . . we had a gathering last week to meet some of the Commissioner people . . . to my surprise several of the schoolmistresses spoke and did it very well.'

Emily never bore a grudge and long ago she had decided to forget the unfriendly attitude of the three leading schoolmistresses in refusing to support her over local examinations. She knew Frances Buss to be, at times, afraid of her own shadow, and that Dorothea Beale, admirable in some ways though she was, could never support a cause that did not directly affect her own school. She was the only headmistress to play a lone game and Emily consequently wrote her off. Lately Frances Buss had become a close friend whose co-operation was worth striving for. Timidity was a terrible weakness which Emily could never understand or forgive. At one time she had thought Henry Robey tainted with it, for it seemed to rule all his actions, but now he was quite changed. Once, after a meeting to discuss whether local examinations should be made permanent, she had called Robey's speech 'the most mischievous of the evening', for every word seemed weighted against her, yet on a later occasion he had impressed her by his generosity and kindness. A little cynically she reflected that nothing gathered support like success. Now, directly after her appearance before the Commissioners, he paid tribute to her enterprise in the warmest terms, saying that he fully appreciated the momentous consequence of her initiative over the Local Examinations and the Royal Commission, but that this impact had as yet affected so few women, adding that the great ferment about the education of women 'would now increase in consequence of what you have done'.

After ignoring her for many months not only were the Commissioners now bombarding her with requests for this and that, but she had even heard Dr Fearon tell Hannah Pipe that as headmistress of one of the top girls' schools she should lead the way in reforming the teaching in order to reach the same standard as that in boys' schools, for a male mind was in no way superior to that of females – a doctrine that Emily had been preaching for years but which Dr Fearon seemed to believe was his own discovery.

6

For Friendship's Sake

When the Commissioners' report was published in 1868 it completely justified Emily's efforts, for it showed clearly the deplorable condition of girls' schools. The report received a great deal of publicity of the kind that would make responsible people stop and reflect in horror at the way the education of girls had been so long neglected. Many a father dwelt with indignation on the deceitful way schools had taken his money and given nothing of value in return. Many remembered with remorse how they had turned a deaf ear to the complaints of their daughters, who had repeatedly said they were learning nothing and had asked to be taken away.

Emily read the report with great care and was satisfied that it set the right tone. There was in schools 'a want of thoroughness and foundation, a want of system, slovenliness showing superficiality, inattention to rudiments, undue time given to accomplishments and those not taught intelligently or in a scientific manner, want of organisation . . . a very inferior set of school books . . . rules put into the memory with no explanation of the principles . . . a tendency to fill rather than to strengthen the mind . . . teachers have not themselves been taught and they do not know how to teach . . . much evidence showing the general indifference of parents . . . a long and inveterate prejudice that girls are less capable of mental cultivation or less in need of it than boys. Over the last half-century a great deal of money had been diverted from the education of girls to that of boys, contrary to the stated intentions of the founders of the charities concerned.'

Even though the Royal Commission had ended satisfactorily (Emily was especially glad to see that it was now acknowledged that girls were as capable of learning as boys) there was still a great deal to be done. Reverting to her original idea that it was higher education that was so totally lacking, and much strengthened in purpose by her many conversations with headmistresses during the period when they had consulted together before the Commission's report, Emily resolved to make another assault on London University and try once more to secure permission for women to matriculate as members of the university. She approached them once again, this time through Dr Plumtree, Dean of Queen's College, Harley Street, but she got little satisfaction. Plumtree wrote to say that all Convocation would be willing to do 'would be to establish an examination for women of an appropriate lower standard . . .' She returned a firm refusal.

For some time Emily had been working on a small but important book on higher education for women, and in 1869 it was published. It showed clearly the kind of education girls needed after school age but could not get, so that their lives were empty and purposeless. But what did she mean by higher education? At that stage Emily meant only a course of more advanced study than the schools of the day could give; she had not yet clearly formulated her later prime objective, university education for women. The book received excellent reviews, and more than one periodical indicated that 'Miss Davies had met the enemy at every point, it was unassailable'. Even the highly critical Helen Taylor praised it warmly: 'I like the book more and more every time I pick it up.' Of course Emily knew that nothing revolutionary would come out of it, it was no more than another step in the slow and often tedious pursuit of justice. She asked her publisher to send a copy to George Fitch, Inspector of Schools, whose ambitions for women were limited to sending them to an establishment where they would acquire 'lady-like manners and deportment'. He had said this to Emily so often that she had come to look on it as a hint that her own manners were not all that could be desired. Nevertheless he lent the book to a friend of Emily's with the following passage marked:

> What society says to them seems to be something to this effect. Either you have force enough to win a place in the world in the face of heavy discouragement, or you have not. If you have, the discipline of the struggle is good for you; if you have not, you are not worth troubling about. Is not this a hard thing to say to commonplace girls, not professing to be better or stronger than their neighbours?

Emily poked fun at the way many mothers really believed that 'book learning', as they called education, 'makes a girl unmanageable'. But what did men look for in a wife? When preparing her book Emily put this question to several young men she knew, and was annoyed when not one mentioned intelligence or companionship. All insisted that 'book learning' took a wife away from her proper duties – looking after home, husband and children. 'Book learning' would make her discontented with her lot.

How long, Emily wondered, would it be before this could be changed?

Emily had come a long way, but she was nowhere near her goal of complete emancipation for women. In her dreams she saw women choosing between marriage and career, even perhaps combining both and doing so with great success. Women varied as much as men, so why should they all be tied down to a life that might not suit some, a life to which they were supposed to be destined before they were born? Progress required women to be educated, and men to change. It was a slow process but she saw some signs of improvement already. Periodicals like *Punch, Macmillan's, Frasers* and the *Spectator* had all begun to show that they approved of educated women. Harold Hutton, editor of the *Spectator*, had published some friendly articles on women's rights or the lack of them, and the necessity for reforms in the law. But one could not be sure that these articles were read by people outside the literary world. The bulk of the population went in for something a great deal less highbrow.

Then quite suddenly the tone of the *Spectator* articles changed. They became almost hostile, and in the very year of the Royal Commission Hutton himself wrote a long and pompous article advocating a lower standard of education for girls, the very thing Emily was fighting against: the strain of hard work was too great for them, mental illness and nervous breakdowns would surely be the result. He added a strong plea that all those with the interests of young girls at heart should accept London University's offer of a special examination of a lower standard than that undertaken by men. Such turncoat behaviour deserved a strong answer, and Hutton received a sarcastic one from an incensed Emily. 'I am afraid that the people who are interested in improving the education of women are a thankless crew. Instead of accepting as a great boon the admission of women to London University in the manner proposed they have come to the conclusion that a special examination is not any boon at all. We will have nothing to do with it . . . we are really obliged to Convocation for their kind intentions in offering us a serpent when we asked for a fish though we cannot pretend to believe that serpents are better for us.'

It was not long before the reason for Hutton's change of attitude became apparent: Emily discovered that he had recently been made a member of the Senate of London University. Thus, having joined the establishment, he forsook his former views as easily as he might have thrown away an old coat. Unwisely Emily continued the correspondence, as did Hutton, long after it should have stopped, and it was developing into a slanging match when Henry Tomkinson persuaded her to put an end to it. London University, he said, was very stuffy and would never give her more: she should put it out of her mind or accept the special examination. But Emily said she would never compromise on that point, and she never did. She did not know it then, but by the time London University opened their examinations to women in 1878 Emily had no further need of them.

* * *

Whatever else it did not do, the Hutton correspondence cleared Emily's mind of many false hopes. She had been wrong to pin her faith on London University; it was a waste of breath to try and persuade them to bend to her will, however reasonable. Might salvation not really lie elsewhere? Had she been looking in the wrong direction all these years? A new idea had suddenly struck her: why should she seek to realise her ideal of higher education for women through London University at all? She had wasted enough time and energy on it already. Why not found a college for women herself, run on exactly the same lines as a college for men? The very idea startled her, yet it seemed only common sense. Besides, she knew that she was always at her best when she relied on herself alone. She tried the idea out on Anna Richardson and was delighted to receive enthusiastic support.

She had no money and little influence (though more than she knew) but many friends to help and advise, and her heart was light as she experienced that wonderful feeling of elation that comes with finding a solution for a long-standing problem. Was such a college feasible or was it a mere vision, with no substance and too difficult to bring about?

Almost breathless with her own daring, she rushed to Scalands to consult Barbara, but the cottage was so full of her lame ducks that although she welcomed Emily warmly it was three days before they were alone long enough for Emily to explain her ideas and ask Barbara for her views. To Emily's delight she at once declared that a college for women had always been her dream. At that time Emily did not know that Barbara's dreams were of ephemeral, insubstantial things that might happen one day in the very distant future and that she always expected someone else to bring them down to earth, while to the practical-minded Emily a college for women was a real possibility, fraught with difficulties but perfectly possible all the same.

That night Emily gave Barbara a full explanation of all she intended to do, and asked for her support. Barbara was hesitant. This year, she explained, she intended staying on in England in order to open up the suffrage question, dropped now for far too long. The idea of a women's college was of course wonderful, but surely Emily would agreed that the suffrage should come first?

Barbara was so full of her own plans that she seemed not to grasp the importance of Emily's, nor that if they were ever to become reality they would require Emily's complete attention, and not only hers but that of everyone that she could draw into her circle for the purpose. Barbara was well aware of Emily's view that education should come first and of her reasons for wanting to delay the suffrage, but she felt that Emily was wrong. She saw the disappointment on Emily's face and immediately used all her persuasive powers to get her to agree – and Barbara could be very disarming when she liked. She knew that once Emily had given her promise to help she would not break it, and without Emily she could never manage at all: Emily was essential to her scheme.

In the end Barbara won. Emily promised to help, albeit reluctantly. She did not mention her college again, nor did Barbara bring it up, but continued to talk of nothing else but ways and means of getting women the vote.

Emily's consent to postpone her own plans while she helped Barbara requires some explanation.

That year Barbara had been very ill with something very like typhoid fever which she had caught while helping her husband with his medical work. She was now recovering, but Emily was not prepared for the sad sight Barbara had become. She had been deeply shocked at the ravages the fever had left: yellow skin, emaciation, her lovely golden hair thin and lifeless. Her tender heart would not allow her to press her own ideas at the expense of Barbara's. Surely it was a sign that Barbara was getting better that she took an interest in the suffrage? If this was so it must be encouraged. Even when she left Scalands she was far from sure that Barbara would recover. Barbara herself made light of her illness, but to Emily it was terrible to see one usually so beautiful and vital lose her looks and her strength.

She was reluctant to leave Scalands because this was the one place where she could get peace and quiet to think about her ideas and put them into some sort of order. She had fallen in love with the place the moment she saw it, and it was exactly the right background for a glamorous woman like Barbara. Set in the heart of the country, simple without artificiality, it was cut off and remote, yet it had riches galore for flowers and fruit grew in profusion. It annoyed Emily to hear the Rossettis and their friends disparage the little house which they used as their own, grumbling at the cold and the draughts and the irregular meal-times, for even painters are human. But Emily was made of sterner stuff and enjoyed all the free and easy ways of her hostess, even the draughts. It has been said that Emily was impervious to her surroundings, but no one could write of Scalands as she did without a deep sensitivity to the beauty of nature. In 1863 Emily had written to Anna: 'Scalands is not a place for all the year round, but in the heat of summer I don't think I have ever been in such a reposeful retreat. There are noises but they are all rural, the murmuring of the wind in the trees, buzzing insects, barking dogs, lowing of bullocks, birds twittering, nothing to remind one of mental labour and stress.'

Emily looked on Barbara as a sister, confided in her, trusted her, tried out her new ideas on her before she ever mentioned them to another soul. Years ago, possibly at that first meeting in Algiers in 1858, Emily had got it into her head that Barbara was a sophisticated being who knew the world, a fearless creature who trod the earth like a goddess and who had every right to be admired. Barbara's beauty blinded her a little to her faults and she excused many a stupid peccadillo on the ground that beautiful women lived in a world apart: 'they don't think in the same way as we ordinary mortals'. The warmth of Emily's affection obscured the lack of it in Barbara, who was generous in material things but quite incapable of deep unselfish love. Nevertheless, though so different in temperament, the two women got on together very well. Somewhat mistakenly, Emily looked on Barbara's judgement as sound, while Barbara admired the strength and determination of Emily's character, perhaps because she knew that these were the things lacking in her own.

That Barbara was not really interested in her startling idea for a women's college dampened Emily's enthusiasm more than it should have done. She had expected something so different, even excitement to match her own. Shrewd though she usually was with people, she was often in danger of attributing virtues to Barbara she did not possess. Loyalty was one of those virtues and lack of jealousy another. Barbara had deluded herself that she thought of a college for women before Emily. She may have thought of it (Emily certainly believed her when she said so) and she may have been right. But even if she had, it is certain that it was only in a very casual way that went no further than dreams. There is not the slightest evidence that she had ever done anything to put the idea into practice. She had certainly never mentioned it to Emily, with whom she discussed many of the problems facing women.

Nevertheless she could write thus to William Allingham, the Irish poet, when Emily's great idea was about to materialise: 'It is absurd of people to say they will do good and establish this and that, the great thing is to find a good worker with good head, good heart and sound health and then just be content to help them do what they best can without furthering any fixed plans of your own which only shackles the best worker.'

Not long after her letter to Allingham, Barbara wrote to Helen Taylor (who she knew would pass her words on to her step-father J.S. Mill) denigrating Emily's idea of a college: 'I felt just a little that you were not in favour of Miss Davies' scheme. Neither am I, but I am so happy to see anyone work with perseverance and good sense that I feel I cannot do better than support her.' Such duplicity in Barbara startles and dismays. It was simply dishonest to tell one correspondent that the idea of a woman's college was hers not Emily's, another that she was not in favour of it but was prepared patronisingly to go along with it because she admired Emily's pertinacity. But this was Barbara all over, blowing hot one moment, cold the next, incoherent in thought and devoid of practical sense. The only possible excuse for her conduct is that she was beginning to be a sick woman, and that she had been out of England so long that she could not appreciate the full impact of Emily's success over local examinations and the Royal Commission, but remained anchored to her theoretical ideas about enfranchising women.

Emily's friends all knew that she had said, 'education first, the franchise second'. It was one of the things that irritated Millie Fawcett (Lizzie Garrett's youngest sister and wife of the blind MP, Henry Fawcett), a life-long worker for votes for women. So much did it annoy her that she really believed that Emily would not work for the suffrage because she could not be leader of a group, a position Millie believed fervently belonged by right to her. Although she had known Emily for years, she entirely misread her character, and this lack of understanding blinded her to Emily's great qualities. She thought it cowardly of her to keep saying that the vote would come when women were better educated, it was merely an excuse not to face up to the issue. Therefore it puzzled her when she heard that Emily was helping Barbara in her bid for votes for women. When Lizzie told her sister that Emily was doing it for friendship's sake, she thought the reason very stupid. If she had known Emily better she would have seen that she helped Barbara in a hundred different ways purely because Barbara was her friend.

She was doing so again now. She had even promised to attend a meeting of the Kensington Society in the autumn to hear Barbara read a paper, 'Is the Extension of Parliamentary Suffrage Desirable?' As she always did, Barbara sent it to Emily for correction – she had no wish to make a fool of herself in public. With some cutting and shaping and alterations to punctuation and grammar, it was very good, as Emily told her encouragingly – 'It is among the best'. Barbara's speeches were often a problem. The most unconventional of women, she could not understand why certain subjects were taboo – free love, for instance, and what today is called open marriage. Nor did she always take kindly to criticism, although Emily, aware of this, dealt with her work as tactfully as she could. Yet she had to risk a tiff when she wrote to say: 'In your paper there are two or three expressions I should like to see altered. For instance, I don't think it quite does to call the arguments on the other side "foolish". Of course they are, but it does not seem quite polite to say so . . . the enemy always maintains that the disabilities imposed upon women are not personal but solely intended for their good, and I find that nothing irritates men so much as to attribute tyranny to them. I believe that many of them do mean well – or, as they say they do, it seems only fair to admit it and to show them that their well-intended efforts are a mistake and not a crime. Men cannot stand indignation and tho' of course I think it is just, I think it is better to suppress the manifestation of it . . .'

When the Kensington Society meeting came round again, Barbara's speech was received with much applause. Immediately afterwards there was an informal meeting at Barbara's house to discuss the suffrage question and form a committee (to which Emily was elected), its object to present a petition to Parliament on the enfranchisement of women. The general opinion was much in favour and Barbara was greatly heartened by so much support (it did not occur to her that it was unenlightened) and many highly unsuitable names were suggested. She did not like it at all when Emily pointed out bluntly that more than half of them would not do and that a committee of 'wild people' would merely land her in trouble. It was clear that Barbara's marriage and residence abroad had cut her off from English ways and opinions. Even during her six months' sojourn in England she mingled only with painters and literary people whose views were like her own, and she had disregarded Emily's warning that votes for women could hardly be a popular cause in a society which looked askance on all social change. Barbara accused Emily of being 'fixated by matters of propriety and convention', yet according to Charlotte Manning, who was present, Emily was the only one not talking hot air and impracticalities. She told the assembled company that they must not be dazzled by flights of fancy. Most women knew little or nothing about politics. It was simply not true, she said, that their indirect influence was great; this was a myth kept alive by men to keep women quiet, and if they believed it they were certainly not ready for the vote. Women were so ignorant of politics that they could not influence a child. Naturally this did not make Emily very popular.

On her return home Emily wrote to Henry Tomkinson to give him a resumé of the meeting and to ask for his opinion, for despite his bachelor state he was one of those rare men who have an instinctive understanding of a woman's mind. He had realised at once that Emily was a highly honest woman who seldom exaggerated in conversation and almost never in her letters. She called the rather acrimonious Kensington Society meeting 'a subdued kind of agitation for the suffrage'. When she mentioned her own part in trying to subdue over-enthusiastic optimism she merely said 'I have rather tried to stifle it – the scoffers do not see how much is involved in improved education, but they are wide awake about the franchise. You see I mean to compromise, though I would like also to keep clear of hypocrisy and the line between the two is rather faint.'

Henry Tomkinson's reply has not been preserved, but from a letter Emily wrote to Lizzie, it seems that it was not entirely satisfactory. She had wanted him to approve all she had said and done, because she knew that she had been foolish to fall in weakly with Barbara's whims simply because she disliked upsetting her. She was now afraid that Henry Tomkinson would think that it was not a good enough reason. He had warned her often not to dissipate her energies by taking on too much and then becoming anguished when she did not succeed. His cool reply made her cross but in the end her sense of fair play reasserted itself and she acknowledged that he was right.

7

A Refusal is Sometimes a Blessing

In 1866, John Stuart Mill became a candidate for election to Parliament to represent the city of Westminster as a Radical. In his election address he talked openly of the necessity to give women the vote as quickly as possible, a bold, even foolhardy subject to raise if he wanted to win the seat. But to some women, who had been told he had influence, this was as good as having the vote already in their pockets. Barbara was one of these, and she felt it her duty to do all she and others could to get him elected to parliament: then the sparks would fly. She hired a carriage, covered it with election slogans, and inveigled Emily, Bessie Parkes and others to drive with her all over Westminster to emphasize the fact that all women and right-thinking men should rally round their hero, which they did. Mill was looked on as the centre and mainspring of the new movement, for most women believed that the election of a single MP could usher in a new era when they would come into their own.

No one was surprised when Mill became known as the 'man who wants girls in Parliament'. Enthusiasm ran high and all but a few believed that Mill would get in. Emily wished she could be so hopeful. She knew Mill to be a stubborn man, not easily moved by argument and not a born fighter despite his great gifts: she could not visualise him swaying Parliament in favour of women's suffrage, however clever and sincere his speech. Even his appearance was against him: his thin gaunt face was seldom softened by a smile and he had never been known to make a joke in public. He always seemed quite unable to descend to the jovial attitude of those whom he hoped would be his colleagues in the House of Commons, where many a harsh statement was turned aside by a kindly word.

Emily voiced her fears to Anna: 'I hope in the future Mr Mill's outward form will be more expressive of the many-sided soul within. It may be that being very shy he does not choose to express anything but what he cannot help, namely refinement.' As soon as Mill was elected, Emily and Barbara and her friends set to work. It fell to Emily to ask this unapproachable man to present a formal petition to Parliament on behalf of women who wanted the right to vote. He consented willingly on one condition – she must collect a hundred signatures. She collected one thousand four hundred and ninety-nine.

There was already a suffrage society in existence, but it was not very effective. Millicent Fawcett ran it, assisted by Frances Power Cobbe; several of Emily's friends belonged, including Lady Stanley of Alderley and her daughter, Lady Amberley. They were both enthusiastic and worked hard to help Emily collect signatures. Millie Fawcett was furious that Emily should 'interfere'; it was an infringement on her rights, and she and her committee would have nothing to do with the petition. Her sister Lizzie thought Millie was absurd and that she should not allow personal jealousy to harm her cause. To make amends Lizzie generously offered her dining room for committee meetings. In her 'Family Chronicle' Emily has left us a description of these meetings and it is not difficult to detect her keen sense of fun in these hilarious gatherings, despite her curiously flat style.

It had been difficult to try and persuade the committee that it would be a mistake to ask Parliament for too much all at once. Reluctantly they gave preference to women of property 'as a beginning', that is, widows and spinsters, as a married woman's property belonged to her husband. This Mill flatly refused to do: there must be no favouritism. It was his intention to ask for the suffrage to be given to all women, married or single. His step-daughter, Helen Taylor, backed him up. When Emily heard that, she was certain that the petition would fail.

At last the day arrived to take the petition to Mill: Barbara was too unwell to go herself, so Emily and Lizzie took it alone. The scroll with the signatures made a bulky package and when they reached Westminster they attracted so much attention that they became self-conscious and, giggling, they begged an old woman to hide it behind her stall. When Mill appeared he was astonished by its size and seizing it in both hands he brandished the heavy package in the air saying 'I can handle this with effect'.

Although Emily had gone to work on the suffrage question with some reluctance since she did not believe that it would succeed, she had to admit afterwards that she had enjoyed herself hugely. Taking the petition to Parliament had been a worthwhile adventure. It had been worth the effort to see the pleasure on Mill's face when he first set eyes on the huge package as they dragged it out from behind the stall. She had been in high spirits when she returned home and related it all to her mother. Later she wrote to Helen Taylor: 'I should like to see the faces of the members when the question is brought forward for the first time in the House of Commons. I think there must be truth in your theory as to the peculiar fitness of women for fighting. I cannot help enjoying it.' It was not long since, in the course of her struggle with Cambridge dons, that she had called this particular type of fighting 'disagreeable work'. Success had changed all that.

She was right of course about the petition. Despite what the press called an excellent speech, Mill failed to move the Commons to action. Everything remained just as it had been before, therefore it was all the more disappointing when Disraeli's 1867 Reform Bill contained nothing for women. Emily took it all calmly – it was to be expected – but Barbara and her followers were deeply disappointed. They had always been more optimistic than Emily and had looked on her pityingly when she had warned them not to expect too much, in order to soften the blow that she knew was coming. She realised now that her words had not sunk in at all. Barbara had even declared loftily that if Emily knew Mill as she did she would not say such things and they were lucky to get such a highly respected man to take up the cause. Emily knew when she warned Helen Taylor that her step-father might not be lucky, that she was courting unpopularity, since Helen worshipped Mill and thought him capable of miracles. With great tact Emily had tried to induce Helen to persuade Mill to change the wording of the demand; pointing out that '"on the same conditions as men" seems to me a little too definite. Commonplace people, women as well as men, have a horror of what they call "women wanting to be on an equality with men". I should like to avoid anything that might possibly suggest that unpleasant phrase.' But Mill did not think the wording unwise, so it was not removed, and the Bill failed.

Nevertheless Mill's speech did make the Commons uneasy, especially the passage where he asked: 'Is it good for a man to live in complete communion of thought and feeling with one who is studiously inferior to oneself?' Because the Commons had listened respectfully many women believed that the franchise could not be long delayed, despite the fact that the House had rejected it. Emily knew better. She had noticed that all their supporters came from the same section of society – select Radical circles. There were still too many women who thought the movement immoral, even impious, while a small proportion believed that because their cause was just it must also be popular. There were a very few like Emily who believed that most women were not yet ready for the vote. Furthermore, she attached the utmost importance to conservative support, hence her cautious approach – nothing must be done to turn public opinion against them. Unfortunately many of those eager for the suffrage were extreme Radicals to whom such a slow policy was uncongenial. In years to come this attitude of Emily's was at the root of the split (although there were other reasons as well) between herself and Millicent Fawcett's Suffragette party.

Henry Tomkinson pointed out to Emily that she had been wasting her time on Mill and his dreams to help women. He knew Mill too well not to fear that his lack of knowledge of the way the human mind worked would tell against him. If something was 'right, loyal and fair'

81

he expected to succeed, and if it did not he was as bewildered as a child. Yet Henry Tomkinson was wrong in one respect: Emily had learned something from the tedious infighting – the importance of timing and preparation.

Emily's dream of a women's college was still with her, perhaps all the more vivid for the rest offered by the suffrage campaign. It was about this time that, when discussing a women's college with a friend, she made a remark that has been sometimes misunderstood, and was to do her some harm later on in the controversy over research. Her aim, she said, was to produce women of the 'best and highest type'. By that she meant women who had been well-educated, and well-balanced, able to stand on their own feet and make a success of a career or of marriage; Emily did not despise marriage in itself, but only when it meant the union of unequals. That was the kind of marriage Emily despised. Since she had never married herself, she was supposed not to know anything about it. But she had observed one marriage (her parents') at close quarters and she knew a very great deal about the way a young girl's mind works, for her own youth with its disappointments and frustrations was still vivid to her. In a talk before the Social Science Association she once spoke feelingly of 'people who have not been brought into intimate converse with young people have little idea of the extent to which they suffer from perplexities of conscience . . . the discontent of the modern girl is not idle self-torture for her case is particularly hard in that she has fallen upon an age in which idleness is accounted disgraceful. The same atmosphere rings with exhortations to act, act in the living present, and the advice given is easy to offer and so hard to follow and presupposes exactly what is wanting, a formed and disciplined character able to stand alone and follow steadily a predetermined course without fear of punishment or hope of reward.'

By 1867 Emily was facing up squarely to the discontented state of mind in young girls – they needed an education corresponding to that given by the universities to young men. As soon as girls' schools were improved and better teaching methods introduced she felt sure that girls would demand more. Nothing would come right in the Women's Movement until university education for girls was properly established. She believed this so firmly that every day that she was at home she made notes on the pad of paper always ready on her desk about what was required that did not at present exist. On reading them over one day she saw that they could all be reduced to one thing – university education on the same terms as men. Her purpose, obscure and confused until now, lay at last absolutely clear before her eyes. She would devote her life to securing university education for women, since this had logically and necessarily to come before the ultimate goal, political equality, could be achieved.

So far – that is, over the reform in girls' schools – things had gone well, but she was too level-headed to let past successes blind her to the greater task that lay ahead. She knew that any scheme to secure education for women would arouse opposition fiercer than any she had yet encountered, but in spite of this she was determined to press forward with what she was absolutely convinced was the only remedy to the present injustice and discontent.

She could not rest until she had shared her excitement with Anna Richardson, who replied enthusiastically; she knew Emily's determination and felt sure that she would succeed. Emily knew it; already she could see the building in her mind's eye: '. . . it is to be as beautiful as the Manchester Assize Court with gardens and grounds and everything that is good for body, soul and spirit. I don't think I told you how intensely I enjoyed the beauty of the Assize Court. I have seen no modern building to be compared to it and the delight we felt in it made one realise how much one's happiness may be influenced and delights enhanced by external objects.'

She soon discovered that the architect of her favourite building was Alfred Waterhouse: she wrote to Anna again extolling his virtues. The building was 'so light with large windows that lend dignity to the whole place and not in the least over-decorated'. Choosing the man to design the first college for women gave substance to her dream and helped her to believe that her vision would before long become reality.

A hurried visit to Cambridge early in December to canvass opinion amongst those dons she already knew, left her with the impression that most of them were in favour of her plan. Unfortunately this was far from the truth. The fact was that dons thought the idea so absurd that it was not worth a second's thought. They behaved politely to Emily, but all the time saying to themselves, 'what a strange woman'. To take such an idea seriously would be to upset their comfortable little world and put their lives in a turmoil. So they ignored it with the comforting thought that it was out of the question. So of course they said all the proper things to Emily; this cost them nothing and sent her away happy.

She lunched with Professor Liveing and his wife and questioned them minutely on details of college life: how many lecturers, how many tutors, and how long would it take to learn enough to pass the first examination? What functions did each college official perform? Very much amazed, Liveing answered her as truthfully as he could, but thought it all really very funny. Mrs Liveing thought differently and marched Emily off to her sitting room after lunch to continue the talk about a women's college. In this private conversation with her guest she learned a great deal about Emily and her aspirations and suddenly felt that her vision could be realised. She wished with all her heart that she was younger.

Emily returned to London in great spirits, a programme half-formed in her head. There was one disappointment: to begin with, college tutors and lecturers would have to be men, as there were not yet enough women educated to teach at such a high level, and the instruction would have to be of the best. She very much regretted that Henry Tomkinson was abroad on business and she could not pour it all out into his sympathetic ears. His advice and help would be needed on a thousand different things she knew nothing about. Until his return she would use the time to sketch out a prospectus, but it gave trouble. Too long at first, it then became too short and not explanatory enough. After several attempts she was fairly satisfied that it stated clearly enough to be understood by even the stupidest people that there was an urgent need for a women's college analagous to the existing colleges at Oxford and Cambridge. In Henry Tomkinson's absence she sent a draft to Henry Robey for comment, asking if twenty copies would be enough to send to close friends. Her plan was to form a strong committee under the chairmanship of Lord Lyttelton, whose interest in education was well known. She calculated that she would need £30,000 at least to build a college, but where was it to come from? 'It is not a large sum,' she told Robey, 'considering that there is to be but one college of this sort for Great Britain, Ireland and the Colonies, and considering how easy it is to raise immense sums for boys' schools, but considering how few people wish women to be educated it is a great deal.'

Lizzie encouraged Emily; the idea was a splendid one, and she immediately promised £100 as soon as she began earning. Emily herself put aside £100 and another £100 came from Barbara. £300 without stirring from her chair! 'Everything will depend on how we start. If we begin with small subscriptions a low scale will be fixed and everyone will give in proportion.' Quite untutored, Emily had instantly seized on one of the basic principles of modern fund-raisers – start big, to encourage other subscribers to emulate the rich.

If only someone really wealthy with women's welfare at heart could be induced to give a large sum, perhaps £1,000 to start them off and act as an example to others, what a morale-booster that would be. She showed how much insight she had gained into other people's lives since coming to London when she told Lizzie that she did not think Lord Lyttelton would like to be chairman of a beggarly concern that would be struggling with pecuniary difficulties all its days. It showed, too, that Emily was not timid; big schemes involving large sums of money did not scare her. She thought 'big' about most things and could plan and tie up loose ends before taking anyone else into her confidence.

The size of her plans, and her firm belief that they could be carried out, her courage and her lack of shyness in asking for help, her meticulous sense of detail, all inspired trust in others and drew people to her with offers of help. During the Schools' Inquiry Commission she had become very friendly with Mark Pattison and they had had many long and fascinating talks on education. When she told him that she was going to found a college for women ('going to' and not 'hoping to', he noticed) he showed no surprise and at once offered assistance. He now knew and trusted Emily well enough to realise that she had considered the plan from all angles before mentioning it to him. Because of her astonishing optimism he felt he must warn her of the many pitfalls that she would encounter and that until public opinion became used to the idea, it would be against her. 'I expect that,' she replied cheerfully.

8

'The trumpet must be blown
with no uncertain sound'

When Emily looked about her for suitable women with common sense and intelligence to sit on her college committee, she could think of only one new name, Fanny Metcalfe, a headmistress of about her own age whom she had met through the School Mistresses' Association. The others were to be old friends who had helped her before: Lady Goldsmid, Lady Augusta Stanley, Mrs Russell Gurney and Mrs Charlotte Manning. The task of selection among her male acquaintances was much easier, but Emily was careful to choose those who had already had some experience of committee work. For chairman she chose Dr Alford, Dean of Canterbury, editor of the new Greek Testament, who could almost be regarded as a professional committee man and who would have no qualms about keeping the rest in order. Others who agreed to serve were Thomas Howell FRS, MP, Henry Robey, the former head of the Schools Inquiry Commission, and three new acquaintances whom Emily had recently come to know: John Seeley, Professor of Modern History at Cambridge, the Rev. John Sedley Taylor, an economist and Fellow of Trinity, and James Bryce, Regius Professor of Civil Law at Oxford, who as Viscount Bryce was later to become Ambassador to the United States. Last but by no means least, there was Henry Tomkinson, whom Emily had come to regard as indispensable. By any standards this was a formidable list, and the fact that such distinguished men were happy to associate themselves with Emily's college showed the high regard in which she was held, while Emily gained for her scheme an air of respectability that only such distinguished names could give.

Barbara Bodichon's name was not on the list, and this omission has been the cause of much speculation. The suggestion has been made that Emily's cautious nature stopped her from putting someone of Barbara's Radical tendencies on her committee. The truth was simple: Barbara had had a recurrence of Algerian fever and had been forbidden work of any kind by her doctors. As soon as she recovered she returned to England and joined the committee at Emily's express wish.

At this early stage the committee's main function was to carry out all the necessary preliminary work for the foundation of a women's college. A location for the college was to prove a problem. Emily of course favoured Cambridge because of her existing connections with the Local Examinations. But she knew there would be fierce opposition from the university were Cambridge to be chosen. Opinions on the committee itself were very mixed, but Emily quickly pointed out that it would be advisable to have some connection with Cambridge, although that did not mean that the college would have to be in the town itself. She asked Henry Tomkinson for his views: 'There has been a question whether to mention Cambridge definitely from the beginning; it seems not unreasonable, as the whole thing has grown up out of the Cambridge Local Examination and it saves trouble to have the matter settled.'

It was impossible not to be irritated when the women on the committee held matters up for a considerable time by asking unnecessary questions and making endless fusses about unimportant details, so that Emily wondered if she had been foolish to appoint any women at all. The kinder side of her understood that it was sheer inexperience that caused the trouble, yet how could they gain experience if she did not give it to them? Feeling guilty because she had been unfair, she unwisely invited two more women to join them, Miss Bostock of Bedford College and Miss Wedgwood of the famous pottery family. To her dismay they only added to the confusion: the second meeting was contentious and, but for some firm handling by Emily, would have become unruly. 'It was not exactly acrimonious, but verged on it,' she told Lizzie: 'Miss Bostock was troublesome and objected to everything, while Miss Wedgwood hesitated about everything, which does not speak well for women.' But the full force of Emily's wrath was directed against poor Henry Tomkinson, who in a vain attempt to pour oil on troubled waters jokingly, but with a straight face, was determined to make the college a paradise, 'insisting that the girls should breakfast in their own rooms . . . and then said that he was quite sure girls could take mathematical honours with very little teaching!' Emily saw that in future she would have to take charge of each meeting although Dr Alford nominally sat in the chair. She kept cool now and asserted her authority, but inwardly she trembled at the size of the undertaking she was embarking on and felt deeply depressed that not one member of the committee backed her or gave her reassurance by a single word. 'It frightens me a little,' she wrote to Barbara, 'to see our castle coming down from the clouds, substantiating itself on the solid earth, for I really think it will be done'. Brave words in the face of lack of sympathy or helpful advice. But she had stood firm before through all the contentiousness, not weakening, but continually pointing in the direction she wished to go.

'On the religious question there will be controversy,' Emily wrote in her memo pad the day before she brought the tricky question before the committee. Painful past experience had taught her to stick to her opinions.

Although a clergyman's daughter and the sister of one of London's most popular preachers, Emily was no bigot and numbered among her friends men and women of all denominations or none, but on one point she was resolved: only Anglican services should be held in the new college, but she would not make attendance at them compulsory as in the men's colleges.

It all seemed reasonable enough, but she would be glad to get this troublesome subject out of the way. As it happened, matters did not turn out quite as expected. There were some murmurings from the male members: James Bryce wanted to know why one denomination should be mentioned more than another but was quickly satisfied with Emily's explanation, and one or two of the other men said mildly that all they cared about was that the college should not seem to be a denominational institution. But the women would not let the matter alone and at one point Emily feared that the whole scheme would fall to the ground over the religious question. Helen Taylor, a new recruit and an awkward customer on a committee, immediately bridled. She had listened to Miss Davies's explanation to Bryce, she said, and was afraid that if Miss Davies stuck to her resolve and made the new college Anglican she would decline to have anything to do with it. She did not think it right that those who were not members of the Established Church should be invited to give money to the college. Even Anna Richardson, the most reasonable of women, wrote to say she was not satisfied. High Church herself, she suggested that Emily should have some High Church names associated with the college, perhaps on the committee, as a start. Emily replied tartly: 'your . . . suggestion is admirable. Please give me some names. I should like Dr Pusey.' High Church names, Low Church names, Roman Catholic names, Dissenting names, all fell round Emily's ears like confetti and she had to call the meeting to order. Whenever a controversial subject was raised, women's inexperience of committees became glaringly obvious. Even a bishop and two deans needed reining in when they forgot themselves and imagined they were in the pulpit. Henry Tomkinson (now much chastened) helped all he could to restore tempers, and fell from grace only once when he wrote 'Polly B.A.' on the back of his agenda paper to make Emily laugh. The disagreement became so heated that Emily proposed that to allow tempers to cool they should leave the matter unsettled for the moment. As they left the room, Henry cheered her up by offering to take care of the finances. Gratefully Emily handed them over to his safe keeping. She was so relieved to have this nagging worry removed from her shoulders that she thanked him in a warm letter: 'I am so much obliged to you . . . I feel very ignorant about it and it would be disastrous to be making mistakes.' Instinctively she knew the right moment to lean on a man for support.

'Dullness is not healthy.' Years ago Emily had written these words with much feeling. Now, when her world was brightening, she remembered with a pang the unhappiness that boredom and lassitude had caused her as a child and young adult. Whenever she was low she would experience again the dreadful feeling of hopelessness that used to be so hard to shake off. But she had put her despair to good use, never once giving way, and although she did not know it, it was this that had set her apart as a most extraordinary woman.

Her diary had never been so full. Nowadays it was late to bed and early to rise in order to fit in all her engagements and attend to her ever-increasing correspondence. Recently Bedford College had made her a 'visitor' and, having accepted, she was in duty bound to take an interest. Of course these commitments meant sacrifices here and there: she could not see her country friends as often as she liked: 'This will not seem much to you country people,' she wrote to Anna, enclosing a list of her duties for the week, 'who pass your lives in the extraordinarily fatiguing process of "spending the day" with each other and talking from morning till night, but to a quiet not to say stagnant Londoner so much working of the jaws is a considerable effort.' She was meeting new people all the time. A recent acquaintance and a contemporary of her brother's, Professor Seeley, was showing great interest in the college. She invited him to dine at Cunningham Place to talk about it and to meet Barbara, who happened to be in London. She was anxious to know, she said, how a college should be run, she was ignorant of so many things that he took for granted.

Like all academics, Seeley was at first full of gloom – 'a most important and difficult business, Miss Davies, the course of studies will give trouble. Female students willing to study hard will be difficult to find. Indeed if I may say so, the difficulties may be too difficult to overcome!' Nevertheless Emily noticed that he seemed very cheerful as he accepted another glass of Llewelyn Davies's excellent claret, when suddenly his gloom vanished and he became most helpful. Since the dinner had been arranged specially to discuss the intricacies of running a college, Emily was determined to make Seeley talk; it was the only way to avoid making a fool of herself when next the committee met to discuss the subject. On the other hand Barbara did not disguise the fact that she was bored with so much talk of how to run a college. It was something she would never have to do and it was monopolising far too much of Professor Seeley's attention. Anyhow, having got into his stride, Seeley proceeded to regale them with stories of his early days at Trinity, horrifying Mrs Davies with descriptions of undergraduate pranks. Before leaving he urged Emily to 'stick at it, that is the only way to succeed'.

With her nose thoroughly out of joint (Professor Seeley was quite unmoved by female beauty) Barbara next day sent Emily a peevish letter. 'There is a frightful coolness about the college,' she wrote untruthfully. 'I felt it at your house that Mr Seeley was bored by it and if I had followed my instinct I should not have mentioned it to him that night at all. Perhaps another time he might not have been slightly oppressed and apposite (if there is such a word). I don't know him, but I felt he was not inclined to discuss. Did not you?'

Emily took her time to answer: 'thank you for your kind words' which, since there were none in the letter, can be taken as sarcasm: 'I thought you were more discouraged than need be by other people's coldness because you expected more from them than I did. You go about bravely talking to people and expecting sympathy from them when I should not open my mouth, so you get cold water showered upon you. I did not think Professor Seeley was nearly so timid of the subject as I was . . . I am well used to that cool Cambridge manner that is not half as pleasant as the kind gushing way Oxford men have, but it comes to more.'

Cambridge soon made it plain that it did not want women in the university: they would be nothing but a disruptive influence. They would have to do without libraries and museums used by undergraduates, yet without them they would not be able to obtain enough books or to examine the specimens in the medical museums. If they made any attempt to attend lectures, undergraduates would be entitled to walk out. Furthermore, no lecturer of any repute would demean himself by teaching women. Despised, neglected, ostracised, the college would not last a term. All this was related to Emily second-hand by those who said they had reliable information. How true was all this? She went to see Professor Seeley, who told her she would certainly have a battle on her hands, but that she might find the battle exhilarating. She wrote to James Bryce, who had always been helpful, but he was not encouraging either: a women's college in a monastic setting where all the power was in the hands of the dons could not but fail. Not one man would stand for it, everything would be barred to women, so she might as well throw her prospectus into the fire. Some place outside London would be more suitable.

She turned to her brother; what did he think? Very much the same. There were too many distractions in a university town for immature young girls who had never been away from home before. Discipline and protection would have to be much tighter and he understood that Emily preferred a certain amount of freedom. Even Henry Tomkinson shook his head: Cambridge was at the moment somewhat unsavoury, somewhere in the country would be much safer. No one had anything helpful to suggest except find a place as far away from Cambridge as possible. It was most depressing not to be welcome anywhere. Where was a safe place to be found? Baldock, Bletchley, Stevenage, Hitchin, Mill Hill were near at hand, but all had something against them. Emily favoured Hitchin after she discovered that in the adjoining parish of St Ippolyts there were two Trinity livings whose incumbents were Cambridge scholars: it might weigh heavily with the committee if she could tell them that both these men might be persuaded to do some teaching. But the committee were still doubtful: divided amongst themselves, they could not come to a decision. Dr Alford suggested a semi-public meeting to advertise the college and to invite opinions on location, and if all went well to appeal for contributions.

These semi-public meetings had recently become very popular as a means of advertising or fund-raising for a good cause. The idea appealed to Emily, her only fear that over something as unusual as a women's college the meeting might become controversial and noisy, yet contention of any kind was to be avoided. Dr Alford offered himself as chairman and Lord Lyttelton, Henry Tomkinson, Professor Seeley and her brother Llewelyn promised to speak. All five were well aware of what was at stake. About a hundred people turned up, some more curious than concerned, but all seemed enthusiastic after rousing speeches from the platform. Seeley spoke like a man who had been in charge of the young for years (which he had not) or like a father of ten (which was remarkable since he was not married), but in a few simple words he made more impact than all the others put together. After speaking of the advantages university life could give, he said that of course the young students would be homesick at first, but since they would only be away about six months altogether (and never all at once) they would be back before they were missed and since the college was to be in the country their safety would be assured.

There were some anxious questions: What was 'Little-go', 'the Previous' and 'the Tripos'? Llewelyn Davies assured the audience that these were just fancy words for quite ordinary examinations, and nothing to be alarmed about. Professor Seeley chipped in to say 'but we don't mean the ladies of our college to stop at that'. This put everyone into a good humour and ready to listen quietly to the amount of money that would need to be raised. Henry Robey struck the right note when he said that £30,000 was a large sum but small when compared to £50,000 raised in a fortnight for the City of London Schools. Sedley Taylor and Professor Sidgwick rocked the boat when they asked if anybody had thought how difficult it would be for busy lecturers to travel into the country two or three times a week to lecture to girls. Cambridge railway station was half an hour's walk away from the two largest colleges in the centre of the town: the journey to any of the places suggested would take another half hour, so that at least two hours would be spent on travelling. A single lecture would take a man away from his college rooms for hours, not to mention the fatigue and the cost of the journey. Professor Lightfoot touched on something Emily had not considered; in the country the college would be quite out of reach of museums and libraries. If that could be overcome he was in favour.

After the meeting the money seemed to be rolling in, but when counted the total was only £2,100. It was proposed that Emily should speak at the next Social Science meeting on 'a certain proposed college for women' giving a sketch of the daily life of the student, which no one knew much about. Emily knew nothing – 'what did a student do all day?' 'One has to steer clear between the temptation to make it look pleasant so as to attract students and the risk of exciting the jealousy of parents.' Some reminiscences of Henry Tomkinson's from his own undergraduate days were most unhelpful; they showed Emily how incredibly ignorant bachelors were of the workings of a young girl's mind. However he did make one sensible remark: 'parents would be sensitive about the dullness of a young woman's life at home'. 'It is the weak part,' she replied, 'I am utterly at a loss to defend. I do not believe that our utmost efforts to poison the lives of students at college will make them half as miserable as they are at home.'

The number of people at the centenary meeting of the Social Science Association at which Emily was to speak was so large that there was not enough room to seat them all. 'There is more interest in the college than in anything else except strikes,' Emily told Barbara gleefully. 'I feel people are much more curious about the college when they have seen someone who is concerned with it.' In her speech Emily managed, without twisting the truth the slightest bit, to make a student's life sound innocently calm and peaceful: the girls were to have a bedroom and sitting room all to themselves where they would be free to study undisturbed and where (when not working) they would be able to enjoy the companionship of their own friends. Peace and quiet were essential to the productive life of a student, she believed. Thus she stressed solitude as one of the most important ingredients that college would provide; it was necessary for the formation of character. Barbara Stephen believed that Emily's desire for privacy was in reality a desire for freedom; this may have been true. Thus in giving freedom to adolescents she was in some way compensating for the hopes and aspirations which she had never been able to realise in her own youth. She forgot that a younger generation might think differently and that too much solitude might mean loneliness. Presumably this was to be catered for by 'tea with chosen friends'. But how were these to be found? She should have remembered the need for community life in some form. The majority of her students would have come from large families and the sudden solitude might prove a rude shock. Emily had taken it for granted that all the girls would automatically become friends. She wound up her speech in style. 'The college is a dependency, a living branch of Cambridge. It will aim at no higher position than, say, that of Trinity College.' This last remark evoked a dry comment next day from *The Times*: 'Such a degree of humility will not be excessive.'

Once interest was aroused, Emily was bombarded with advice as to where the college should be. Much of it was most unhelpful, so that she wished that she had never mentioned the difficulty of finding the right place. A poverty-stricken laird in the Highlands offered his crumbling castle at an enormous rent, and other equally foolish offers poured in daily. James Bryce (an Oxford man) had been to look again at Cambridge (he complained that he had never had time to see it when he was working on the Schools Commission); it reminded him, he said, of Suffolk, so quiet and peaceful and utterly delightful. Of course he had forgotten that he had paid his visit out of term-time when the place was almost empty.

At a meeting of the Executive Committee Henry Sidgwick advocated Grantchester, near but not too near Cambridge. Sedley Taylor had nothing new to offer but was against every suggestion. If money was a consideration, then it must be in Cambridge. Barbara, attending her first committee meeting, chipped in to say that she was against the country; no one could be sure that the place they chose would have all the necessary amenities such as tap water, gas lighting, decent roads and a railway station. No one liked to be reminded that such a practical thought had never entered their heads. Emily's own head ached with all the various arguments. Then suddenly she heard of a suitable house in Hitchin, with a beautiful garden and a delightful view of the surrounding country. It was only twenty miles from Cambridge, not isolated, yet secluded from the bustling little town by a private road. There was an excellent train service. When consulted, Professor Seeley advised her to take the house at once in case it was snapped up. Emily rushed to see it, liked it on sight and after a tussle with the landlord took the house for three years and not five years for which he had asked. Things were moving at last. Benslow House was now hers and she was really and truly committed to starting the first women's college. Pleased and proud though she was, she was also a shade fearful: 'It does worry me a little,' she confessed to Barbara, 'but I try not to be depressed about it.'

She might well be depressed: money was not coming in fast enough, in fact it was not coming in at all, and since they had planned to open in October 1869 this was serious. Even when Benslow House was being prepared, the rent would have to be found and many different things bought. Barbara advised opening first and getting it ready afterwards, beds etc. could be paid for out of the fees: Emily had to remind her that there were also no desks, bed linen or saucepans and many other things they had not yet thought of. She knew it was prudent to begin small and grow but some things would have to be bought, otherwise the girls could not work. The fees would have to be kept to pay the lecturers and their travelling expenses. Most worrying of all was the reticence on the part of the lecturers to tell her how much they were going to charge. Emily had asked, in her forthright way, and was told that they would let her know. Since then there had been silence.

A letter from Professor Seeley brought good news: he offered himself as one of the lecturers but again not a word about charges. He had been elected to the Chair of Modern History at Cambridge since Emily had got to know him, and she had taken it for granted that he was now too grand to teach girls. The day his letter came she happened to be lunching with Mrs Russell Gurney and asked her if she should accept Seeley's offer. She was at once reassured: to have such a man associated with the college would be worth more than £1000 a year. This set a high standard; Emily said that she was determined not to look lower.

Seeley's offer touched Emily deeply. He had always supported her, despite never being enthusiastic about the college. 'I do not feel able to judge,' he had written, 'whether a university education would be good for women generally. There are evidently some for whom it would be good, and the experiment is worth trying for the others.' Emily hoped that his common sense would be catching. She was beginning to learn that dons were an exceedingly nervous race: they minded what people thought and were terrified of innovation, lest it disturb the tranquillity of their comfortable lives. Besides, none wanted to be her only supporter, lest he look foolish and lose face. Dr Whewell, Master of Trinity College, was as anti-feminist as a man could be. Most dons stood in awe of him, for his bite was even worse than his bark, which alone was enough to send shivers down the spine. If only he could have contented himself with saying that her college for women was a revolutionary but excellent idea, her prospects would have been rosier from the start. Sedley Taylor was like a barometer: whenever he had been to see Whewell he returned finding fault with everything Emily had said and done, and told the committee that this or that would not work, so that Emily longed to throw him out. On one occasion she did lose her temper, and accused him of disloyalty – 'you change course like the wind'.

Some were staunch. Lady Goldsmid, Lady Stanley and Mrs Gurney were advertising the college in confident tones among their friends and acquaintances, praising the foresight of those in charge for placing it in the country. Lord Lyttelton too was very much for the college. Meeting

Emily one day he inquired kindly if her plans were progressing well. 'How much money do you think, you will need?' When she replied £50,000 he nodded and said: 'Well, we shall see.'

9

A Cat and Mouse Game

It gave Emily a strange feeling of unreality to find herself seated in a train on the way to Hitchin to hand over the first quarter's rent and take possession of Benslow House. She only half believed that her 'vision in the clouds' was about to come down to earth. There was still a long way to go: the real conundrum which she would have to solve was how to make a little money go a long way. If only there were just a few hundred pounds more to play with, what a difference it would make! But like all pioneers she was not foolish enough to let the lack of it deter her; money would come, of that she was certain, even if it was only from the students' fees.

It was a lucky chance that she really did like Hitchin and that the liking grew the more she saw of it. An important point in its favour was the cheapness of everything; a walk round the town had given her a pleasant surprise – fish, meat and vegetables at half the price of London and Cambridge. At least there would be a saving on food. Recently Emily had persuaded Barbara to pay Hitchin a visit, but it had not been a success. Barbara disliked the place on sight, found fault with the house, the furnishings and the few arrangements Emily had already made for the girls' comfort. She saw nothing in the surrounding town that smacked of culture and would not be pacified even when Emily told her that the house and the town were only temporary. Happily nothing she said could dampen Emily's spirits. Barbara would be won over in time. With her it was always a question of getting used to an idea. When Benslow House was filled with busy students, she would soon change her mind: 'I think you would not long so much for Cambridge,' she wrote on Barbara's return to London, 'if you stayed in Hitchin enjoying and admiring it. It helps to reconcile me to not having quite everything. Then the weather is a great point, I grew stronger while I was down there than I had been for years and all that about the difficulty with the lecturers is quite fictitious. Mr Malton is delighted to come and no one is better than Mr Stuart. I suggested the troublesomeness of the journey and he said "Oh yes, but it is so short".'

To add to Emily's happiness a large box of Barbara's own paintings turned up to brighten the walls of the empty house. Emily supervised their hanging, taking great care not to have them 'skied'. She chose some of the best for the Mistress's room to welcome the new occupant whoever she might be. It was a little worrying that the right person had not yet been found, but Emily was optimistic that she would emerge before long.

She spent every spare moment writing to friends and acquaintances, especially those with a large number of girls, asking 'Have you a daughter for us?' Mrs Bradley, the wife of the Master of Marlborough, had so many that she was like the old woman who lived in a shoe, although she refused to admit it. Emily had met these daughters, cross-looking girls singularly lacking in charm, whom Emily longed to transform by means of higher education into lively contented young creatures. But would Mrs Bradley listen? She would not hear of 'my girls' being sent away from home. What good did education do except make them unfit for marriage? Mrs Bradley fondly hoped that all her sweet girls would make a good match, so she did not want them changed. Emily could see plenty of room for improvement: 'of course education changes everybody,' says one of her letters to Mrs Bradley, 'but for the better'. If it made girls dissatisfied she hoped that it would be with the tiresomeness and boredom of home life. How painfully timid women were: because a thing was new it could not be good. Tough as Emily was, she could bear anything except arguing with stubborn mothers; it made her ashamed of her own sex to hear ignorant opinions uttered with such self-confidence – and these women thought they ought to be given the vote! That young women should be happy and fulfilled did not trouble most mothers in the least. Unfortunately the success of Emily's college depended on women like Mrs Bradley being willing to 'give up my girls' (as they referred to getting their daughters turned into useful human beings). One day they would regret keeping these discontented young women tied to their apron strings, becoming sulkier and more bad-tempered and quarrelsome with the years.

'The real difficulty is perhaps to decide which is the duty, as in some families the most trifling and useless faddles put on the airs of home duties and are considered of more importance than any other possible claims of any other sort . . . it looks like a consciousness of weakness and unsoundness when there is so much fear when the home ties will snap at the least pull . . .' This letter brought no response and Emily wisely dropped this unfruitful friendship. Like some other women Mrs Bradley was all for higher education until it came to her own daughters, then the college was at too experimental a stage for them to risk it: while those who had no children like the Rev. Frederick Denison Maurice earnestly assured her that if he had any daughters he would not hesitate to entrust them to her care, for he had the greatest confidence in her, he said. He had, however, several sisters, two at least of whom were still of an age to benefit from three years at college. Emily noticed he did not mention them. Lady Stanley was a great believer in education but all her numerous daughters were now married. Her youngest, Lady

Amberley, a highly intelligent and gifted young woman, told Emily, with real regret in her voice, that if she were younger and single she would love to be a student at her college. Five minutes later she was confiding in a friend that she had no intention of sending her daughter Rebecca to Miss Davies's college.

Emily had come to understand that 'book-learning' (as education was erroneously called) frightened the untutored, and that when a woman went in for higher education a metamorphosis took place and there was an instant and alarming change, so that the thought that their daughters were to be educated above themselves was terrifying. 'What should I do,' wailed one mother, 'if my daughter should return from college and address me in Latin or Greek?' Emily's Quaker student Anna Lloyd had to go through fire and water to get to the college at all. Her family were furious that this sister and aunt, who was so useful to them all when babies were born or illness struck, had shown a desire to be educated. Why was her life at home not enough for her? Her much younger niece went so far as to call Anna 'unchristian'. Was not Christianity all about thinking of others? This attitude was laughable, of course, and Emily was not without a sense of humour even when she was contemptuous, but she also felt bitter that intelligent girls like Anna Lloyd were expected to devote their whole lives to others because they were unmarried.

It was gradually beginning to dawn on her that opposition to her college was growing. She had been so taken up with arrangements for the opening day, so anxious to attract suitable pupils and also so busy coping with the constant worry (it continued for some years) of making both ends meet when funds were low that she had not noticed that support was falling away. The moment it was known that a house had been rented and that a date for the opening would shortly be announced hearts became faint and the college was suddenly 'too revolutionary to succeed'. When two pupils cried off for that reason Emily was alarmed. She had gone to such pains to get the best that Cambridge had to offer in the way of tuition, too. Teachers without pupils! Whoever heard of such a thing and the teachers of the best! How could she bear it? She unburdened herself to Adelaide Manning who, she knew, would see things as she did: 'It seems to me that we do want to charm people by an animating view of the studies and the names of the teachers. We want to attract the students. For myself I feel decidedly more heart-broken at not being able to start after realising what the teaching will be and also we want to enlist support by making people feel that what we are going to offer could be of a higher quality than women will have the least chance of getting anywhere else.'

Then the villain of the piece turned out to be *The Times*, which had, in an article that Emily had not had leisure enough to read, denigrated

98

in scornful terms the very idea of putting girls through a course of study equal in mental strain to that of men. It warned parents to expect breakdowns and nervous collapse which could incapacitate a girl for her proper duties as wife and mother. In a burst of fury Emily wrote to the editor: '. . . is it because of a poor woman's lack of strength that they are employed as beasts of burden in mines and factories and are condemned to sweated labour from the age of six . . .?' Not unnaturally the letter was not published. The day was not far off, however, when every letter that Emily wrote to that newspaper (and she was a prolific letter writer to the end of her days) was not only published but placed in a prominent position.

The following week the *Manchester Guardian* took up the theme: 'a girl's proper university is her own home in the bosom of her family . . .' This too Emily answered: 'Why should intellectual excellence be incompatible with the domestic virtues . . .?' She knew this nonsense to be written by men, possibly bachelors with no knowledge of the female mind and a selfish love of their creature comforts. Not one of them would exchange the luxury and freedom of their own lives for the dullness and drudgery of a woman's lot.

But there were some who were beginning to see the light. Recently, at a dinner party in London she had sat next to Professor T.H. Huxley and found him most agreeable. She quickly made use of her good fortune to ask him if he believed the theory that because a woman's head was so much smaller than a man's, her brains must also be smaller? In reply Huxley stated quite categorically that there was no truth whatsoever in such a theory. She boldly asked him next if he found learned women abhorrent? Again his answer left no room for doubt: 'There are not nearly enough learned women about.'

In May Emily went to Oxford for a few days to discuss college business with the Brodies. She was very well aware that isolation had its dangers: it was important to mix as much as possible with all kinds of people to keep a proper balance. She was coming to believe that it was because Cambridge was so segregated from the real world that dons behaved childishly in defence of their rights. One don whom she was introduced to said with brutal frankness that he would fight to keep women out of the university ('over my dead body'). To see only one side of a question showed a shocking narrow-mindedness that education ought to have eradicated. The practical good sense of the Brodies never failed to restore her sense of values as well as her good humour. It was a relief to find that not all academics were against education for women. One young Oxford don confessed shamefacedly to Emily that he had never given the question a moment's thought, but as soon as the unfairness had been explained to him, he wanted to bring about changes at once but had no idea how to begin. After a long conversation with Emily in the Brodies' drawing room, he became her firm ally.

She enjoyed herself so much in Oxford that she was persuaded to stay longer and talk to people about the college, a temptation Emily could not resist. She returned refreshed and full of energy, only to learn that some members of the committee, which was acting as a provisional governing body, had met informally to compose a first draft of the constitution which they now submitted for her approval. Whose idea it was to commit such an act of discourtesy behind her back is not known, but it was probably meant kindly, as Henry Tomkinson was always warning them not to allow Emily to overwork. It was unfortunate that they had not paid enough attention to the reasons Emily had given for wishing to compose this herself and then submitting it to the committee for approval. Their draft had been cobbled together so badly that it seemed to connect the college in a loose way with three existing universities – Oxford, Cambridge and London – but to aim ultimately at a separate university for women, something Emily had said more than once that she would not have at any price. Henry Tomkinson admitted somewhat sheepishly that the draft was rough and ill-thought-out when he brought it to her for approval.

Emily read it in silence; then, still silent, she tore it up. When she had composed herself a little she wrote Henry what he called a 'fundamental letter': 'As to the composition of the college,' Emily wrote coldly, 'it seems to me that the proposal to represent three universities departs altogether from the fundamental idea of the college which is to be at the earliest possible moment a constituent part of the university of Cambridge . . .' At the next committee meeting all mention of the offending draft was deleted from the minutes. Nevertheless, still angry, Emily did not mince her words at the members' foolishness in thinking that they could settle such an important issue without her. When she had cooled down she wrote Henry a disarming letter of apology, reminding him that she was 'one of the unfortunate people of an ill-assorted compound of Celtic and Anglo-Saxon, who by nature of their constitution are continually compelled to say and do what they are sorry for afterwards . . .'

No sooner was the little fracas over than Emily was again being prevailed on to let her students take a separate examination specially geared to the needs of women. She instantly rejected this insulting suggestion: 'nothing is more calculated to lower the tone and drop the level of female education . . .' She made her views very clear to Henry Tomkinson in case he too should have picked up some wrong ideas: 'It seems to me that there is an increasing disposition to give women fair play, there is also some tendency to increasing separation, we have not yet come to it in religion but with Ladies' Committees, Ladies' Associations,

Ladies' Lectures and the rest one does not quite soon see why there should not also be ladies' churches and chapels in which the duties of women as such should be especially inculcated. We have the principle already in the double moral code which most people believe in . . . perhaps I exaggerate but we think it is discouraging to see so many of the new things for women started on a basis of separation . . .'

The question of the special examination for women was discussed in the Cambridge Senate in October 1868. When the scheme was passed, Emily was determined that neither she nor her college would have anything to do with it, but the best policy for the moment was to be silent. No doubt when the time came to declare herself, she would know what to do. She would play it cunningly and continue to see that her girls were prepared to sit the same examination as the male undergraduates before asking anything for them and then to go ahead in small steps carefully timed.

It was expected that the college would open in the autumn of 1869 with about fifteen or twenty pupils, but by the summer of 1868 the number had dwindled first to ten, then to six, and ultimately to five. Emily blamed the effect of the newspaper articles on nervous mothers but did her best to keep up her spirits; pessimism never paid. In one way she was thankful that she had gone into this momentous plan without realising what difficulties and troubles lay before her.

By the spring of 1869 she was struggling with the syllabus of studies, trying desperately to get it settled. Had she been able to fund her college fifteen or twenty years earlier or that number of years later, she might have encountered fewer obstacles, for the reform of the universities' teaching and examination system would either not have started or have reached a stage more suited to her needs. 'Not until the early 1880s,' wrote D.A.Winstanley, was 'the stagnant atmosphere which had hung over Cambridge in the eighteenth century at last completely dissipated'. By sheer ill-fortune Emily founded her college in a period of transition.

Under the stimulus of the Prince Consort as Chancellor – he had experienced the new and progressive German methods while a student at Bonn – Cambridge began to break the ancient and restricting mould in 1848 with the foundation of two new triposes; Moral Science (which included some history, law and jurisprudence) and Natural Science, in addition to the existing two, Mathematics and Classics. But in spite of the Royal Commission of 1852 and the Cambridge University Act of 1856, which dealt with administration rather than learning, little more was done to modernise study and teaching before the new statutes of 1882, save the opening of college lectures to members of other colleges (a change of which Emily was able to take great advantage) and the foundation of the first university laboratories in the 1860s and 1870s.

The world of Cambridge was in a state of flux in the 1860s when Emily set to work. In the age of Darwin, knowledge was expanding in every field. The Cambridge Board of Mathematics reported in 1867: 'The progress of science is continually enlarging the field of mathematical knowledge.' The same applied to other subjects, too. The university was in a turmoil, and bitter feelings divided the reformers from the conservatives. The two new triposes – which had not proved popular – were already being denounced as rigid and superficial. The reformers found the Ordinary or Pass degree antiquated and elementary, while the Previous or Little-go (in effect an entrance examination) was almost universally condemned as academically valueless.

It had been Emily's intention from the start to make her girls follow the same course of study and take the same examinations as men so that, when the time came to seek full membership of the university, adherence to some specially female course of study could not be advanced as a barrier against the admission of women. Yet to copy the men was in the 1860s and 1870s to follow a course far inferior to that which Emily's reforming friends were at that moment advocating. The dilemma could not have been more serious, for both possible lines of action had drawbacks which might eventually prove extremely damaging. Which was preferable – to aim for a superior education and risk failing to secure membership of the university, or to accept lower standards which might carry full membership but would very likely ruin the future of higher education for women? In 1867 it was impossible to say, and Emily was pestered by the problem for many years.

The conflict of views stands out vividly in Emily's correspondence with two members of the sub-committee she appointed to recommend a curriculum for the college. 'Stop and reflect,' James Bryce begged her in 1867. 'I doubt rather as to the propriety of holding examinations exactly similar to the Cambridge examinations for a degree. These examinations, Pass or "Poll", are really very bad and quite unworthy of the university. Those at Oxford are just as bad, in fact they are little better than a farce. It would be much better for a new institution not only to set up a higher standard than the contemptibly low one at Oxford and Cambridge. Let the examinations be in subjects and on text books better chosen and of more educational value.'

Here was Emily's dilemma starkly outlined. True to her principles, she stood her ground, so Bryce tried again. Girls should take the same examinations as men, he agreed, but 'we think it a pity to load a new institution at starting with the very vices whose existence we deplore in an old one. In my view the course at your college ought to be a model for men's colleges to follow instead of a slavish copy of their faults.' This was an estimable ideal, but Emily knew that only in dreamland could Cambridge dons be induced to follow a woman's lead. She was still unmoved twelve months later when Professor Seeley added his voice to Bryce's. He tried a somewhat different approach, emphasising that he looked forward to the not very distant time when the teaching of logic, English, political philosophy and science would replace the outworn discipline of the classics. Much as Emily sympathised with his long-term objective, she was insistent that if her girls did anything different from the men it would be construed as inferior and might be held to disqualify them from degrees. Her answer was therefore firmer: 'I shall stand up to you as long as you continue the controversy'. The girls at Benslow House embarked on the same studies as the majority of Cambridge undergraduates. It was a risk, but one Emily had to take. What would come out of her firm stand she did not know, but philosophically she consoled herself with the thought that since she was already up to her neck in risks one more, however large, made little difference.

10

Life will Never Be the Same Again

Christmas 1868 came and went, but Emily did not stop work. No public announcement had yet been made about the college, although many of the arrangements had been finalised. But she was in fact relaxing a little more than she appeared to be doing since she was tired after the gruelling weeks when everything seemed to be going wrong. She confessed to a friend that she was unusually apprehensive – 'once the college is announced there will be no going back' – an admission of nerves quite out of character.

During the winter a compromise had been reached between Seeley and herself. After their disagreement he had repented and asked for a meeting to sort things out, and he had behaved so well that Emily's heart warmed to him. This time they got on splendidly, for next day he sent her a friendly note which put her fears at rest: 'I am well content. It puts the stationary and progressive principles side by side. I am not afraid of the result if justice is done to both . . . let the education of the sexes be the same if you will. I only want to anticipate by a short time the change which I see coming over the education of men . . .'

It is plain that Seeley was one of the genuine reformers, that he was willing to accept women on the same level as men, and also that he did not agree with Emily but was prepared to let her have her way. This meant that the controversy which had made them both unhappy was over. 'There could not be a better start to the New Year,' Emily told Barbara.

There were other blessings too: it had come to her suddenly that Hitchin was the right place for her college, and with this realisation all doubts had vanished. She liked the little town more and more. If only Barbara could feel the same: she tried to convince her that the choice was right, at least to begin with. 'Cambridge is not a healthy atmosphere into which to plunge young girls used to family life and the society of their fathers and brothers. There would have to be too many restricting regulations . . .' A conversation with Llewelyn when he was a young fellow of Trinity had made a deep impression on her. She had longed to visit this favourite brother and be shown over the college and

104

walk with him in the beautiful Backs (the gardens between the colleges and the river) of which he had talked so often. When she asked him if she could visit him during the summer term, his consent had been so lukewarm that Emily had not gone. Later she remembered that he had once told her that his friends were ashamed of being seen with their mothers and sisters too near their own college. Emily had been deeply upset, for it did not speak well for education. She would not like the girls at her college to have the same experience. Painful as it had been at the time, Emily was glad that she had not embarrassed her brother by visiting Cambridge. She knew his world and how he hated the breaking of conventions; she cared nothing for them herself, but understood that if she wanted her college to succeed she must accept those that were reasonable if she wanted to avoid insuperable opposition. Of course she agreed with Barbara that mixing freely with young men broadened a girl's mind – but at what a cost! She reminded Barbara of the influence of novelists like the celebrated Charlotte Yonge, whom everybody read and whose false sentiments ruled the lives of far too many females. Cambridge would be a shock to young girls brought up on Miss Yonge's view of life as rosy and protected.

Perhaps unwisely Emily had sent Charlotte Yonge an invitation to become a member of the Executive Committee, thinking that perhaps her name would inspire confidence, and had received a snub in reply. 'Nothing,' Miss Yonge said, 'would induce me to be associated with such a project,' and proceeded to show how harmful the evils of university life could be to young girls. Of course she had to rely on her vivid imagination for every word she wrote. 'A college would mean the loss of the tender home bloom of womanliness which is a more precious thing than any proficiency in knowledge' was nothing but ignorant prejudice. Emily showed the letter to Barbara, who shook her head gravely. 'It will do the college much harm and start a furore among the very people who should be behind us: the sacrifice of Cambridge for the college would not be worthwhile.' But Barbara was not always of the same mind as Emily. She wrote to Emily, 'You must see besides that to spend money on a hired house is not good husbandry.' Again Emily had to explain that she had not given up the idea of building on a permanent site somewhere else eventually: '. . . but I think that it may help us to get the money to come into existence in some shape as soon as possible if we had a certain number of students actually collected together and at work. We could proclaim the astonishing fact and show that the thing is actually begun . . . we want by every possible means to make ourselves look substantial. As you see I only proposed the hired house plan for a year or two while the college is building.'

In one respect Barbara was right. The existence of the college must be announced as soon as possible, the place where it was to be located, the fees to be charged and the way the periods of residence were divided into three terms, and so on: 'It is no good putting it off until we have a certain number of students.' A little frightened but also a little elated, Emily hesitated no longer. She would make her announcement as soon as she had consulted Henry Tomkinson on one or two points.

Nevertheless news of the new college for women had leaked out, and before the end of March 1869 two prospective students had come to Emily for interview. The first, a bright-eyed intelligent eighteen-year-old, Emily Gibson, from Hannah Pipe's school at Laleham (that explained how she had heard) was not in the least abashed at the idea of an entrance examination; the second, a Quaker friend of Anna Richardson's, Anna Lloyd, who considered herself almost middle-aged at twenty-nine, wanted, she said, to do something useful with her life. Two such promising applicants raised Emily's spirits at once: 'more are in prospect,' she wrote happily to Barbara.

By April the prospectus was ready. Emily gazed at it with satisfaction; she particularly liked the way the names of the distinguished examiners stood out clearly under the date of the entrance examination and below that the announcement of two scholarships of £100 each to help meet the fees of £105 a year. Both had been donated by friends who wished to remain anonymous.

The amount of the fees had been a worry. Many middle-class families with intelligent daughters might not be able to afford them. The committee had tried to keep the fees as low as possible, but Henry Tomkinson assured them that the college could not manage on less. Since he was the man who had rescued Marlborough College from bankruptcy they trusted him. Of course a college run on pinch-penny lines could never be popular, but if they charged too little they would soon find themselves in a predicament.

The day fixed for the entrance examination was 3 July 1869. Emily had not wanted to have this examination at all. Young men wishing to enter a Cambridge college were not required to sit one, yet she saw reason when Henry Tomkinson pointed out that they would look very foolish if they accepted a girl, however charming and well-mannered, and it turned out that she could not read or write properly, or did not possess even a smattering of other things as well. It had been a shock to discover how many girls were like this.

The invigilation of this simple examination was done by Emily, who was surprised to find that there were far more candidates than she expected: 'Eighteen young women are under examination,' she informed Barbara. 'They vary widely in attainments. Some of the French and Latin papers are extremely bad and some I thought very good. This morning is devoted to the struggle with arithmetic . . .' They had not long to wait for the results: ten candidates were successful, better than Emily expected: a talk with the lucky ones gave much satisfaction – they were all eager to try the honours degree.

Before opening day on 6 October Emily travelled continually between London and Hitchin. It was no great distance but the journey was slow and tedious, the train stopping at every station and even between stations. In order not to be driven mad with impatience Emily read or wrote letters and made notes of last-minute decisions which she had not had time to record before. Now and again she gazed at the countryside which was neater and prettier than expected. She was very happy.

Not one of Emily's many letters in Girton College Library gives the slightest sign of regret at the momentous step she had taken, or indeed of anxiety or fear at the responsibility she was shouldering. Of course the Executive Committee shared the burden, but the one who would suffer should the whole idea collapse was Emily. Ever since the opening day had been announced (prophetically the same day exactly as the university) she had been full of confidence and hope.

In consultation with her mother Emily planned menus; they chose good plain food, milk, bread, beef and mutton, with vegetables of which Emily noticed a plentiful supply in Hitchin market. Fruit was not on the list, but this may have been because there was no imported fruit in the days before the invention of cold storage, and English fruit was seasonable and expensive. This was rectory nourishment all over again, which the Davies children had once consumed in large quantities without complaint, but which the first Hitchin students were to come to detest. To like food, to be a gourmet, especially for a woman, was considered 'not quite nice', almost a flaw in her character. With the Davieses the reason was different: it was wrong to keep a lavish table while hundreds were starving, and in any case self-denial was good for the soul. The Rev. John Davies only picked at his food and the meals his wife provided were more than enough. It would never have occurred to Mrs Davies to titillate her children's appetite, that would have been putting too much emphasis on things of the flesh. Emily, her sister and brothers, ate what was put before them and were taught to be thankful.

The pioneer students at Benslow House thought differently and complained that the food was tasteless and inadequate. In a letter to a friend that first term Emily said that 'all the food disappears very fast'. It did not occur to her with her small appetite that its rapid consumption might be because there was too little of it. The puritanical side of Emily abhorred what she called 'fancy food' and she certainly never allowed it to be served while she had a say in the running of either Benslow House or Girton. It seems that Henry Tomkinson did not care for the food at Cunningham Place either. 'Mr Tomkinson dined with us' was soon replaced by 'Mr Tomkinson called after dinner'. As a rich bachelor, Henry Tomkinson liked good food and wine, and even for friendship's sake he could not endure Mrs Davies's mutton stew.

Emily's friends had never been more helpful than now when she needed them. Annie Austin (the former Annie Crow) offered to prepare Benslow House for its first term, no mean task since the place had not been lived in for some time and smelt of damp and mildew. Emily had been bridesmaid at Annie Crow's wedding to Thomas Austin and, when Thomas died tragically young, Emily had been the first to take his widow under her wing. Henceforth Annie, practical and cool, made herself useful to her friend in many different ways, not least in her support for the new college and of Emily herself when things went wrong.

In July, Annie with her two maids opened up Benslow House, received and saw to the arranging of the furniture, the stocking of the kitchen and the purchase of all those things that the undomesticated Emily had not thought of. In late September Emily joined them at Hitchin, prepared for a long stay and with an enormous quantity of luggage for a woman so frugal in her dress. Nevertheless, she believed it expedient to be ready for every eventuality, and since there was no precedent to follow, anything might happen. The first term might be tricky.

She still did not quite trust the lecturers to teach the subjects agreed on in the syllabus. For someone who was not suspicious by nature she showed a surprising lack of confidence in these academics who had offered themselves to teach her girls. The course of studies was directly geared to Little-go, which Emily decided all the girls must take. With the eyes of Oxford and Cambridge on her, Emily was determined to make the opening smooth and free from mishaps, though what could go wrong she did not know.

The sixty-five-year-old Charlotte Manning had been persuaded to become the college's first Mistress. The widow of Sir William Spear, she had married Sergeant Manning, the distinguished lawyer, in 1857 as his second wife; she was not only cultured but a woman of great charm. Unfortunately she was delicate and could only stay for one term. A suggestion of Emily's that her step-daughter Adelaide, an old friend, should come, too, as the new Mistress's secretary, was gratefully accepted. Adelaide was to receive no salary. In deference to her age, Mrs Manning was forbidden to set foot in Benslow House until all was ready to receive her, but Annie Austin had worked miracles, turning a dusty house into a spick and span home with which Emily could find no fault.

The day after Emily's arrival Henry Tomkinson turned up complete with suitcase, announcing in a cheerful voice that he had come to inspect his property (which of course in effect Benslow House was) as a member of the Executive Committee. He went on to say to the two astonished young women that he wished to test the comfort of the guest room and to make history as the first man to sleep in a women's college. He had not been in the house an hour before Emily was thanking a kind providence for his presence. With jacket off and sleeves rolled up he moved furniture, opened boxes, hung pictures, fixed screws and made curtain rails fit, all in a spirit of great hilarity. Emily had not laughed so much for a very long time. With his experience of college life, they let him advise them on the best room for the dining hall – in the basement to avoid the smell of cooking.

He assured Emily that it was a waste of good space for each girl to have her own room, and he kindly offered to move the beds himself, but here Emily was firm: she had promised. After some good-humoured wrangling Henry gave way: 'Women have no idea how to economise.' When Emily told him it was nothing to do with economy but her anxiety to create an atmosphere of peace and calm so conducive to work, Henry burst out laughing. He could see that she had got it into her head that scholarly girls needed solitude in which to meditate and it had not occurred to her that even intelligent girls who are also healthy could enjoy 'larks' and be just as high-spirited as stupid girls. How was he to tell her that too much peace and quiet was resented by the young adolescent, and that if she did not change her ideas there would be trouble? When later on Emily was forced into becoming Mistress, the quietness of Hitchin after London made her nervous, but she excused this on the ground that she was no scholar.

At last the longed-for but dreaded day arrived. Emily awoke at daybreak apprehensive yet excited. She did not dwell on her own feelings but let her mind linger on the fears and hopes of her prospective students. Were they lying awake in the half-light as she was, longing for the day to begin, yet half afraid? Would they enjoy college life, settle down to real work, and experience that sense of achievement that is so important when one is young? Of one thing Emily was certain. A new dawn was breaking for women everywhere and, although she might not live long enough to enjoy the full results, life was changing for the better.

11

'Everyone needs a purpose in life'

The five students were told not to come before the afternoon. Emily Gibson arrived shortly after one o'clock had struck, fearing that she was a little early; but she was so eager to start that to wait even an hour longer would have made her feel quite ill. It was just the right note to strike, the ice was broken, and Emily was so amused by the look of mock distress on the young girl's face that she laughed outright as she took both her hands in her own and made her welcome. She would have been even more amused had she read her first letter to her parents: she described Emily as a 'keen little lady, quivering with excitement thinly veiled under a business-like manner'. She was in no doubt that it was because of this 'little lady's' courage and enterprise that she was going to college for a delightful two or three years of study and freedom.

By the time all five girls had arrived Emily was amazed at the noise their chatter made and how even that small number seemed to fill the house. Two days later Mr Clark travelled from Cambridge to give his first lecture. Because Emily did not quite trust him not to deviate from the syllabus she went in with the girls and sat through all of it, notebook and pencil poised ready – not to catch the pearls that fell from Mr Clark's lips, but to note every deviation. She excused this outrageous conduct by coolly telling Clark that his lecture was so fascinating that she had not been able to drag herself away. Privately she did not think him as good as she had been led to believe, but put his nervous manner down to her presence – 'he had not expected it'. Indeed he had not.

Of course Emily was not qualified to teach but she quickly saw how she could be useful to the girls in a number of ways. She offered to hear them recite their Greek and Latin verbs and encouraged them to come and talk to her if something puzzled or upset them, an invitation they eagerly accepted. They came in twos and threes, talking naturally and openly about their frustrations and aspirations and their ambitions after they had become better educated. They asked endless questions, which Emily was able to answer. She had some questions of her own to ask, too. How had they heard of the college? Two had read an article by Llewelyn Davies in *Fraser's Magazine* and knew that this was what they had been waiting for. Two had academic fathers with friends in Cambridge, while one had Lord Lyttelton for a relation. All agreed that it was too good a

110

chance to miss. Emily Gibson pleased her by enthusing about Hannah Pipe's school at Laleham which she had attended – 'her teaching was inspired'. It was gratifying to learn that the school was using her book *Higher Education for Women* and that it had opened the girls' eyes to the many possibilities that life held for them.

An older student, Louisa Lumsden, impressed Emily with her serious outlook on life. She was twenty-eight years old and had always lived with her parents in Edinburgh, bored, restless, even friendless; she longed for some purpose in her life. She knew of girls as unhappy as herself, whose only recreation was to walk to the edge of the cliff and 'watch the Edinburgh express slip its carriages'.

Emily had made the basement dining room as like that of a man's college as possible, an arrangement that surprised the girls, who without a word took it upon themselves to alter it. '. . . the plan proposed', she had written to Charlotte Manning, 'is a students' table and a Mistress's table, the first long and narrow to sit only on one side with their faces towards the Mistress's table, the other a rather smaller table for the Mistress and supernumerary [possibly Adelaide Manning] and the College Secretary' (Emily herself). It looked too silly, as Louisa Lumsden pointed out, and was not conducive to conversation. 'We quietly ignored the rule and insisted upon comfortably facing each other. We might have been fifty undergraduates instead of five harmless young women.'

It was necessary to make some announcement about religion, as loose and free as possible, allowing the girls to decide for themselves. Her own feeling of rebellion against her strict evangelical Anglican upbringing was still very vivid to her. There was already among her five a Quaker, a Scottish Presbyterian and an Anglican, so she must tread carefully. As soon as possible she gathered her little flock together and told them they could attend any place of worship they liked in Hitchin – the parish church, the Congregational Chapel or the Friends' Meeting House. Although Benslow House had no chapel, she or Mrs Manning would hold simple morning devotions – a custom they were used to at home – at which passages from *The Book of Common Prayer* would be read, but there was no compulsion to attend. This proved acceptable to all.

Charlotte Manning was an immediate success as Mistress. Her gentle manner and obvious affection for young people made a great appeal. Her step-daughter, Adelaide, got on splendidly with the girls too; she made an efficient secretary, was so quick and methodical that she was able to help Emily with her work as well. Furthermore, her presence in the college meant that Emily had someone of her own age to consult whenever a tricky problem arose, and someone with whom she could gossip in rare leisure hours.

Like Emily, the Mistress was not qualified to teach, so her role was threefold: housekeeper, chaperone and bursar, for the simple household accounts were her responsibility. The Executive Committee had somehow managed to scrape together enough money to give Mrs Manning a small salary, but neither Emily nor Adelaide was paid.

It had been suggested that Emily should be the first head of her own college, but she had refused and for good reason. Until the college was well-established she would have to be here, there and everywhere, outside or in, working at the less glamorous but vitally important tasks of ironing out difficulties, keeping close watch on the teaching and getting the right people interested in higher education. She would, of course, have to be often at Benslow House, so a small bedroom – much less luxurious than the students' – was permanently reserved for her use. She would come and go as she pleased, commuting between London and Hitchin for committee work and to keep an eye on her mother.

With her dream a reality, albeit as yet only in a small way, she allowed herself the luxury of thinking of the future – a constant flow of girls coming and going, taking their degrees and then going out into the world properly equipped to make a career. How the teaching world would profit from these girls, eager to pass on their knowledge to others! Perhaps that was the most selfless career of all. She had the pleasure, indeed the great satisfaction, of seeing some signs of this manifesting themselves already. She had noticed how very quickly those who learned rapidly helped those slower than themselves. She had seen them go in and out of each other's rooms, piles of books under their arms, to share something that they had discovered or to read together. It was a cheering sight.

Emily did not imagine for one moment that her troubles were over. There were still battles to be fought, women to be roused, money to be raised and men to be made aware that women could not give of their best in an age of sex-discrimination and injustice. All the same, she had never been so happy. As the days passed she showed no sign of a violent reaction or depression, rather the reverse. Her euphoria did not lessen; she simply became more used to it and liked that state of mind all the more for familiarity. To wake up in her narrow iron bed in her little bare cell at the top of the house gave her an indescribable thrill. She would rouse herself slowly at six o'clock and murmur over and over again: 'this is college life'. It gave her a delicious feeling of fulfilment to go into the Mistress's room after breakfast to discuss the business of the day and see if there were new applications for admission. There frequently were, but a large batch of inquiries produced few with serious intentions, for far too many had been made out of curiosity.

While exploring the Hitchin bookshops one day, two of the girls discovered an indoor swimming pool with a 'Ladies only' afternoon and they decided – Emily and Adelaide too – to learn to swim. Competition was keen and they all agreed that they felt better for the exercise. They found an old croquet set in a shed, and although it was getting rather late in the year, the weather was so mild that they set it up and played between lectures, rushing out shouting to each other full of sparkle and fun. Henry Tomkinson, a frequent visitor, taught them how to play fives and showed no surprise when Emily at thirty-nine was quicker and more skilful than the younger girls. An old garden roller was dragged out of retirement, and some of them tried to balance on it while it was moving. Here was a game that Emily had often played with her brothers, frequently beating them with light rapid steps that they could not emulate. After each girl had had a turn she said casually, 'I believe I could do that', and holding out her hand to Louisa Lumsden she jumped lightly onto the roller and began her 'walk'. 'She seemed small and lightweight as I helped her to mount, then without the least mistake, she went from one end of the lawn to another,' Louisa wrote many years later.

But Emily had to draw the line at football which she caught the girls playing one day: when living in the rectory at Gateshead Emily had played the roughest football with her brothers every autumn and winter, and thought nothing of it. But here the circumstances were very different. At Gateshead the field where they played was well hidden from the house and the road, so no one knew of it, but if it leaked out that she allowed her girls to play football the gossip would cut through Cambridge like a keen east wind and she and her college would be swept away. She was well aware that to put a stop to harmless fun, purely because it was a male sport, could not be justified, yet she knew the world she had to deal with, so it had to be done. Of course she instantly lost popularity but she did not think of that; she would have to live it down without surrendering her authority.

The girls' reaction was just as she expected: in a second the atmosphere became electric, they seized their ball and marched off, muttering under their breath 'there is no harm in it'. They sent Emily to Coventry and she was almost tearful when she related the incident to Henry. She had been so pleased at the way the girls were progressing and so happy to prove the dons wrong by demonstrating that intellectual work did not unbalance girls and cause nervous breakdowns, and had even felt that she would like to invite a few of the most crusty and critical to watch the girls as they chased each other round the lawn.

She tried to explain why everyone at Benslow House had to be extra careful but they muttered sulkily that they did not care what people said, they were doing nothing wrong, and for that Emily had to rebuke them. Later she felt guilty that she had criticised them so sharply even to a man as kindly as Henry. They saw things differently because they were young: she could not rest until she had explained her

113

feelings to Henry in case she had given him a wrong impression: 'I have been sorry since for disclosing any part of the imperfect side of anyone here, but you will not think more of it than was meant . . .'

There were few distractions at Hitchin but the girls were amazingly good at making their own amusements. Everything was fun. They had formed themselves into a club, 'the college Five' and, elated by success in the practice Little-go which Professor Seeley had set them, decided to celebrate by trying their hand at acting a selection of scenes from Shakespeare. They hunted in the attic for discarded curtains and bed covers to turn into improvised costumes and stage properties. When all was ready they invited everyone in the house for a performance in the library. Perhaps rather thoughtlessly, for they considered themselves sophisticated young women who understood the distaste in which acting of any sort was held in the conventional society of the day, two of them wore boys' clothing and came tripping onto the makeshift stage full of confidence and expecting applause. Instead the outraged audience watched this scene in stony silence, and when all was over Emily trounced the girls roughly for jeopardising the good name of the college. Emily Gibson has left a short account of this painful scene: 'The ringleaders amongst us took umbrage and disputed the right of the college authorities to interfere in such matters, and relations with Miss Davies became strained.'

Behind these disagreements there lay one simple fact. So alien to the society of the day was higher education for girls that, as Emily later realised, only the bravest and most unconventional dared to undertake it. This was probably the reason why so many of the first applicants had withdrawn at the last moment. The first five were therefore in effect almost revolutionaries against society. Emily too was a revolutionary, but only in one way: women must be lifted out of their current state of ignorance and educated to play their part in the world. Thus Emily and the pioneers did not see eye to eye in every particular. No wonder that there was occasional friction between them.

The Shakespeare incident was, Emily said, nothing but 'a storm in a teacup' and rather laughable by present day standards. Its importance lies in showing how backward English society was in this respect. At that date (1869) acting was not allowed in Cambridge at all; undergraduates who wanted to act had to do so in secret and had to be very circumspect, since discovery might mean expulsion. On the other hand, ten years earlier Victoria and Albert had encouraged their children to give *tableaux vivants* to celebrate birthdays and the Queen was very proud of the 'perfect boy' that Vicky (the Princess Royal) made. There was no nonsense at the palace about not wearing boys' clothes.

By some curious quirk these outdated conventions were particularly

114

slow to change among the professions. Not long before the football incident Lizzie Garrett, who had to tread warily in matters of convention, had written to Emily about a somewhat similar dilemma. She had invited a colleague (Ellen Drewy) to read chemistry with her. Ellen duly came, but as Lizzie wrote to Emily: '. . . after the arrangements were made for her to come I was almost afraid it was unwise on my part. She looks awfully strong-minded in walking-dress, short petticoats and close round hat and several other dreadfully ugly arrangements, but as my room is out of the way I hope she will not be supposed to belong to me by the students.' Lizzie was full of courage, afraid of no one and the least conventional of girls, yet even she was alarmed that Ellen Drewy's masculine attire might reflect badly on her and harm her career.

After the acting incident the atmosphere at Benslow House was heavy with resentment, although Emily would have been glad to forget the whole affair once the rebuke had been given, but the girls felt ill-treated and misunderstood and would not be easily appeased.

Barbara Bodichon was due to pay a visit and as soon as she arrived, Emily, who hated quarrels and looked on Barbara as a peacemaker, begged her to speak to the ringleader Emily Gibson and make her see reason, which Barbara willingly agreed to do. When Barbara went along to her room, Emily was making a dress for herself, 'a preacher's robe', a style Barbara favoured. Indeed she liked it so much that she begged to be given the pattern and in her enthusiasm for a new kind of dress she forgot all about the scolding she had come to give and did not say even a few words to stop this stupid feud. According to Emily Gibson she never mentioned the transgression. Yet that night at dinner she unblushingly told Emily that she had used 'strong words' and that the matter was at an end.

12

No Second Chance

The Lent Term of 1870 did not start well. The girls returned after too much cossetting at home, full of grumbles about all sorts of things. The food was too fattening, the beds too narrow, the sheets too short, the mirrors too high on the wall, and they thought it childish to have to ask permission for leave of absence even for one night. Calmly – for the atmosphere was becoming heated – Emily explained that the Mistress was *in loco parentis* and if their parents wanted to get in touch with their daughters quickly it would look very bad if she said that she did not know where they were. It was a rule very strictly adhered to in men's colleges and she was afraid that they would have to put up with it. Not all complaints were settled so easily: why were the gates closed at 10 p.m.? Again, they were told that it was the same in the men's colleges and they would have to accept it.

By the end of term tempers improved with the onset of spring, which showed itself early in the sheltered garden of Benslow House. After consultation with two of the lecturers, Mr Clark and Mr Stuart, Emily was able to tell the girls that they had praised their work and the admirable diligence and courage (for none had the slightest experience of intellectual discipline) they had shown in getting down to study. In private Clark told Emily that four of the girls had a good chance of attaining Tripos standard later on if they worked steadily. (Discreetly she does not name the fifth girl who 'lagged behind'). In addition at Emily's instance all of them had shown a growing interest in current affairs, a closed book to them hitherto, and were now assiduously reading *The Times, Manchester Guardian* and the *Spectator*.

A wooden hut with an iron roof had to be built hastily in the garden the following October to accommodate three new students. It was the best that could be done in a hurry but it was not popular with the unfortunates chosen to sleep there. Hot in summer, cold in winter, cramped and draughty, the rooms divided only by curtains, it was a nightmare to those sensitive to noise; rain falling on the tin roof was particularly irritating. The girls loathed it, christened it 'the tabernacle in the wilderness on the way to the promised land' and grumbled incessantly. Curiously enough, Emily quite failed to understand why it was so hated. Creature comforts meant little to her and she possessed that iron endurance which sent many a gently nurtured Victorian woman to wild and distant lands in search of adventure, enduring privation and hardship without complaint. She did not want to be unsympathetic, but in her heart she thought it a fuss about nothing.

But the grumbles and cross looks produced one good result. Emily began to realise that with few outside interests and few girls of their own age to mix with apart from those in college, the students were becoming too inward-looking, too absorbed in themselves, so that small incidents became enlarged and discomforts magnified out of proportion. But what remedy was there in a small country town?

When winter was past and the weather improved, the girls took to going for long walks in the unspoiled countryside, returning tired but glowing with health, their arms full of wild flowers, laughing and joking together. Emily was amazed that such disparate characters, boxed up together in a small house, could find so many common interests. Their conviviality found expression too in reading aloud together in the evening, sitting round the fire in happy contentment, their day's work done. One wet and windy week-end one of them introduced charades, and very noisy and hilarious they were: the merriment was sweet to Emily's ears. She took comfort from knowing that their troubles did not go very deep and were soon forgotten.

Emily was not the only one to see Charlotte Manning leave Hitchin at the end of the Michaelmas Term with real regret. She had turned out to be everything that the head of a woman's college should be and the girls immediately sensed this, treating her with the greatest respect, even with awe. Not the least part of Emily's regret was the departure of Adelaide, who had been a wonderful prop and stay, but her stepmother's increasing infirmity meant that she could not be left alone for long and Adelaide had to be constantly in attendance.

Another Emily, daughter of Rear-Admiral W.H. Sherreff, was chosen to succeed Charlotte Manning and, although nervous at the thought of change, Emily felt certain that the right choice had been made. The youthful Emily Gibson described her in a letter to her parents as 'elderly', yet Emily Sherreff had only just turned fifty and looked young for her age, as her photograph shows. She had a sense of humour and seemed at her interview both tolerant and authoritative. For many years her interest had centred on women's education and her book *Thoughts on Self-culture for Women* caused a stir and sold well in its day. Emily, who always relied on first impressions, warmed to her on sight, while the Executive Committee much liked the modest way she accepted the post, calling herself privileged to belong to this remarkable new college and saying how much she looked forward to the chance of observing the effect of higher education at close quarters: 'Her view of coming here,'

117

Emily told Anna Richardson, 'is simply that if she is wanted and can do it, she ought.'

Another addition to the college staff was Julia Wedgwood of the pottery family, a friend of Emily's, who had offered to come in a temporary capacity to help out as tutor. Her experience of girls had been gained through teaching in the village school her father had set up, and she had liked it so much that she wanted to gain experience of another class of girl, engaged on far more difficult work. Like Emily she was self-educated, highly intelligent and quick, with a keen sense of what was fitting: that was all that could be asked for until the present generation of students was ready to teach. Julia Wedgwood had one other advantage: she was deeply interested in the Women's Movement and held many of Emily's views on the necessity of awakening women to the need to help themselves.

Living on the spot as she had done for several weeks, Emily could see what other changes were needed. Domestic affairs were still under the care of the Mistress, but Emily saw the necessity for releasing her from mundane jobs and giving her more responsible tasks better fitted to her position, lest the post sink to the level of a domestic servant. The past division of responsibility for domestic affairs between three inexperienced women (the Mistress, Adelaide and Emily) had not made for a smoothly run household. A housekeeper was required, but how could one be induced to leave London and incarcerate herself in a small country town with a bunch of unappreciative girls?

Emily Sherreff was settling in well as Mistress. Emily Davies felt that it was a great advantage that she came from quite a different background, because this would mean that many new people would hear of the college and begin to send their daughters. The great disadvantage of not advertising was that only a small proportion of people had yet heard of it. Emily felt that only ignorance of its existence kept prospective pupils from hammering on the door for admittance. As it was, numbers increased too slowly to induce confidence in doubting parents. Here Miss Sherreff could be very helpful in telling her friends of its existence. She had another asset too: she had scholarly interests and encouraged the girls to read more widely, lending them her own books and discussing different points with them afterwards.

All the girls had bravely consented to take Little-go without any pushing from Emily; as they said, what had they to lose? But as the time approached nerves became frayed and tempers strained; here again Emily Sherreff was a great help in calming them down. The chief complainer was Louisa Lumsden, who said (most unfairly) that the students only existed for the college and that Emily cared nothing for their welfare. 'We were mere cogs in the wheel of Miss Davies's great scheme, we counted for little or nothing as long as we furthered her plans,' she wrote much later in her acid little book *Yellow Leaves*.

Happily Emily was not fully aware of the extent of these grumbles or how insidious they were. In their hearts the girls knew that they had benefited greatly from all that Emily had done and was continuing to do for them, but because they were young and privileged, a little spoilt and not quite as comfortable in Benslow House as they were in their prosperous middle-class homes, they blamed her for luring them away. Their parents would never have forced them into hard intellectual work which might in the end prove fruitless.

Since the girls were suffering from examination nerves, this was the worst possible moment for Professor Seeley and the other lecturers to behave badly. In Emily's opinion they had chosen it in order to wear her down when she was already low. In fact there was no truth in this at all. They had not the imagination to stop and reflect on her feelings, and they had not given the timing a thought. They had something to say and they said it. Poor Emily had thought that the disagreement between herself and the lecturers had long been at an end and Seeley's letter came as a shock. Had he only acquiesced because it was convenient for him to do so? His letter was probably meant to be businesslike and not as unkind as it sounds, but it caught Emily unprepared: 'Just at the moment when education is taking a new shape, I cannot take any pleasure in attending to the details of a college where the old and to me obsolete routine goes on. I cannot do more than passively wish you well. I do not feel prepared to give my time to you . . .' This was indeed a severe blow. Seeley was an excellent teacher, and to get someone as good to replace him seemed impossible. What was more, the girls loved his teaching since he possessed the knack of firing them with enthusiasm. Who could replace such a man?

Emily had long know that, by insisting on the same examinations as the men, she had chosen a rough and stony path and that she had to walk it alone. But she was convinced that it was the right path and to turn back now in the face of discouragement was impossible. She had never aspired to popularity and cared nothing for it now, but it did seem hard to find so few who believed in her. Recently, with all the turmoil leading up to Little-go, she had felt that she was entering into the bleakest and most discouraging stage of her work to bring women out of the darkness into the light. It was only possible to bear it because she knew that her steadiness and resolution were being tested to the utmost of her endurance: she sensed that if she faltered now all that she had gained so far would be lost for ever. There would be no second chance.

Many years ago when Emily had first begun to work at improving the lot of women, Llewelyn had given her some good advice: take your troubles as they come and do not dwell on them when you go to bed, otherwise you will soon be worn down and you will lose your judgement, so essential for taking important decisions. Emily felt that she had already lost not only all judgement but all ability to foresee trouble. She ought to have realised that Seeley and she could not agree at any point. She was wondering what to do about a replacement for him and getting nowhere when she received another shock: a letter from the Council of the Senate to say that since her college was not part of the university she must not take it for granted that her students would be allowed to take Little-go. Permission would have to be asked for but would not necessarily be given, although the authorities had no objection if she cared to make a private arrangement with the examiners. These private arrangements were not easy to make, and after trying to find help and getting nothing but refusals, in a fit of despair Emily threw herself on the mercy of Dr Cartmell, the senior examiner, pleading ignorance. Dr Cartmell responded with the greatest goodwill in the world and arranged everything, even a room in the University Arms hotel, because the girls would have to sit the examination in Cambridge.

When the day came, Emily took charge of the girls herself. The train from Hitchin was late and to Emily, used as she was to the journey, its stoppings and startings and slow progress between stations became very nerve-racking. Nevertheless she managed to conceal her nervousness from the girls who were white and trembling with apprehension. They knew very well that the eyes of Cambridge were on them and that they were not kindly eyes: naturally this added to their misery.

To Emily's relief, all went well. Dr Cartmell looked in from time to time to see if anything was needed and in the end what was dreaded as a terrible ordeal turned out to be a pleasure: 'everything has gone quite smoothly,' Emily informed Anna that night, 'the kindness shown on all sides has been exhilarating. We have managed to see a great deal during our leisure intervals and the three classical students went with me to dine at our Greek lecturer's, where we met a pleasant party.' The girls delighted in Cambridge, and found everything wonderful. Their hostess invited other young people to meet them who instantly offered to show them the sights. It was all so different from what Emily had expected.

When all the girls passed there was general rejoicing. *Punch* did not allow such an historic event to go unnoticed: 'Out of all these flowers of loveliness, not one was plucked. Bachelors of Arts are all likely to be made to look to their laurels by these spinsters.' As had happened over the mock examination, such unexpected success gave the girls courage to believe that they could work for a Tripos. This was all very well, but Emily had to remind them that unlike boys they were starting from scratch and that although the long pull of elementary work for a small examination like Little-go had ended in triumph, it had been a strain for girls unused to study to work at their desks for four or five hours a day. Nevertheless it was a challenge that the girls were eager to take up. They begged Emily to tell them just what it involved, which she did as well as she could, warning them that it would be better if they took classics and mathematics instead of other subjects (moral science, for example, which very much intrigued them), because there were far more university teachers in these well-established subjects who knew the ropes. Classics and mathematics could be learned in three years, natural sciences and moral philosophy could not. (The girls took only classics and mathematics. There were as yet no Tripos examinations in history, English and economics, for instance.) Some of the lecturers (James Bryce, for example, whose lectures were so popular that even Emily attended them) were more acceptable than others who tended to try out their own pet theories on the girls rather than keeping strictly to the Tripos syllabus. Emily had to be forever on the watch for these sly tricks.

Because the new Mistress was turning out to be efficient and helpful, Emily spent less time in Hitchin and more in London, advertising the college and recruiting new pupils as far as she dared without appearing too blatantly partisan. Thus she failed to notice that Emily Sherreff was becoming restless, despite the fact that once she told Emily wistfully that she would like to have more to do with the academic side of the college. Hints having failed, she then asked Emily outright if she might be entrusted with the 'arrangement of studies', saying that it would give her pleasure to relieve Emily of a tedious and time-consuming job. Emily knew very well that this intelligent and well-read woman could do this as well as she could, but it happened to be a task that Emily much enjoyed since it brought her into direct contact with the dons. She had spent many happy hours discussing the merits of various subjects that might be most useful to her girls, and she was loath to give this up. She made some lame excuse: it was expedient to keep this in her own hands at present, adding vaguely that some time in the future she might be glad of help. Thus the matter remained unresolved.

A little later when she asked Emily Sherreff if she would like to stay on, the Mistress made conditions: she wanted two things: 1. to direct studies 2. to become a member of the Executive Committee. Here she touched a sensitive spot. Long ago Emily had explained to the Committee that it would not do for one of the paid staff to be a member. It might give rise to acute embarrassment, and complications might follow when their own appointment or tenure was under discussion. That was why the Committee consisted entirely of outsiders (except for Emily herself), most of them resident in London. There was some point in this, but it had the immense disadvantage (which Emily does not seem to have realised), that as things stood there was no link between the college and the committee which ruled it except for herself, and that only so long as she was part of the time resident in Hitchin.

There is no doubt that Emily felt a little guilt in denying this natural request. She wrote Charlotte Manning a somewhat lame explanatory letter: 'She evidently thinks that the power of active help depends more than it does on the committee.' It was now quite plain to Emily Sherreff that the Committee and Emily were willing to wait until a member of the college itself became qualified to take over the job of resident tutor who would manage the girls' studies, therefore she was not surprised when both her requests were refused. But the consequence was that in the summer term of 1870 Emily Sherreff resigned and Emily, who did not want to lose her, was taken aback. Only two months previously she had told Charlotte Manning that the new Mistress was '. . . an amiable affectionate woman warmly interested in the college . . . I feel inclined to persuade her to stay on if she is willing . . .' But Emily had not cared to bend her rules a little to allow the 'amiable' woman to stay on. So Emily Sherreff packed her bags and left, and Annie Austin took her place at short notice. Thus Hitchin was denied the help and advice of a sensible and intelligent woman when she was most needed.

13

'Preposterous things sometimes get done'

In October 1870 Emily received an excited letter from Lizzie Garrett with the astonishing news that she had been invited by the Working Men's Association to stand for the newly established School Board as the representative in the Marylebone division. Lizzie had become highly thought of by working-class people after opening her dispensary for sick women and children in the area, a clinic that she was able to finance herself because she also carried on a flourishing private practice from her own house, which proudly bore a brass plate with her name, 'Elizabeth Garrett M.D.'.

She had been practising as a doctor since 1865, after passing with high marks the final examination of the Society of Apothecaries, but her MD degree was taken in Paris since the obduracy of London University had prevented her from acquiring a doctorate in England. Therefore she refused to use the title 'doctor', a self-imposed prohibition with which Emily was in complete agreement. 'I should not consider it an act of friendship,' Emily explained to Barbara, 'to present anyone to strangers under a title which excited repugnance.'

The invitation to Lizzie, which came from the husbands and fathers of her dispensary patients, posed a real dilemma. Would her medical work suffer were she to accept the distinction of being the first woman ever to be the member of such a body? 'It's queer why they want me,' she wrote to Emily. 'I wish you were here to advise.' Four days later Lizzie followed this light-hearted letter with a more serious one; enthusiasm for the honour that had so unexpectedly come to her swept her along faster than she cared. A deputation of working men had told her that it was her duty to accept, since no one was better qualified. 'I suppose I ought not to refuse,' she wrote a little doubtfully, ' 'tho' I am sorry it is so. I dare say when it has to be done I can do it . . .'

Almost at once it was Emily's turn to face the same dilemma. Before she could reply to Lizzie, she was invited to stand for the City division of the School Board by an uncle of one of her Hitchin pupils. Like Lizzie, her first thought was to refuse. The invitation had come by the same post as yet another letter from Lizzie telling Emily that she had been asked to speak on the same platform as her rival for the seat, Professor Huxley, and that she trembled at the very thought, although she accepted the fact that, if she were to stand, speech-making and publicity were unavoidable: 'We must be ready to go into the thing as men do, if we go at all,' she wrote, 'and in time there will be no more awkwardness on our side than there is on theirs . . . the first of these trials is to be some time next week. I hope you will be up in time to go with me.'

This letter decided one thing for Emily; she could not plead too much work as an excuse if Lizzie, who was slaving away from dawn till dusk, did not. Perhaps it might make matters easier if she and Lizzie spoke at each other's meetings and thus gave each other more support. On reflection she felt that there was a strong reason why neither she nor Lizzie should refuse – it was a unique chance for women to take part in public life. If they did not accept it would be held against them and never forgotten: it would be said of women that they get the chance but are too timid to seize it.

Emily did not want to give a definite answer until she had consulted Henry Tomkinson, although it is plain from her letter to Lizzie that she had already made up her mind. 'I am torn in two between rival advisers,' she told Henry. 'My mother and Miss Garrett urge that if a woman is wanted, I ought not to lose time by holding back. My brother insists that it would be too audacious to stand for the greatest constituency in the world [the City of London] without more invitation. What do you think? If one could be absolutely sure of respectable failure it would be enough. An ignominious and ridiculous defeat would do harm. Do please give me some advice about the City. It strikes me as preposterous . . . but preposterous things sometimes get done.'

Henry's reply was a shock, it was so discouraging. He neither congratulated her nor said 'well done', but stated bluntly that she would be taking on more than was good for her and would soon wear herself out. He advised her to refuse. Because it was not what Emily expected or wanted to hear, she was incensed: how dare Henry be so cross-grained? She had not expected congratulations on being singled out for such an honour but neither had she expected a douche of cold water. And this was the one person above all others whom she thought she could rely on for comfort and support. She replied crossly: 'we have not any of the crafty designs that you attribute to us'. How different was the letter she received from the public health pioneer, Edwin Chadwick, urging her to accept since 'your name has been proposed by others as well as myself . . .'

Because of the burden of responsibility it would entail, Emily thought it wiser to refuse the City and to stand instead for Greenwich, which was proposed as an alternative. She made sure that Henry heard of the change, although she told herself that she did not care what he thought. Once having taken the plunge she had no intention of looking back with that uncertain feeling which she knew to be so bad for progress. With the decision taken she went straight ahead and prepared her election address.

In recent months there had been some acrimonious comments in the papers about the lack of religious instruction in schools. Emily was strongly in favour of religious instruction for the young and insisted in her address to the electors on making her position clear, even if it turned the voters against her: 'I believe that religious instruction suitable to children may begin without entering into doctrinal differences and that for practical teachers "the religious difficulty" can scarcely be said to exist. However I am willing to accept the parliamentary provision of a purely secular education for those who prefer it.'

It would have been natural for her to show her address to Henry Tomkinson for criticism and comment, had he not already tried to discourage her from the whole enterprise. It gave her confidence, on the other hand, to know that she had written her speech entirely on her own and that she had not said a word that might offend. But she was still angry with Henry, who was still standing his ground and refusing to change his opinion – that she was grossly over-doing things and that her latest venture was madness. He had become a typical male in her eyes, refusing to pay any attention to her plea that she would be shirking responsibility if she turned such an offer down. She told herself that it did not matter in the least what he thought, his disapproval meant nothing to her . . . Nevertheless the thought that she and Henry had quarrelled prevented her from feeling happy. She told herself that she knew that the work would be arduous, proper work well done always was, but she would have people to help her even in planning her campaign. 'It cannot be worse than those terrible drawing-rooms about the college at Mrs Russell Gurney's which I did survive.'

She wrote to Henry in an effort to soften him, enclosing a draft of her letter of acceptance, but without any effect. He answered with another stiff note which she replied to with firmness: 'I am sorry you and Mrs Tomkinson [Henry's mother] do not approve, but I think you would if I could explain exactly with what intention I am going into it. You ignore the philanthropic period of my history: the twenty years at Gateshead were all schools and district visiting, and I feel that the experience counts for a good deal as a qualification for the School Board.' The result of this letter was silence.

The address read quite well, but it would have been nice to have been told that it was really good, as praise from Henry was always sincere: 'I have had some experience in the management of schools for the artisan and labouring classes and in other ways have had opportunities of becoming acquainted with the homes of the poor. I believe that the education of neglected children can only be secured by compulsory measures . . .' In conclusion she reasserted what she had said earlier to the Social Science Association – that she would be sorry to see religion excluded from schools.

No sooner had she posted this important letter than Barbara wrote to say that she, too, thought it a mistake for Emily to accept the School Board invitation, but if she insisted on standing, could she not use this golden opportunity to stress the importance of good health? 'The way to good health is to have it taught in schools and a catechism of health should be compiled and taught.' Emily's heart sank when she read this letter, for she knew that once Barbara was off on her hobby horse, nothing but compliance would stop her. She would return to the subject again and again, possibly because she had lost her own glowing health and knew that she would never regain it. Emily treated this request, as she did so many of Barbara's suggestions now, with good humour and tact: 'Lizzie Garrett does not believe in teaching health in schools . . . the great thing would be to approve healthy habits. I would think it possible that some little teaching might also be useful in elementary schools, the ignorance of the class from which the children come being so very great . . .'

From the beginning of her public life Emily insisted on writing and delivering her own speeches: it was a matter of pride. It encouraged her that her first to the voters of Greenwich was a success, but her speech the following week at Blackheath was a disaster. Confronted with row upon row of apathetic female faces, their dull eyes fixed on the platform, Emily almost dried up with dismay: 'I had an uncomfortable sense of failure,' she wrote to Henry (whom she had vowed never to speak to again, but from whom she had now received a charming little note apologising for his bad temper: 'caused only by concern for you' made everything right again). Nevertheless he kept away from her meetings, and now she was glad since she did not want him to see her make an exhibition of herself. 'I felt myself nervously hurrying on to get it over,' she wrote, 'and I am afraid the audience must have felt the same. This chilly reaction to the opening speeches was depressing but one ought to be able to resist such influences . . .'

A week later Emily went to Marylebone to speak for Lizzie. Her campaign was going well and she was on sparkling form. Lizzie had never cared for public speaking but she seemed to have overcome her abhorrence of it, for she held the audience of a thousand spellbound and they cheered her at the end. She dealt easily with hecklers and stood up to a not unkindly barrage with remarkable aplomb. When it was Emily's turn they immediately started to question her on religious instruction in schools. Later she heard that since it was known that she was a clergyman's daughter, they were surprised to find her so broad-minded, in particular her boldly uttered belief that parents should not be forced into letting their children sit through religious instruction of a different creed from their own. When the speeches were over the women came crowding into the committee room to shake both speakers by the hand as they promised their votes. But would they remember on the day?

Emily and Lizzie had to be honest with each other and confess that if they had known the work involved they might have thought twice before taking it on, but as Lizzie reminded Emily, 'failing conspicuously will do us as women so much harm that it must be avoided at all costs'. Emily's schedule was heavy. The organisers were merciless and arranged not one meeting an evening (the only time at which working people could attend) but several, sometimes many miles apart. As well as this she had to fit in at least one three o'clock meeting at the Crystal Palace. Henry was right, Emily thought wearily as she made her way home, it was tough going, tougher than even he had guessed. But if men were beginning to believe that women were needed and could do a job well, it was worth it. She longed to go straight to bed as soon as she reached home, but that was impossible. There were the next night's speeches to prepare, letters to answer, and questions about this and that from Benslow House to look into. All her speeches had to be checked again in the morning and facts verified, for she knew from experience how quickly one could be felled by ignorance. Fortunately her experiences at Gateshead had sharpened her gift for repartee. When asked by a hostile member of the audience why schools did not teach cooking, needlework and washing, Emily replied that to teach these subjects in school hours would be doing a very right thing in a very wrong place. 'I am glad the Board has not sanctioned anything of the sort.'

She defended compulsory school with knowledge and skill, qualifying her statement by saying that she knew and sympathised with the difficulties of mothers. There might be many reasons why a mother did not send her child to school: no warm clothes in winter was a common reason and in cases like these, women would be much more understanding than men. She claimed that although she believed in compulsory school, she did not believe that there should be penalties for non-attendance. In many cases persuasion was more effective.

Once again *Punch* was to the fore with support. Emily's answers to these questions were praised in glowing terms: 'the ladies possessed no strong-minded doctrines, only those which all rational people could teach'. A great point was made about the impression left by Emily and Lizzie on the audience: 'it was womanly'. Not to be 'strong-minded' but to be 'womanly' was praise indeed. Far too many males of that period feared that education would make a woman masculine.

Since 1862, when Emily had first started work for the women's movement, she had gained greatly in stature. It was not that her manner had changed; she was still demure and smiling, but so clear-headed and decisive in conversation that those who tried to trick her into submission on a point where she had no intention of giving way often found to their cost that it did not pay to challenge her without first making sure of the facts. Her self-confidence and her conviction that she could handle the opposition and lead her troops to victory had developed continuously since her first battle five years earlier. She was at her best as leader taking sole responsibility, and when her passion was roused she was often feared.

It was she who first thought of the idea of having district agents, whose job it would be to visit the homes of schoolchildren to find out why they were not attending school. On one point she was adamant: these women were not to seem to be acting like police but only as women (preferably mothers themselves) who would be sympathetic and gain the parents' confidence by showing at once that they had come to help and advise; they should keep their tempers under pressure, for parents often became belligerent through fear. After her experiences at Gateshead there was little Emily did not know about the bad effect poverty had on morale.

All sorts of people came forward and offered to speak on Emily's behalf, among them Thomas Hughes, author of *Tom Brown's Schooldays*, and Henry Robey, the Cambridge don once highly critical of her but now quite won over. Some were so enthusiastic about the special gifts women possessed for this work that they communicated their enthusiasm to the audience, whose response became overwhelming.

All was going well for Emily and Lizzie. The meetings were no longer the cold affairs that they had been to start with but became noisy with laughter and good humour; but Emily missed the warm words of praise that Henry had always given her when she did well. She always spoke better and was less nervous when he was on the platform clapping vigorously or silently supporting her, and the fact that she could not discuss the proceedings with him afterwards (as she always had done) took away some of her zest for public speaking. She confessed to Adelaide Manning, who came with her as often as she could: 'Speaking does not get easier as time goes on. The chief feeling that I get through it all is a kind of sense of being half asleep and having nothing to do with it.'

As the days wore on and the election loomed nearer Emily began to experience a sinking feeling that perhaps Henry was right after all; the work was almost too much for her. Yet she must have concealed her feelings and spoken with more confidence than she thought, for the audiences had come to respond well, listening and clapping in the right places.

When the election took place in late November both Emily and Lizzie were successful, winning by comfortable majorities, Lizzie topping the poll in Marylebone. Both women went bravely to the count. While waiting for the result, sitting in a dark deserted corner of the platform, Emily said she experienced the strangest feeling that she had 'moved forward a century in time': for a moment she could not imagine what she and Lizzie were doing in the Guildhall. She was nervous, too, and this surprised her, especially since Lizzie seemed perfectly composed; she wondered whether perhaps her strange sensations were caused by fatigue.

At the first Board meeting after the election there was some talk that Lizzie, who had polled the greatest number of votes, should take the chair. After persuasion she laughingly agreed and later was severely rebuked by Emily for levity. Emily treated her roughly, making no allowance for the excitement of the moment, which was great and must have been felt by Emily too, otherwise she would not have acted so out of character. She was still angry when she reached home that night, and in this mood, as though her instantaneous rebuke was not enough, she wrote poor Lizzie a harsh letter, the first and last of its kind that she was ever to write to a friend so close to her heart: 'I should be sorry that you should do anything that might give colour to the charge of being "cheeky" which has been brought against you lately. It is true that your jokes are many and reckless, they do more harm than you know . . .'

That Emily should lose her temper in this childish way is inexplicable; she must indeed have been not only tired out but unwell. But her remarks to Lizzie are put more clearly into context (though they cannot be excused) by a letter sent to her by Henry Skelton Anderson, a successful young businessman who was deeply in love with Lizzie and whom she was shortly to marry. After a meeting at which she had made an indiscreet reply to a heckler, he wrote angrily 'you have lost yourself thousands of votes by your carelessness . . .'

Lizzie knew very well that she had transgressed through high spirits and that she had been brought up short by two people who really loved her and cared deeply about her welfare. In other less exciting circumstances she would have understood that any lack of decorum by a woman at a vital stage in their fight for freedom would be held against them and greatly exaggerated.

The work of the new School Board was as heavy as Henry Tomkinson had predicted, but having taken up her position as women's champion it was impossible for Emily not to do what was asked of her – to serve on two of the six standing committees – just because she was a woman; yet these alone involved hours of preparation. In addition she paid her regular visits to Hitchin and coped with the many difficulties waiting for her there.

When in 1872 she was compelled to become Mistress of her college, first at Hitchin and then in its permanent site at Girton, the double (or rather treble) burden became overwhelming and she was forced to resign from the School Board and its many committees the following year. At last she understood what Henry had meant and that his severity had been, as he said, caused solely by concern for her.

Nevertheless she did not regret her three years' hard work: all she had learned in that time enormously increased her knowledge both in education and human nature. As she said to Lizzie: 'I would not have missed it for the world.'

14

'A prey to all sorts of fears'

The lease of Benslow House was due to expire in the Michaelmas Term 1872. Soon a decision would have to be made as to where the new college site should be. It was because Emily hoped that the numbers would rapidly increase that she had refused to be bullied into signing a lease for more than three years; she wanted to be free to move as soon as the college looked like becoming firmly established. Three or four extra students in a moderate-sized house gave a look of overcrowding. The makeshift building in the garden continued to be most unpopular and this proved, as nothing else could, that a permanent site must be found as quickly as possible or students would have to be turned away. Her dreams had always been of a college large enough to hold three or four hundred, all in the greatest comfort. Barbara Bodichon with much good sense advocated an immediate move to Cambridge where there was plenty of space, and land could be bought cheaply. In her heart Emily longed for someone to push her towards Cambridge, the rightful place for the college to be. But the feeling of hostility towards women generated by the dons was so fierce that she could not subject her girls to such an atmosphere; therefore under the circumstances it did not seem a serious proposition.

It was very tedious to have to reopen the old arguments as to where was most suitable for the new building. Mrs Russell Gurney, an influential member of the Executive Committee and one of those saintly women who see evil everywhere when the sexes are mixed, was absolutely against Cambridge, and others acquiesced in her opinion without giving the matter much thought. Even someone with as much sense as Lady Augusta Stanley, Dean Stanley's wife, was swayed more than she liked to admit by Mrs Russell Gurney, and she said (a little doubtfully, it is true) that mothers of daughters were a prey to all sorts of fears and the idea of a women's college in Cambridge might frighten them. A letter from the wife of the Master of Marlborough, Mrs Bradley (a short-sighted mother who had already been unwilling to give up any of her many daughters to Emily's care) angered Emily by its ignorance. She knew nothing at all about Cambridge, yet was determinedly against the place for 'innocent young girls'. Emily asked her boldly if her prejudices were well-founded: 'I think you may sometimes afford to defy prejudice

131

and find courage the best policy, but if the objection has no real weight it is worth nothing.'

Nevertheless, the prejudice did affect Emily too, although she tried to be impartial, as this letter to Anna Richardson shows: '. . . without actually seeing something of University life, you can scarcely understand how distracting it would be to have two thousand undergraduates, most of them idle and pleasure-loving, close to your doors. I am only speaking of English human nature as it has been made by social habits and by the system of segregating boys and girls from childhood, but we cannot wait ten or twelve years for our building, we shall want it next October . . .'

Between desire to place the college near the university for educational reasons, and a certain reluctance to expose girls to the dangers (whether real or imaginary) of proximity to so many young men, Emily was swayed first one way and then the other. Never before had she found it so hard to make up her mind. In the end she opted for boldness, as always, and never had the slightest cause for regret.

By the summer of 1871 the Executive Committee, at last aware of the urgency to build quickly, decided on a site 'near but not in Cambridge' and to purchase it as soon as they could raise £7,000: '. . . I should like to be in a position to judge whether at a distance of three or four miles it would be tolerably secure from the ravages of Cambridge under-graduates . . .' Emily wrote with a touch of her old humour. 'I am not so much afraid of undergraduates. We might protect ourselves from them while still giving the students as much freedom as at this age (eighteen to twenty-one) would be desirable for them.'

On the whole she was content: 'near' Cambridge was good enough. Land was cheaper outside the town even than at Hitchin, and the salaries of lecturers would be less because there would be no travelling expenses. Moreover, in time the girls might be allowed to go to the regular univer-sity lectures in Cambridge itself, thus saving a great deal more money. Emily wrote hopefully to Anna Richardson: '. . . as soon as the sum of £7,000 can be raised the committee resolve to purchase an adequate site and to build on a plan capable of future additions, rooms for a Mistress and thirty students with the necessary lecture rooms, kitchens etc., the site to be near Cambridge but not in or close to Cambridge itself . . . but about three miles off . . .' At the same time a note went to Henry Tomkinson, who had been unable to attend the meeting: '. . . three miles from Cambridge was fixed on . . . I told the meeting that all that mattered was that Benslow House was bursting at the seams and while we can only take twelve students we can scarcely speak of the college as a national institution without being laughed at.'

It was a great humiliation, after aiming at £30,000 (even £50,000 at one time) to have to face the sad fact that £7,000 was proving difficult to raise. Barbara offered to send another £100 at once to get the subscription list going. Emily gratefully accepted it, while reminding herself how many more such cheques she would need before reaching the least amount which would permit a brick to be laid. Henry Tomkinson suggested another fund-raising public meeting, and it took place in May 1871. Lord Lyttelton, the Bishop of Peterborough, Emily and Lizzie spoke, but only £600 was raised. Yet the meeting did serve another useful purpose: it made people think seriously and for the first time about women's education, a subject which had never troubled their heads before, and because of that Emily felt that it could be looked on as a success.

In the end another suggestion of Henry Tomkinson's – to raise money by private guarantees – was adopted; it would at least fill the immediate need to raise enough money to buy a site for a new college. That was why long before she expected it Emily was travelling to Cambridge with him to find and buy the land on which England's first women's college was to be built. Before driving out to Girton, where the agent assured them there were several suitable plots for sale, Henry took her for a walk along the Backs which were so beautiful and serene that for a moment Emily felt that it would be a mistake to build her college so far out and so far away from this delightful spot. But once out at Girton common sense reasserted itself, for they both liked the piece of land that had been provisionally reserved. It was flatter and a little bleaker than Emily had expected; nevertheless she could see the new building in her mind's eye, and on that golden day she could picture it warm and welcoming and filled with laughing merry girls. Henry brought her back to earth with a reminder that it might be a different story in winter when the wind howled and rain belted down in great torrents. But he spoke too late, Emily had fallen in love with Girton and refused to relinquish her dream. They came again the following week to sign the contract, bringing Alfred Waterhouse, the well-known architect, with them, for Emily would have no other to design her college. The Assize court building in Manchester, which he had designed in 1859 and which she much admired, had laid the foundation of his fame as an architect. At the time of his work at Girton, he was also engaged on substantial buildings at Caius and Pembroke Colleges, Cambridge. Although it was only August the wind blew and Emily felt quite chilled in her thin dress. She had to reassure herself that she had not made a mistake, and was glad to hear Waterhouse say that a good brisk wind blew away many an epidemic and that she had chosen a healthy spot.

The moment she let the Executive Committee know that a site had been bought there was a general exodus to Cambridge, with Henry as guide. Mrs Gurney was unappeased – it was still too near a university town filled with young men. Henry quickly reassured her: men's colleges kept strict rules and she must think of the financial advantages – the saving would be large. With a high wall around the building (perhaps with broken glass on top) the girls' virtue would be safe and she could thus recommend the college to her friends with an easy conscience.

When tenders for the privilege of building the college began to arrive, Emily was radiant to find everything cheaper than she expected, even Mr Waterhouse's fees. For one busy week nothing marred her happiness, then, all too soon, troubles began. The buying of the site, the many things needed to make the building habitable and the move from Hitchin had absorbed Emily to the exclusion of everything else, so that she had not taken the slightest interest in the many other details that had to be settled. A chance remark by Sedley Taylor as they were walking into the committee room together shook her considerably. He said (as though it was not news) that now a site had been purchased she should think seriously about joining forces with Miss Clough and Mrs Butler who, with Henry Sidgwick's help, were hoping to bring their popular Ladies' Lectures down from the North to Cambridge, where he felt sure that they would be just as well attended.

Emily knew all about these Ladies' Lectures, which recently had become more widespread than ever before. Large towns like Birmingham, Manchester and Liverpool encouraged them and let rooms in their town halls to the organizers. The lectures gave many an idle woman a purpose in life that she had lacked before, but they were not intended to give serious and systematic instruction. Never for one moment did Emily think of these lectures as a rival to her own college; they were a totally different thing, their standard far lower than she was aiming for. But it gave women a feeling that they were becoming cultured if they could rattle off a few literary names with ease and assurance.

The prospect of Ladies' Lectures being given in Cambridge did not disturb Emily at all. But she was extremely angry to discover the perfidy of Sedley Taylor and Sidgwick. Both were members of her Executive Committee (Sidgwick was also Professor of Moral Philosophy), but both were now playing a leading role in promoting these lectures and neither had said a word to Emily about their double loyalty. Sidgwick was a man whom Emily had particularly relied on to help her with much she did not understand, and at first she thought it very noble of him to bring the lectures to such an anti-female place as his own university. It seemed to show that his heart was in the right place, but the idea that her college should be allied to these lectures was outrageous. Such a thing had never crossed her mind, and to be invited to amalgamate the two schemes was a shock. She felt deceived by such treachery. Very reasonably she complained to Anna Richardson that she could not help wishing that the introduction of the lectures into Cambridge could have been postponed until her college was firmly established: '. . . it is working against the college in Liverpool and Manchester . . . At Sheffield, local examinations which have been successful for two years have gone up the wall . . . they have no candidates at all this year. . . It is better frankly to acknowledge that at present, the lectures stand in the way of the college . . .'

There was at the time some confusion about these lectures, and whenever they are mentioned in modern publications the words 'higher education' invariably creep in. In fact the standard of these lectures was not at all high. How could they be with such a mixed audience, the intelligent rubbing shoulders with the unintelligent, the old with the young, and the subjects so eclectic and not welded together into a coherent course? Emily was absolutely right to point out that the good was here the enemy of the best.

Not content with merely bringing the lectures to Cambridge, Professor Sidgwick was renting a house at his own expense to act as a hostel for those who came from afar. Jemima Clough, sister of Arthur Clough, the poet (who had been at Trinity with Sidgwick), was put in charge. Miss Clough had once had a school of her own in the north, but she had given it up in order to arrange the lectures with Josephine Butler, the social reformer. Her intentions were good but she was not a pioneer of Emily's quality, nor had she the burning desire to improve the lot of women; moreover she was very much under the thumb of Professor Sidgwick and his wife.

Once the hostel was opened it would be no longer possible for Emily to disregard the lectures: many of those attending them would be domiciled in Cambridge under one roof in a kind of pseudo-college. While she was staying with Professor and Mrs Liveing in Cambridge for a few days, she was told (again by chance) that a voluntary test was to be established for those attending the lectures and that the papers were to be set and marked by dons. This was serious. At once Emily sensed that this 'test' could be none other than the inferior examination for women which she had been offered for her college but which she had indignantly rejected.

Not long after the hostel opened, a small group of girls, chosen by Miss Clough as especially intelligent, sat the Local Examination. They failed dismally. Their failure enabled Emily to take their measure, for her own girls had sat this Local Examination a year or two before taking college entrance and all had done extremely well. A very different standard indeed. Because she was in Cambridge and the Liveings advised it, Emily went to see the examiners who were to set the papers for the voluntary 'test'. They were extremely helpful and assured Emily that the 'test' was nothing but a stop-gap and certainly not as high a standard as the Local Examination: Miss Davies had nothing to fear. It was therefore plain that it was of an infinitely lower standard than

135

the degree course, with which nevertheless it would be equated by the uninformed.

Soon after Emily opened her college at Hitchin in 1869, the Ladies' Lectures were well established and the 'inferior examination' (Emily's words) flourishing, since it was cheap, undemanding and popular. Emily was being cruelly pressed to adopt it but she fought it tooth and nail: 'I will never agree that everything for women must be separate and inferior,' she wrote angrily to Henry Tomkinson. The real barrier between Emily and Sidgwick was the latter's total failure to understand her aims and ambitions for women. She could not make him see that while his scheme might be admirable in itself, it was totally different from hers and fundamentally hostile to it. Sidgwick entirely failed to understand this, and in his memoirs argues that any differences did not matter since both would produce more educated women.

By 1881 Sidgwick had made so much money out of the lectures that he was able to move the hostel from the small house in Regent Street and to rent a large and attractive house on the Backs spacious enough to hold more than twice as many women. It was another blow to Emily; there were still only a handful of students at Hitchin and money remained a perpetual worry. The Ladies' Lectures were therefore a very sore point indeed. It was irritating to hear Lady Stanley, usually the soul of tact, talk enthusiastically of the widespread appeal of these lectures, and urge Emily to accept their lower standard. Her daughter, Lady Amberley, was telling everybody how sad she was that she was not going to spend the winter in London where the sponsors of the scheme were running a series of special lectures: 'I am longing for some system in my education . . .' It made Emily despair that a young and intelligent woman could not see the difference between the two systems. The Stanleys and the Amberleys were the sort of people on whom the college depended for money and support. It was galling to be so poor and to have to listen to praise of something that was far from praiseworthy.

It irked her that Sidgwick and Sedley Taylor had not offered to resign from the Executive Committee, now that they were supporting a rival system. It hurt too to realise that others must have known of their perfidy but had never once warned her. Both men had every right to change their minds, but they were honour bound to tell Emily what they were doing and to let her decide whether she wanted them to continue as members of the Executive Committee. Perhaps of the two Sedley Taylor was the more guilty. In 1871 when the new lecture system was expanding, he wrote to Barbara to ask for her support, despite the fact that he knew that she was a great friend of Emily's. 'You will see by the circular I sent you, how much more comprehensive and how much cheaper are the lectures being given at Cambridge than what we can by any possibility offer at Hitchin.'

Drawing of Emily by
Annabella Mason, 1851

Painting of Emily by
Rudolph Lehmann,
presented to the College
by past and present
students, 1880

Photograph of Emily, about 1866

Photograph of Emily in academic robes, after honorary degree conferred by University of Glasgow in 1901

Reading a letter, 1901

First building, Girton
College, 1873

Original entrance hall,
about 1873

Original dining hall,
about 1885

'The College Five', 1869: standing, L. to R., Woodhead, Lloyd, Lumsden; seated, Gibson, Townshend

Students with Professor Clark at Hitchin, 1870–71

College Fire Brigade, 1887

Henry Tomkinson

Painting of Barbara
Bodichon by Emily
Osborn

Elizabeth Garrett
Anderson

Sedley Taylor

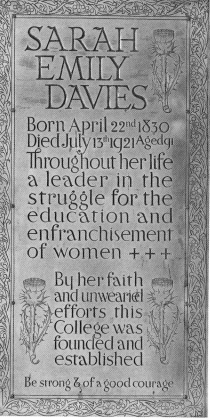

Memorial plaque, Girton
College

Perhaps it was as well that Barbara did not tell Emily of this letter until later, possibly from kindness, for she knew all about Emily's difficulties and did not want to add to them. As it was, Emily saw that Sidgwick was committed heart and soul to his special lectures. As she said 'people so easily get to love the thing that they are working at and think it the best thing possible'. Nevertheless she condemned in the roundest terms the way he had gone about things. Nor did she allow him to get off scot-free, as this letter shows: 'I am sure it is generous consistency and not cruel mockery that makes you say you are willing to help us when your scheme is the serpent that is gnawing at our vitals. It glides in everywhere. As soon as interest is awakened people are told there is something else as good or better and which does not ask for money. I dare say it does not end in them doing much for the lectures but it is enough to hold them back from doing anything for the college. We meet this hindrance at every step and lately it has seemed to me that it bids fair to crush us. However we are not going to give in yet.'

It is a measure of Sidgwick's and Sedley Taylor's total incomprehension of Emily's objectives and of their unconscious presupposition that women were inferior, that they could complain loudly all over the university that Emily was a thorn in their flesh. Cambridge High Tables talked of her 'unjust and incomprehensible conduct' and that she was forcing Sidgwick 'into a state of antagonism'. Emily and Sidgwick were diametrically opposed on a fundamental issue. Sidgwick was quite sincere when he said that he wanted to see the education of women improved, but he did not say – what was also true – only up to a point. For Emily, on the other hand, it was her purpose to give women equality of opportunity with men through equal education, and nothing in the world should stand in her way.

The gulf between them was unbridgeable. But so strong has the prejudice against women always been that the blame for the quarrel is always laid at Emily's door and she is accused of making Sidgwick's life a misery. It has been forgotten that she was always scrupulously fair and open, making it plain that she could understand him changing sides but not his doing so without warning her in advance, and that it was he, not Emily, who behaved in an underhand manner.

In May Emily was notified that at the end of the term she was expected to present her girls for the special women's examination, the examination that had been devised for Miss Clough's girls at Sidgwick's instance. The letter gave Emily the feeling that officialdom was commanding her to toe the line – their line – but since she was never alarmed by authority she came to the conclusion that the notice was a mistake, or perhaps merely a reminder that should she change her mind the examination was open to her. After pondering on the matter for an hour or two, she decided

137

to ignore it and there and then threw the 'royal command' into the fire. She knew that this defiant act might mean that authority would threaten to chop off her head or blow her college to the four winds, but she had always taken the view that one should never give up one's principles because of the difficulties involved.

Henry Tomkinson was visiting Hitchin at the time and he gave Emily some sound advice. He had heard that Dr Gunson of Christ's College was very favourably disposed towards education for women and had said in a speech that it was a disgrace to the whole university that Emily was left to struggle alone. Tomkinson advised her to see him, explain her difficulties and ask his advice.

Happily Gunson turned out to be a delightfully talkative man, unself-conscious and with a fund of amusing anecdotes. It was easy to see that he liked and got on well with women. Emily sensed that he was a fighter, and her confidence came flooding back. Gunson was full of schemes to get his own way and offered to propose a Grace (Act of the university 'parliament') authorising the examiners in all university examinations to admit students of Hitchin College (as he called it) and to allow their class in the examination to be published along with the names and classes of undergraduates. Anonymity was absurd: 'I feel the time has come for having the question openly settled,' he wrote to Emily, 'and that the policy of shilly-shallying and connivance [he meant 'by the examiners'] which has openly prevailed is unworthy of the university.'

On 16 November 1872 the senior examiners for the Little-go, E.H. Morgan, W.M. Gunson and others, brought the question of the admission of women to university examinations before the Council of Senate, but their motion was rejected by ten votes to six. Gunson declared himself thoroughly dissatisfied with the result and wrote to Emily to tell her 'the same unsatisfactory method of getting your students examined will have to go on for at least two years more . . .' Even more awkward, the custom of collecting the papers from the Senate House one hour after the start of the examination had been discontinued without warning. Emily thought quickly, and had a talk with Mr Morgan: perhaps it might be possible to suggest that the papers were the property of the examiners who set them 'and that at some later hour, to which we should accommodate ourselves, they might be handed over'. Miraculously, this worked, and with the minimum of fuss and Mr Morgan's help, the crisis passed and the girls knew nothing of it, to Emily's profound relief. All five candidates were successful.

An identical problem faced the three candidates who were now ready to sit for the Classical Tripos, and it was solved in the same way. Emily's relief was all the greater, for the three were her first Tripos candidates, and Emily was anxious that nothing beyond the natural nervous tension should disturb their peace of mind.

As in 1870, Emily went with the girls to the University Arms Hotel, where they were to sit the examination. But her trials were not yet over. The messenger who was to bring the papers from the Senate House went to the wrong address and the girls were kept waiting for over an hour: 'My nerves were all a-quiver,' Louisa Lumsden tells us in *Yellow Leaves*, 'and work was almost impossible . . . it settled my class, a Third.' It was amazing that not one of the three failed. When the news of their success reached Hitchin the students went mad with joy. Several climbed onto the roof and tied three flags to the chimney, singing *'Gaudeamus Igitur'* while others rang the alarm bell so loudly that the police thought Benslow House was on fire and ordered out the fire brigade.

The examiners turned out to be quite human after all. They took the trouble to let Emily know that 'Rachel Cook's translation of Aristotle was the best in the whole examination and the two examiners who looked over it are in raptures' and that Louisa Lumsden's paper on Roman history was 'one of the prettiest shown up'.

15

'The way to kindle faith is to show it by taking risks'

The last year at Benslow House began disastrously. No sooner had Annie Austin settled into her new office in October 1872 than she fell seriously ill with pneumonia, and had to be taken home as soon as she was well enough to travel. The widowed Lady Stanley of Alderley was persuaded to step into the breach and proved an instant success. The mother of numerous daughters, she possessed humour and tolerance, but when necessary she was not afraid of asserting her authority and administering a rebuke. Managing young girls had been her life and she fitted the peculiar situation like a glove. While she did not take her new duties exactly lightly, the fact that she was temporary made her less strict and more inclined to turn a blind eye to minor misdemeanours. The college was so happy under her regime that Emily wished that Lady Stanley was younger and could stay for a very long time.

Finding suitable women to be Mistress was not getting any easier, and with a sinking heart Emily could sense the way the wind was blowing: she would soon have to take on the job of Mistress herself, an 'honour' she did not much relish.A strong argument against becoming Mistress was that her job as Secretary could not be done by anyone else and there were many other jobs that only she could do really well – that of fund-raiser for instance. She was the only woman member of the Executive Committee who was used to standing on a platform and making a speech appealing for money. There was another reason, too, one she had never used: she knew that she would find living permanently in Hitchin too confining for someone as active as herself, and she could not leave her mother alone for too long. Annie's sister Jane Crow solved this last problem at once by offering to live with Mrs Davies until Emily's term of office was over. A progressive young woman, who was determined to be independent, she had got herself a job in London and until Lizzie Garrett's marriage to Skelton Anderson in 1870 had lived with Lizzie, for it was considered not quite proper for a young unmarried woman to live alone. Emily accepted the offer gladly, for even as things were she had to be away from Cunningham Place frequently. She knew too that Mrs Davies would never be happy living away from her home for as long as two or three years in a house filled with noisy young girls.

On 2 August 1872, with a haste Emily often wished they would show when discussing college affairs, the Executive Committee appointed Emily Mistress. Now she was confronted with it, she accepted her fate with a good grace. For the first time for years she would be tied down for an unknown length of time. The prospect filled her with gloom.

Her excuses for not taking on the job of Mistress were genuine enough, for unlike her predecessors she was in a peculiar position. Her work as Secretary was heavy even without other commitments and compelled her to attend many committee meetings in London – and yet the new building was bound to take her often to Cambridge to confer with Alfred Waterhouse. In addition, there had to be visits to Greenwich in connection with the School Board. The list of her duties would have been formidable, even with modern equipment and a secretary. If Emily sighed at the inevitable, she did not quail when it came to the point. She had not yet found a competent woman to run the domestic side of the college, to her the most distasteful job of all, so she must continue to shoulder this task as well. The salary offered for such a woman was too small and Emily was trying desperately to squeeze a little extra from her own income to add to it.

In the middle of sorting out and giving priority to all the new tasks that would fall to her lot and trying to fit them into a day that was not long enough, she received a delightful letter of congratulations from Mrs Russell Gurney who was 'resting' in the country after a busy season of balls and dinner parties, and who had not the slightest idea what hard work meant. She was full of pleasure that Emily was at last 'driven to take on the Mistress-ship'. Even Henry was pleased, repeating that of course she would do the job so well, until Emily was forced to scold him for having so much confidence in her: 'it is rash of you . . .' she told him severely, 'nothing but the impossibility of getting a really fit person for the college could bring me to consent to my own appointment, but perhaps it is a good thing to be too much believed in . . .' She was not reassured when Henry pointed out that she was doing much of the Mistress's work already: the arrangement of lectures and the girls' studies had never been out of her hands. Work never killed anyone, Emily replied tartly, but incarceration in Benslow House for long periods might put an end to her.

She had asked for £100 a year as salary in order to allow her to afford first-class travel when on college business. This the Committee readily granted, but not long after she was bewailing the fact that she might have to give it up to a housekeeper in order to free her from those hateful domestic chores: 'It has often occurred to me,' she had written to Henry when the question of her becoming Mistress was first mooted, 'that if I were dead or in some way entirely prevented from doing anything here, it might be easier to find a solution of our difficulties. If that is true, the wise thing for me would be to keep away and to leave everything in the hands of the best person we can find.'

But she was not nearly so downhearted as she sounds in her letter to Henry Tomkinson: it was her way of getting her own back for his part in making her Mistress. Secretly she believed that Henry and Mrs Russell Gurney had talked the Committee into making the appointment, and that once the die was cast they expected her to settle down into what they would keep referring to as her 'rightful position'.

There is no doubt that Henry did not handle Emily very well at this time. Although he was used to women generally, he was not accustomed to a close friendship with a highly emotional woman who was being pushed into a job she did not want. It was unsettling for him to see how hard she worked. He was used to looking on women as fragile creatures, so her toughness never ceased to surprise him: he was always expecting her to collapse with overwork, and when she continued to show no sign of fatigue he was amazed. Nevertheless he was quite pleased when he noticed that her reaction was not so cool as he had expected. On the other hand, she found herself fussing about small things, something she had never done before, and wondered whether her new position would change her attitude to the students. Until now, she had been praised openly for the way she handled them; Mrs Manning had said that she used just the right amount of friendliness and firmness. Now for some reason she did not feel she could do that any more. A few weeks after taking up her post she was worried because she did not think that she was as genuinely sociable as the Mistress ought to be: 'I always said I could not be as much to them in this way as Mistress as I could as Secretary, and it is so. One cannot play with them on equal terms as I used to do and maintain authority as its sole representative . . .'

She may have felt uncertain how to deal with her girls fairly, but she must have kept these uncertainties to herself, for a little later she told Henry that they showed quite the usual cordiality and 'respond with smiling faces when I am trying to compose a timetable to meet all their needs'. It was not the girls who had changed, but Emily: she had forgotten that she had always had authority over the girls and most of the responsibility of running the college, but it was new and not very pleasant to be tied down: the delightful feeling of freedom that she so treasured was quite gone, because she was shut up with a dozen young girls in a comparatively small house. There was no getting away from them. She had to admit that sometimes they irritated her by their childishness and lack of appreciation of what was being done for their good. This made her feel ashamed, but in no way lessened her impatience.

Of course all sorts of mishaps occurred that first winter of Emily's headship. The gas lighting system failed, and the ground was so frozen that the workmen could not get at the pipes until a thaw set in; pipes burst in the kitchen, which was flooded for one whole day so that cooking was out of the question; the parlourmaid slipped and broke her leg, and four of the girls took to their beds with chills. Worst of all everyone looked to Emily to find a solution to this horrible discomfort as, candle in hand, she hurried after dark from one sick-room to another, bringing little more than words of comfort that sounded hollow to her own ears. 'Oh why did things have to change' was comic, coming as it did from a woman who had already brought about revolutionary changes and had every intention of bringing about more. But, like Florence Nightingale, she never denied that she had moments of despair.

Whenever she could Emily escaped to Cambridge to see how the new building was getting on and to extract promises from the lecturers to come out to Girton to teach as they had done at Hitchin. When trying to persuade the lazy ones she referred to Girton as a 'stone's throw away', although when talking of the college to prospective parents it was 'a full three miles from the drive to the centre of the town'. She felt a little guilty at the frequency of these jaunts but salved her conscience by working on letters and papers connected with the college as she travelled in comfort in her first-class carriage.

It always seemed to be raining when she reached Cambridge. Nevertheless it gave her immense satisfaction to see the building rise from the mud in all its majestic beauty higher every time. She could find no fault with Alfred Waterhouse's design which seemed to get better and more beautiful at each visit. Besides, he was such a delightful and understanding man, consulting her at every turn and always ready to listen to non-professional suggestions – of which he got plenty. At Hitchin his plans for the new college were pinned onto the walls of the Mistress's room and the more Emily studied them the more delightful and elegant they seemed. In this case familiarity did not breed contempt. They were wonderfully practical too, for Waterhouse had designed the building to allow for expansion as money became more plentiful, while cleverly avoiding the look of 'bits and pieces tacked on' which Emily so much hated. He managed this by allowing for a series of courts to be added from time to time until the college reached the required size.

As Emily had predicted, the moment the first brick was laid interest was aroused and curiosity got the better of both dons and undergraduates. A succession of eager walkers tramped each afternoon to Girton 'to take a look', and stories about the place circulated through Cambridge for months. Masters of colleges were seen climbing up ladders to take a 'peep' at the Mistress's rooms, while those more youthful who wished for immortality, however obscure, wrote their names on a brick for sixpence and were allowed to lay it themselves.

The private guarantee fund that Henry Tomkinson had organised to raise £5,000 was working out very satisfactorily. Nevertheless, more had to be done. Since they were to move to Girton before the lease of Benslow House ran out, Henry asked the landlord for permission to sublet. As a good business man he measured off the land at Girton that the college did not yet need and let it to a neighbouring farmer. He had handled, of course, all the negotiations for the purchase of the site at Girton, procuring a most valuable piece of ground on very reasonable terms. Sometimes Emily wondered how she could ever have got on without him.

In order to carry out these plans the college had to be brought into legal existence, and James Bryce kindly offered to see to the formalities for Emily. All she did was to add two clauses to the completed deed in order to put on record her ultimate aim – to make the college part of Cambridge University: 'That the college should if possible be connected with the University of Cambridge and that efforts should be made to obtain ultimately the admission of the students under suitable regulations to the examination for degrees of the university. That the religious services and instruction shall be in accordance with the principles of the Church of England but where objections are entertained such services and instruction shall not be obligatory.'

The two burning issues were membership of the university and religion, and Emily had every right to feel nervous when she presented the document to the Executive Committee. Although she had no wish to have a religious test like the men's colleges (religious tests were not abolished until 1871), Emily had always felt that the college should adhere to the Established Church, because she did not intend religion to be a barrier to future membership of the university. At Benslow House the Mistress was in the habit of using *The Book of Common Prayer* for a simple service every morning, and although there was no compulsion all the girls attended regularly, since Anglicans and Dissenters alike were used to the custom of family prayers. But when Emily proposed to the Executive Committee that Girton should be formally Anglican there was an immediate furore. The controversies following the publication of Darwin's *On the Origin of Species* a dozen years earlier were still raging. Skelton Anderson, a Scottish Presbyterian, who had been put on the committee to help with the finances, was so offended that he immediately resigned, despite the fact that he knew that Emily was his wife's closest friend.

Christina Rossetti, too, withdrew her support; as a Catholic she could not accept that the college should be Anglican. Nevertheless Emily stuck to her guns that the college could be no other, and in the end her draft was accepted. She explained her position to her brother Llewelyn: 'It is not possible in the nature of things that the college can be entirely satisfactory either to strong Churchmen on the one hand or to Dissenters on the other. My own feeling is, in a case like this, differences which one feels to be serious may be submerged in view of the pressing necessity of diffusing knowledge . . .'

Wisely Emily decided to do no more explaining; feelings would soon die and the whole question taken for granted – which was exactly what did happen.

Girton College was opened in the Michaelmas Term 1873, although the building was far from complete. The move had been a nightmare. It had rained continuously during the two days that it had taken to remove all the household paraphernalia to Cambridge, and Emily had been trying frantically to protect books and Barbara's pictures from being ruined. The sight of an unfinished building was not welcoming, and a very tired Emily longed to turn tail and run. Inside, chaos reigned everywhere, nothing seemed ready, and Emily had to brace herself to find her way round piles of sand, empty cement tubs and builders' benches to reach the first floor which she had been assured was ready for occupation. The ground floor was still lacking windows and doors and the wind swept through the open spaces carrying dust and rubbish to every part of the building and reducing the atmosphere to Arctic temperatures. The main staircase was only half-finished and to Emily's horrified eyes looked thoroughly dangerous. All the corridors were piled high with sawdust and shavings while the sickening smell of new paint permeated every corner. A little further inspection showed her that efforts had been made to get the girls' rooms ready, and they looked clean and fresh though very cold; but once fires had been lit they took on a different aspect altogether and brought a little warmth even to Emily's chilled heart.

A great deal of care had gone into choosing the new furniture, curtains and covers. Emily had spent many anxious hours poring over catalogues and pattern-books in order to make the small rooms look attractive. Carpets and covers toned in with the colours of the walls and even the bedrooms fitted together in a harmonious blend of paint and fabric. Nothing had been left to chance. Emily had not forgotten the piercingly cold wind that had chilled her to the bone when she and Alfred Waterhouse first walked over the site before a brick was laid, and with this in mind she had bought very cheaply in a sale several yards of white glazed cotton to line the curtains as a protection against draughts. She had seen some pretty trimmings at a greatly reduced price (twopence a yard) and had bought enough to edge the curtains; and she noticed now with great pleasure what a charming effect this little extra gave. She had remembered other things, too, that would make a difference to the girls' comfort: desks with plenty of drawers, chairs and tables the right height, a comfortable armchair in which to relax, and bookshelves wherever possible. She had brought from Benslow House all the looking-glasses that the girls had so disliked, and they were to groan again at the frustration of never seeing both the tops of their heads and their chins at the same time. To most of the girls these rooms were to be the first of their own that they had ever had, and Emily had remembered this when she deliberately left ample scope for individual decorative schemes.

The Mistress's set was conveniently placed on the first floor overlooking the front drive, with another similar but smaller set close by for a resident tutor, a college officer whom Emily was determined to have as soon as such a woman was qualified and the college could find the money to pay her salary. Three of the rooms were to be used as lecture halls, and, as Alfred Waterhouse had promised, space was left for a library, chapel and laboratory at some future date. Gas pipes had been laid but as yet there was no gas, and no one had remembered to tell Emily to order paraffin lamps, so for the first week or two the girls carried candles to light up the corridors when they went calling on each other. With draughts from paneless windows and piles of loose shavings, it was a miracle that the college was not burned to the ground.

It had needed courage of a high order to move into a half-finished building. One of the first Girton students, Emily Gibson, described the state of the college to her parents with an accuracy that they must have found disconcerting: 'It is a red raw building among bare fields with windows and doors still being fitted into their frames. . .' She could have added that Miss Davies was living up to her reputation as an optimist for she said, when she decided to declare the college open on exactly the same day as the beginning of the men's term, 6 October 1873, that 'the way to kindle faith is to show it by taking risks'. Everyone knew that she was not afraid to take plenty. The opening of a half-finished college with a mere handful of students and no money would have been far too much for most people.

The high wall topped with broken glass, a necessary chastity-preserver in Mrs Russell Gurney's imagination, was still unbuilt. As yet there were no proper doors and no gates, and rumour had it that undergraduates were frequently found wandering the corridors as large as life masquerading as workmen. The rumours even reached London, and Parliament became so curious that they sent John Morley the historian to see Miss Davies to try and find out if there was any truth in the stories: 'the throng of visitors has been exhausting,' Emily wrote to Barbara at the end of the summer term.

The land surrounding the building remained bare fields long after the college was finished. This 'neglect' was the subject of much barbed comment by all sorts of people who ought to have known better, and Emily has been blamed for not tackling the grounds and turning them into a beautiful garden as soon as the main building was completed. It was not a pretty sight, they complained, to see a Waterhouse building in the midst of such desolation. Why did she not plant trees and shrubs at once or make some effort at tidying up? Of course Miss Davies had no eye for beauty, they said. They had obviously no right to assume that the derelict appearance of what was meant to be a garden was not as much an eyesore to Emily as it was to them. But she had not one penny to spare: the making of a garden, even a small one, is a costly business, and Girton's grounds were large by any standards. Letters in the college archives bear ample testimony to her anxiety to have a garden as soon as possible. Nevertheless the talk spread: 'Miss Davies does not realise how awful the place looks surrounded by mud and unploughed fields'. She did notice, but she took a practical view of priorities. In 1872, when the college site was first measured and she saw how many trees and shrubs would be needed, she had realised that so huge a task would have to be tackled by stages but that a small beginning was better than none. As she told Barbara: 'Don't you think that we had better at once order the planting of the corner opposite the farm buildings? Any trees anywhere would be better than none.'

Lady Stephen says that a beginning was made in the winter of 1874 with the erection of fencing and the planting of some shrubs, but that not much more was done. Yet a year earlier Emily had written to tell Barbara she was much elated to hear that Mrs Russell Gurney 'is going to give us ten large trees such as may be sat under next summer and I am much occupied with considerations as to the planting of them and where they should go . . .' Yet Lady Stephen continues to insist that Emily cared little about a garden. Emily's thoughts, she writes, were necessarily fixed on finance and building and that a garden was a luxury which had to give way to more pressing needs.

Emily did care about the state of the grounds very much, but she had not a minute to do anything about it, nor the money to hire a garden designer to convert it. Several members of the Executive Committee who had a passionate interest in gardening merely shook their heads and looked grave. The real trouble was that everyone had become so accustomed to Emily organising everything that it did not occur to them that she could do with some help. She had no secretarial assistance with her work either as Mistress or as College Secretary, and she had to answer every letter in her own hand. She often sat up far into the night trying to catch up on her correspondence. One wonders why those who criticised her for not making a garden did not get together and see that trees and shrubs were planted. Emily might have been very thankful to have this one chore taken out of her hands. Fanny Metcalfe would have been a suitable person to do this. The record has it that when she visited Girton as late as 1881 she was appalled by the state of the grounds.

Fanny was an excellent gardener but felt shy about interfering, so she consulted Barbara, who discouraged her: 'I am quite of your opinion,' Barbara replied, 'but it is useless to give gifts to a garden utterly uncared for . . .' Fortunately Fanny persisted, for she could see that the college might be in danger of losing prospective pupils if the grounds gave too bad an impression. Furthermore, strangers from overseas were coming to see the college in increasing numbers, and one American had called the grounds 'scanty and rough'. He was wrong on one count, for 'scanty' they were not. That was part of the trouble: the amount of land was so large and so flat that the small area that had been cultivated was almost invisible.

Before 1881 was out Fanny Metcalfe and her sister with energy and goodwill raised £4,000 towards improving the grounds, hoping that others would follow. They said, very rightly, that not everything should be left to the foundress.

16

Endless Winter

Unlike others of her sex and generation, Emily never wasted time when writing to friends and relations by discussing the weather. It is so rarely mentioned that when her letters become spattered with references to 'hail and sleet', 'arctic conditions' and threatened snow, one wonders what is coming. By April 1874 Emily felt that they all had a right to feel warmer, and that the bleak days of winter were receding, with the promise of better days to come. But it was not only a freak spring but one of the worst winters on record and it loomed large in Emily's life. Her letters to intimates tell of aching bones, and in order to combat this she had sewn cotton wool into waistcoats, sitting up in bed at night wrapped in a shawl, her feet on a hot brick covered with flannel.

The girls suffered too, and not in silence. Desperation fired Emily's imagination: she turned an empty room at the top of the house into a makeshift gymnasium with equipment hired from the town's sports club. Lifting dumb-bells and twisting and turning in Swedish drill and jumping over a leather horse soon got circulation going. Barbara hastily designed a simple sports dress that barely reached the knees and wide enough to allow freedom of movement; it could be run up quickly and cheaply on the village dressmaker's new treadle sewing-machine, but it did not please everybody. Some of the girls complained that it was too long, thus hampering movement, while others found it embarrassingly short; they felt self-conscious, they said, when showing so much leg walking back to their rooms. A little crossly Emily told them to shorten or lengthen the dress to suit themselves. How outrageously unco-operative the human race could be at times. Not a word of thanks, only criticism and discontent. 'When I see such a spirit it makes me feel terribly out of heart . . .' Emily in her turn complained to Henry: 'the doubt arises, is it worthwhile to produce such results as these?'

None of it went deep. The real explanation was the bitter cold, the weird sound of the wind as it howled round the building that winter, and a chapter of accidents that could have been avoided. The chimneys did not draw properly and quantities of soot fell onto the new carpets. The windowframes fitted badly and rattled unbearably at every gust of wind, spoiling sleep and irritating nerves. Draughts lowered the temperature of rooms that should have been cosy and warm, so that the girls stuffed the windows with newspapers and put mats against doors. For a time the boiler failed and there was no hot water; and when the gas pipes were finally laid the jets were continually going out and, when they did burn, made such a noise that the girls preferred to use their candles. Emily took the builders to task but they blandly denied all responsibility and blamed the shape of the chimneys and the new-fangled windows. Alfred Waterhouse had to be called in to put things right.

Emily did her best to hide her real feelings and show a cheerful face. Nevertheless hard work, discomfort and anxiety took their toll. 'She has boundless energy,' said one friend admiringly. 'She never seems to tire,' said another. On the surface this was true. She had never been in the habit of complaining about her feelings; this would have been self-indulgence and was not encouraged at the rectory when Emily was a child. As things were, it was just as well that she had little time for introspection. The post of Mistress – which Henry in his ignorance believed would give her some rest – had greatly added to her burdens. It was not false modesty that made her refuse it in the first place (someone as honest as Emily was incapable of that) but the knowledge of what the job involved. She had really meant it when she said 'nothing but the impossibility of finding a really fit person would bring me to consent to my own appointment'. Henry Tomkinson's secret theory that she felt inadequate to take on the job of Mistress because she was no scholar is nonsense. Her self-confidence and common sense were too great for that. The real reason was exactly as she explained to Adelaide Manning: 'I have only one brain and one pair of hands and jobs that at present no one else can do.'

That year winter seemed endless; but Emily awoke one morning in May to find that the wind had gone, the sun was shining and the aconites which she had planted beneath the window of the Mistress's sitting room had not been killed by the snow and ice but had suddenly appeared strong and healthy. As she gazed at the wonder of it all, it was as though a great burden had fallen from her shoulders, and she was herself again.

The effect of warmer weather on everyone was miraculous. Tempers disappeared, cheerfulness abounded. Emily celebrated the transformation by asking the girls to coffee in her room. In that friendly atmosphere tongues were loosened, questions were asked, and for the first time the girls began to understand the tenacity, courage and self-denial that had gone into establishing a college for women. Feeling that now was the moment, she explained that adhering to tiresomely rigid principles was one weapon that she was using to win her fight to bring women into the light. She talked quite naturally of the shock it had been to her when she first learned that 'all the cultivated thought of the country was occupied by considering and discussing what was best for men . . . and that the same attention was not given to women's education'.

Anna Richardson had died at Grasmere in the summer of 1872, much to Emily's distress. They had been friends since Gateshead days and shared an eager and unquenchable desire for self-improvement. They had worked at Latin and Greek together, studied politics in the pages of *The Times*, and read aloud poetry, history, French plays, even novels, since there was no censorship in Anna's home and her father possessed a large library. Feeling it their duty, both girls had tried their hand at teaching in local girls' schools and both had been appalled by the poverty of what passed for education.

For all her maturity Anna was only two years older than Emily and far too young to die. If she had followed her inclination she would have helped Emily establish her college, but as the eldest of a large family she was destined for nothing better than home ties. It made Emily feel very bitter that Anna had never had a chance to cultivate her intelligence and perhaps shine in the world as she ought. Her death made Emily realise that her own hold on life might be fragile and that it was folly to concentrate on petty and useless things.

Over the years Anna had given Emily much sound advice. It was she who had warned Emily bluntly that she would harm her reputation if she refused to become Mistress, and that she was wasting precious energy fighting the inevitable: if she avoided her duty now, the same situation might come up again in a few years' time when she might be ageing and unable to cope. Anna's wise warning to treat the young students as adults and take them into her confidence when there was a tricky problem to solve returned to Emily's mind at the beginning of the Lent Term 1874 when some of the students came to her to ask if they might drop Little-go and work straight away for the Tripos. Little-go was a useless examination, they said, and took up too much valuable time. They wanted her to know that even if she was unwilling, they were going to send a petition to the Executive Committee asking them to grant their request. Emily guessed that Clark, one of the 'reforming' lecturers, was the instigator of this particular rebellion. He had become very popular. Emily could tell from the rebellious talk that they had not given the matter much thought but were reflecting his views word for word. How often had he told Emily that Greek was useless to ladies and that Little-go was worthless? He had been so sure the girls would back him that he had told her he did not intend to stick to the 'Cambridge Curriculum', having devised a better one of his own.

Emily had gone into this very thoroughly with the lecturers and they knew her views on the subject very well. Moreover, they had agreed to do it her way, so this was merely another battle over an old issue that she thought settled. The girls' request was superficially reasonable, but despite explanations they did not realise its dangers, as Emily had done some time ago: namely, that since no one could be admitted to a Tripos examination without having previously passed Little-go, they would forfeit the possibility of becoming members of the university and condemn themselves to the inferior women's examination which Emily had so furiously rejected.

Clark had written to inform her that the examination for Girton students was to be the special one devised to suit women and that Miss Clough had accepted. 'This, Clark says, is the right one for us,' she told Henry. 'About the best thing that could be said for this examination is that it is probably just a step above the Senior Local i.e. above our entrance. It was created to suit struggling governesses with no time for study except the evenings. But we and their students are alike females and beyond that Mr Clark fails to discriminate.'

As calmly as she could (for she was very irritated) Emily carefully explained to the girls that not only was Little-go indispensable as the portal of entry to the university, but that it was also positively useful to them because it gave much-needed practice in mental discipline, which through no fault of their own they lacked. It taught them, too, how to conduct themselves in examinations. 'It is all very vexing,' she wrote to Henry, whose strong arm she was leaning on more and more, 'to see such a spirit shown. I feel very vindictive generally.' Recently Henry had accused her of dividing everybody into two categories – friends and enemies – and denouncing the latter, in this case Clark and the other lecturers. She had defended herself stoutly: 'It is the fierceness of fear. If I felt more confident of victory, I might perhaps be more amiable.'

It was difficult to be 'amiable' when Miss Clough was held up before her as an excellent example of a woman with common sense – *she* was making no difficulties about the examination. Why was it that nobody seemed to understand that what she and Jemima Clough were doing had nothing in common? Of course she exaggerated when she complained to Henry that every hand in Cambridge was against her; nevertheless some hands were, and that was enough. But although she felt resentment, she must have managed the girls and their complaints better than she thought. The revolt died a natural death, and soon she was telling Henry that she harboured no ill feelings and that the girls were all smiles and affability.

With the death of Charlotte Manning and Anna Richardson the number of Emily's correspondents was sadly reduced. Consequently she valued her exchange of letters with Barbara more than ever. Nevertheless she could not deny that it was not a very satisfactory exercise since she had to sift and sort her thoughts before committing them to paper, for

Barbara did not have a very clear idea of what went on in Emily's life. But the habit of seeking opinions and advice from friends – although she by no means always followed it – was too strong a habit to suppress easily. She continued to write intimately to Adelaide Manning, the friend closest to Anna in intellectual interest, but happily in the early years at Girton Adelaide was often so close at hand that few letters passed between them and her advice was given verbally.

When Emily was harassed she sometimes forgot that Barbara was not Anna and was the most undomesticated of women, so that to ask her for help in solving a household problem was a waste of time. 'Tell me,' Emily wrote, 'by return of post if you can, whether you think it desirable to put the hot-water furnace under the gyp-room instead of in the housekeeper's room . . .'

Because Emily's difficulties were outside her experience Barbara had no understanding of them whatsoever. She was not intentionally unkind, merely unimaginative and too self-centred to put herself in another's shoes. For instance, when she visited Girton in the spring of 1874 and came across Emily writing at her desk in the Mistress's room, she was delighted 'at the honour bestowed on you'. Yet her husband Eugène Bodichon, who happened to be at Scalands when Emily was there for a few days in the vacation, showed the deepest concern at the huge workload Emily had taken on after becoming Mistress. Of course he did not have an exact idea of what it entailed but he was sensitive and imaginative enough to guess what 'another little job', as Barbara called it playfully, could mean to Emily.

Eugène and Emily got on splendidly; in fact Emily was the only one of her friends whom Barbara would allow in the cottage when her husband was there. Emily always addressed him as 'doctor' and conversed with him unselfconsciously in her schoolgirl French, while the Frenchman replied in broken English. Nevertheless they understood each other perfectly and Emily picked up many curious facts with which Eugène's head was stuffed: 'the legal position of women is far worse in England than in France' – 'Frenchmen are more broad-minded than Englishmen, they are willing for their wives to use their maiden name after marriage' – 'Working French women are members of a society for mutual help. Is there something comparable in England?' – 'There are 36,000 unmarried women over sixty in England with no means of support.' Laughingly, Emily told Barbara that the 'doctor' would be far more use to her on the college committee than a dozen dons, and if she could persuade him to stay in England all the year round she would see that he was elected.

Because Barbara was often ill and irritable, she and Eugène had grown a little apart. Barbara was glad to have someone as good-tempered and cheerful as Emily around as a bulwark against Eugène's many eccentricities which had once attracted her enough to marry him, but which now sadly got on her nerves. While Barbara rested, Eugène and Emily went for long walks into the country around Robertsbridge, both talking all the time – for her part, Emily told Barbara later on, 'learning such a lot'. In the evenings Emily with great skill kept the conversation on an even keel when the three of them were together. She was quick to notice signs of strain on Barbara's face, never failing to make excuses for her when she became irritable. When she wrote to Henry from Scalands she would mention Barbara's bright moods, never her bad ones, since she knew that Henry was critical of this friend: 'she is so dear and firm, at the same time so winning and bright'.

Illness made Barbara lethargic, which meant she did not visit Girton as often as Emily would have liked. As the number of students increased, Barbara was hardly known to them, which Emily felt was a pity. She had always over-estimated Barbara's influence on the girls, just as she had her enthusiasm for the 'cause'. Her artistic temperament had always tended to be mercurial, and she quickly got bored with certain aspects of the 'woman question' as her health declined. Even when well she would promise to support Emily on some controversial question to do with the college, then instead of turning up would disappear on a painting expedition, her promises and obligations quite forgotten. But no matter what she did, Emily always found excuses for her.

None of this would have mattered in the least had not much of the work done by Emily later been wrongly attributed to Barbara. It may have been partly by Emily's wish that Barbara was called her co-foundress. Yet in the true meaning of the word she was nothing of the kind. When Emily urgently needed help, it was always Adelaide, not Barbara, who came to the rescue, without making a parade of it. Adelaide's scholarly tendencies pointed plainly to the fact that Girton was her natural home; Emily wanted her to return after her step-mother's death, but she had severed connections with the place when Charlotte Manning's term of office was over. To bring such a useful person back into the fold, Emily asked Henry to propose her for the Executive Committee, and in order to make the link more intimate, Emily arranged for Adelaide to be appointed Girton's 'official visitor'.

17

'Men like this have done much harm'

In the autumn of 1874 Emily asked Lizzie if she would be willing to examine Barbara and perhaps suggest a course of treatment that might eliminate the worst features of Barbara's strokes even if she could not cure her. Emily's faith in Lizzie was so strong that she had hopes that a partial cure was possible. Lizzie was willing on one condition: Barbara must come to her London clinic for treatment. This Barbara refused to do, so her health slowly but steadily declined.

Although Emily and Lizzie did not see each other as often as in the old days, their devotion and loyalty was as strong as ever. Lizzie had been worried that Emily would not approve of her choice of husband and that her marriage to Skelton Anderson would come between them. Nothing of the sort happened. Emily was quick to show her delight at Lizzie's happiness: 'it is very sweet to me to be able to be so happy about it,' she wrote unselfishly to Lizzie on hearing of the engagement. 'It does not make me feel as though I shall lose you . . .' Over the years the two women had gone through so much together, never failing in support when the need arose. Lizzie's difficulties had been Emily's apprenticeship for greater work to come, and in her darkest hours she did not forget that Lizzie had succeeded in the end.

In an unofficial way Lizzie had been connected with the college from the beginning and her interest had been invaluable in many different ways, especially with tricky problems that were partly medical. The great advantage that Lizzie had over other doctors was her experience with women who were really sick: she could spot a sham at a glance, although in her thorough way (unusual for those times) she always made sure by examination.

A year after moving to Girton Emily had to consult her on a matter that might turn out to be serious. The popular periodical the *Saturday Review* published the first of what was intended to be a series of articles by the well-known mental specialist Dr Maudsley. He had made his name by advocating completely new treatment for those who were insane enough to be committed to a lunatic asylum. He particularly condemned the Willis 'chair of restraint' which had made George III's life such a misery. He also abolished strait-jackets and other forms of torture for violent patients. Instead he advised doctors to treat mental illness like any other malady.

Emily was quite familiar with Maudsley's views, since she had often read his articles in Lizzie's medical journals and admired him for his humanity and common sense. Yet it now appeared that there were some areas where he was just as backward and unreasonable as other doctors. He had recently returned from America where the freedom allowed between the sexes had disgusted him: girls went about unchaperoned and were allowed the same freedom as boys. At school they were put through a rigorous course which he warned would end in nervous breakdown or worse.

His first article in what was intended to be a series on 'Sex in Mind and Education' appeared in May 1874 and took for its theme that 'study is the cause of ill-health in women'. Emily bought a copy and read the article with mounting indignation. She noticed at once that it was packed with dangerous half-truths difficult to refute but which every woman with a daughter would believe since it came from such a reliable source.

'Because of the severe educational system to which she was subjected,' Maudsley wrote, the American girl was 'becoming physically unfit for her duties as a woman', a truly terrifying pronouncement coming from such a source. How could a mother with her child's welfare at heart ignore it? How would it affect Girton? Would it slow down or even stop recruits? Recently Lizzie had brought Dr Elizabeth Blackwell to Girton, and during a long talk she had assured Emily that her brisk and commonsensical attitude towards young women students was both healthy and wise and that she wished more women would follow her example. Now Dr Blackwell was back in the United States and Lizzie was in Switzerland enjoying a well-earned holiday, and there was only Frances Buss to consult. Miss Buss was not a doctor, only a headmistress with years of teaching experience behind her, and what she did not know about girls was not worth knowing. 'Girton suffers from the determined opposition of medical men,' Frances Buss wrote. 'As for me I scarcely expect anything else if a medical opinion is asked in the case of any girl. The smallest ailment always proceeds from brain work (!!!) never from neglected conditions of health, from too many parties, etc. etc.'

When Benslow House was first opened Cambridge dons were forever insisting that too much study was ruinous to the health of girls. Since they were unmarried men who knew nothing whatsoever about girls, they were plainly talking through their hats. But Maudsley was different; as a doctor, he spoke with authority. Emily knew, and so did Frances Buss, that Maudsley was making a delicate reference to menstruation, which was supposed to drain a young girl of strength. Of course he did not mention such a taboo subject openly, but everyone knew what he meant. The article was rubbish but Maudsley's confident tone carried great weight. 'Why could he not have waited until Girton was on its feet?' Emily wailed to Barbara, who was being made quite hysterical by the articles – 'Girton is ruined'.

There was another reason for Emily's alarm. If Maudsley's strictures had a widespread effect, the plan by the newly established Girls' Public Day Schools Trust to build twenty-five schools in the next fifteen years might have to be abandoned. If so this would be a tragedy of the greatest moment. Emily was very much involved with these plans because they were the direct result of her efforts to have girls included in the Royal Commission's inquiry into schools. Thus she was vulnerable on two counts and had no means of redress on either. 'Men like this have done much harm before,' Emily wrote to Lizzie on the latter's return to London. Yet as she walked to the pillar-box to post her letter it suddenly occurred to her that of course she did have means of redress, and to say she had none was nonsense: there was still the power of the pen. She and Lizzie together would answer Maudsley in another article in the *Saturday Review* over Lizzie's signature as a doctor. Lizzie had now become almost as well known as Dr Maudsley. The cholera epidemic of 1866 and the brave way she dealt with it by opening free clinics in the most vulnerable parts of London had seen to this. The bristling reply composed by these two friends, which the *Saturday Review* published without a murmur, won the day. Maudsley's articles were immediately discontinued and no more was heard of them.

Emily and Lizzie were braver and more outspoken than Maudsley: they defied convention and called a spade a spade, the first time such a thing had happened in a non-medical journal. 'Is menstruation really an incapacitating affliction? If it is, why should this "illness" only attack women of a certain class? Working women are forced to ignore it. Whoever heard of domestic servants resting from their labours one week in every month? The indignation of the mistress of the house would be too great to be borne. Nothing is more unhealthy than lying on a sofa in a stuffy room at these times. It is not education but dullness, boredom and loneliness that are frequent causes of breakdown.'

There were no adverse repercussions from their article. Such a frank reply quickly put an end to the whole affair and it was soon forgotten, although there was no doubt that, because of Maudsley's reputation, great harm might have been done if the *Saturday Review* had printed the other five articles.

Barbara was overwhelmingly glad that the matter was settled 'so easily'. She had been greatly perturbed because an attack from such a famous man might cost more than pupils. What if he were to take Emily and Lizzie to court for defying him? That would not only cause a scandal but bankrupt Girton. Emily did not think it would come to this, but she could understand Barbara's reasoning. Since her illness Barbara had become much too ready to fly off the handle at something she did not agree with and too inclined to show fear. Emily had soothed her down as well as she could, telling her that the affair would never come to court, since a lawsuit would harm Maudsley more than Girton.

There had been other changes in Barbara since her illness; her mind seemed to dwell more and more on people's morals, mostly sexual morals. It is possible that she was regretting her carefree attitude when she was younger. She had so often laughed at Emily for her stuffy old-fashioned attitude, but Emily had stuck to her opinions, although she never allowed Barbara's actions or views to change her feelings towards this dear friend. She was not blind to Barbara's shortcomings – how could she be when Barbara was so open about her affairs? Nevertheless she managed to convince herself that it was 'circumstances' that made Barbara so free with her affections. Perhaps it was because she blamed her present afflictions on the carelessness of her younger days that Barbara preached about morality and its importance to the lives of young girls in long letters to Emily at this period. Could not Emily arrange for some 'direct moral teaching' at Girton? It was a bad thing, she wrote, that there was no religious instruction in the college and no plans for it. Could not this gap be filled? How nowadays were young girls to get an ideal of life if nobody cared? A lapsed Unitarian who had never bothered her head before about orthodox religion, Barbara now urged that a chapel should be built with all speed at Girton so that distinguished Churchmen could preach the necessity for moral tone to the girls. She had discussed this with a young Jewess, Hertha Marks, whom Barbara looked on always as her adopted daughter. She was very clever and had recently become a student at Girton; Barbara hoped that if Hertha said she agreed with her, Emily, who thought well of the girl, would do what she asked.

It was difficult for Emily not to laugh a little inside herself that of all the women whom she knew the only two who now so earnestly preached the value of morality were George Eliot the novelist and Barbara; the first had lived openly with another woman's husband and the second had taken a married man as her lover. Moreover it was difficult for Emily to understand what both meant by an 'ideal of life' and quite what she was supposed to do about it. Did Barbara wish her to invite the girls to her room for coffee and buns when, in between stuffing themselves with food, they would one by one relate their religious experiences to a rapt audience?

Such public soul-searching was very popular in the 1870s and was indulged in freely, but Emily distrusted it, believing that it was most unhealthy. She had no intention of interfering in the religious life of the students. At the best of times young girls were too emotional about religion; it was a subject their parents must deal with, not the college. Whenever she saw signs of over-intense religious feelings she felt it her duty to damp them down, not to re-kindle them with more fuel. Religious fervour was catching, like hysteria; she had witnessed scenes of weepings and hand-wringings while on parish work in Gateshead, and she did not want to see it among her students.

It had been deliberate policy on Emily's part not to spend money on a chapel yet. Eventually she hoped to have one, and Waterhouse had planned for it, but with so very little to spend he had agreed it was wiser to wait. There were plenty of places of worship close at hand and the girls went wherever they liked on a Sunday. Most of them were rigid sabbatarians and some had offered their services as Sunday School teachers to one or other of the missions run by undergraduates. Emily neither encouraged nor discouraged this, but if asked replied that she thought it very noble of young girls to work so hard for others. She supposed that until the chapel was built, Girton, like Benslow House, would be known as 'that infidel place'.

In Girton's second year, when the students had more confidence, some began to hold mission meetings in their rooms and from time to time invited Emily to join in, but she always refused. She did not interfere in any way, but not unnaturally her detachment from all religious matters was noticed. When questioned, however, she had her answer ready: she did not wish to act as guide and mentor on religion – that was a parent's prerogative.

Lectures on morality were of course a ridiculous suggestion of Barbara's, but Emily had to be tactful – it was not possible to get teaching on any but Tripos subjects. That seemed to satisfy Barbara and the matter was dropped, but she soon picked on another, equally controversial and more difficult to explain away. She wanted to turn her Blandford Square house into a meeting-place or club for Girton students, past and present, a comfortable home where they could entertain their friends. Unwilling to go through the same sort of fuss all over again, Emily wasted no time in pouring cold water on this scheme – it would take them away from their work. As it was, Girton students loved nothing more than dashing up to London on the new express for social functions of one sort or another. She would have done the same at their age had she had the chance, but it was not a habit she wished to encourage. Recently one or two girls had taken French leave (Emily called them the 'flirts of Girton') and had to be reminded sharply that an evening out required permission. Even the nicest girls were easily tempted: Constance Herschel was carried off by friends to a ball in the country when Emily herself was attending a meeting in London. She told no one and there was no information as to her whereabouts. On her return she was severely reprimanded and told in no uncertain terms that for safety's sake the Mistress was to be regarded as *in loco parentis*.

In the end Barbara lost interest in her plan for converting the Blandford Square house. Emily had tactfully explained that for the present, wonderful though such a scheme seemed, the upkeep of such a large house would be too much for Girton to bear. But her rejection of this 'generous offer' leaked out and Emily was criticised. She was a kill-joy spinster who grudged young girls a moment's fun. Some of the girls wrote to Barbara offering to back her and Barbara roused herself enough to repeat the offer, but not with the same enthusiasm. Emily stood firm. How she wished the girls would not appeal to Barbara behind her back whenever something irked them. Barbara encouraged this, especially with girls she knew well. Nothing happened in the college that her niece (now a student) did not tell her, but Barbara's life was so dreary that out of sheer kindness of heart Emily did not attempt to stop the girl keeping her aunt up to date. If Barbara had been a well woman she would have treated her very differently.

Sometimes Emily longed to shake Barbara for making life so difficult, but always when her anger died down she found some plausible excuse for her. There was no malice in her, but from time to time she liked to remind Emily that she too had some influence in the college.

18

A Family Composed of Women

One of the original five, Louisa Lumsden, was Girton's first resident tutor. Just as Emily had predicted, a start could now be made with recruiting the teaching staff. If some thought it a disadvantage to be home-bred, Emily was satisfied that they would be the best the country had to offer. She had always thought well of Louisa and had hoped that when the time came for her to take up a career, she would look no further than her own college; Girton was the right milieu for a scholarly girl. The college was still at Benslow House when Louisa took up her post for one term only, as she said, in case the job was too heavy for her. But she enjoyed the work and the company of the girls so much that one term became one year. When the second year started Louisa said nothing about leaving, and Emily took this as a good sign that she was happy and would be going with them when the move to Girton was made in the autumn of 1873.

At Benslow House Louisa had impressed Emily with her intelligence and character and her care of the girls themselves. She had watched her carefully for a definite reason: did she possess the necessary qualities for leadership? As an older student – she was twenty-eight in 1869 when she came first to Hitchin – she sought the company of Adelaide Manning and Emily herself rather more than her contemporaries, and Emily took this as a sign of her greater maturity. She was old for her years. When the question of a tutor for the girls came up Emily took the trouble to prepare the Executive Committee for her interview, telling them in confidence that Louisa possessed qualities that might well be suitable for a future Mistress. She explained that Louisa had passed a severe test with high marks, she had lived for two years in a small community where irritations and quarrels often sprang from nothing, and she had shown both good temper and enterprise.

It is strange that a woman as intelligent and perceptive as Emily did not realise how deeply critical Louisa was of almost everything Emily did, and that she did not like the Mistress of her college very much, if at all. But Emily possessed an unsuspicious nature which, while it protected her from hurt, did at times lead her into making mistakes. Louisa had reason to be grateful to Emily. At first she was, for up to the time of the move to Girton, Emily had encouraged her in her work and, what was more important, done a great deal to give Louisa confidence in herself. Yet steadily and surely the gratitude had worn off and something less praiseworthy (jealousy perhaps?) had taken its place, and was to eat into Louisa's heart and mind. On Emily's part there was thankfulness that fate had placed in her path a young woman with very obvious teaching qualities, and from the beginning she had marked her down as someone she hoped would want to use her gifts for the benefit of others.

Unfortunately Emily did not know that Louisa had emotional problems. Among a great many more complex difficulties, she had some years before shown that she had no confidence in her looks and felt herself too plain to attract men. This was the reason she affected a dislike of men that bordered on the ridiculous and when in their company took care to appear sullen and rude. She gave in to her feelings and wore her antagonism like a protective mask, and she misrepresented Emily by alleging that she constantly preached that men must be propitiated because nothing could be done without them. Of course Emily did not quite say this, but Louisa chose to misunderstand her deliberately. What Emily had really said in a speech was rather different: 'to improve our status we need the support of intelligent and sympathetic men: . . . equality of the sexes has nothing to do with spurning men.' These remarks and others like them made Louisa sniff with disdain. She could do perfectly well without men, all she cared about were things of the mind, compared to that everything else was of little account. Yet she had none of Emily's passionate concern for women, but showed a barely veiled contempt for all the hard work and self-sacrifice which she saw before her eyes daily both at Benslow House and Girton.

Emily was quite unaware that Louisa bore grudges. This was not because she was insensitive but because in her busy life there was no time for such nonsense. Once Louisa was offended she never forgave, the culprit was cast off for ever, spurned and derided no matter how grievous the loss – indeed the deeper the loss the more satisfaction she got out of hating. Her obstinate nature (which she mistook for strength of character) kept her from recognising the good things of life that passed her by and she often felt ill-used and neglected, while her lack of humour meant that she took herself too seriously and often saw slights where none were intended.

For a long time Emily chose to ignore this side of Louisa's nature and to concentrate on her genuine interest in young girls and her remarkable teaching abilities. She often put in extra hours with a slow pupil and Emily was quick to note this kindness of heart. Therefore when Louisa accepted the tutorship Emily was overjoyed. It seemed a splendid appointment. In her pleasure she deluded herself into thinking that Louisa's over-sensitivity about herself would disappear when her energies were directed into proper channels and she saw that she was appreciated. She saw a rosy future with Mistress and tutor working in harmony, helping girls to become women who were to be some use in the world. Louisa had proved that she could be full of common sense and right ideas when Dr Maudsley's article was published: she wrote to Barbara defending a girl's right to be educated and tearing to shreds all the specialist's forebodings about strain. 'Would Dr Maudsley and his friends recommend that women should learn nothing? . . . a vacant mind revenges itself on the body . . . I cannot see that girls ought to be prohibited from all hard mental work because it is possible to have too much of it . . .'

At first all went well between Mistress and tutor. When time allowed, the two women had long talks together and Emily was happy to report favourably to Barbara: 'When I talk things over with her as I have been doing constantly, more and more we almost invariably agree.' Quite without guile herself, Emily did not realise that Louisa agreed with her lips and not with her heart and that although these talks mattered so much to her they were a mere waste of time to Louisa and one of the ways in which she humoured Emily. One of Emily's habits got on her nerves and she could think of no way of stopping it: Emily used the personal pronouns 'I' . . . 'my' . . . 'mine', very much too much for her liking when referring to the college or college matters. Occasionally she said 'my students' – 'as if she owned us', Louisa complained crossly to a friend. No doubt Emily had become a little proprietorial but since Girton would not have existed without her unremitting efforts over the years, this is hardly to be wondered at, and should have been forgiven. As it was, Louisa read a world of hidden meaning into these words where absolutely none was intended.

The relationship might have been easier had Louisa confessed that she had been deeply distressed by an incident that had occurred two years previously. She held Emily responsible for her 'bitter humiliation'. Someone on the Executive Committee had the kindly but not altogether wise idea of congratulating Rachel Cook and Louisa Lumsden in person after their success in the Tripos. It was unfortunate that Rachel mistook the address and never arrived, so that Louisa was kept waiting in an ante-room for a considerable time for Rachel to join her. When it became clear that she was not coming, the Committee foolishly decided that since they could not see both girls, they would see neither. Barbara Bodichon, the bearer of the message, tried to soften the blow by presenting Louisa with a bouquet of flowers, but she was so angry that the moment she stepped outside she threw the flowers into the gutter. When the Committee made a new arrangement Louisa ignored the invitation and, as far as the Executive Committee were concerned, there the matter ended. But

Louisa never forgave the hurt to her pride. It rankled for years, and her anger was particularly directed against Emily because she was convinced (quite erroneously) that it was she alone who had done this cruel thing to her. Just about the time when Emily was writing to Barbara describing how well she was getting on with Louisa and what a help she was proving to be, Louisa was telling Constance Maynard how irritating she found Emily and that she was such an impossible woman to work with ('so selfish, so opinionated, always wanting her own way') that she had made up her mind to leave and find a job elsewhere.

It never seems to have occurred to Constance, who adored Louisa, that if Louisa detested Emily to this extent, then it was a funny thing to take on a job directly under her and to stay in it so long. She was a free agent and could please herself. But Constance was so adoring that she questioned nothing that the loved one said or did, and Emily never suspected that matters were taking a turn for the worse. The following letter to Barbara shows that she thought that everything was all right: 'So far as I can see things have gone more smoothly and happily this term than ever before. I attribute this to various causes and to having had Miss Lumsden who has been a great help to the students and me.'

Louisa hid her feelings well. Evidently Emily suspected nothing. Her blindness could have been due to various causes. This was the year of freezing winter weather and spring ruined by gales and floods. There was much illness about, several of the girls went down with influenza, and at times even Emily felt far from well. She had narrowly escaped breaking a leg when trying to walk into Cambridge for an important meeting. She had been diverted by the unfamiliar sight of a frozen Cam and had slipped on Trinity Bridge, hurting her knee. She made light of the accident but nevertheless it caused her much pain. Happily both the girls' illnesses and her fall gave her the opportunity to see more of them under congenial conditions. She made her room as warm as possible with a roaring fire and closed curtains, and let them know that she was free for tea every day while the bad weather lasted. It was an invitation that was accepted with alacrity, and she was surprised how many of them were glad to come. 'Sometimes I feel I can do so little for them,' she wrote to Barbara, 'that when I do chance on something by accident it gives me such pleasure . . .'

Louisa was especially invited but she refused; she had 'too much work'. She had a new grudge against Emily; she believed that Emily had ordered her pupils not to call on her in her rooms. The truth was very different. It never occurred to her that they did not come because her room was cold and uncomfortable – the fire always going out, lukewarm tea and stale buns – whereas there was warmth, an excellent tea and amusing company at the other end of the corridor.

*   *   *

Louisa's appointment had never been confirmed. When the job had been first offered to her she had been reluctant to accept because she felt that she could not work happily with a woman she did not like. In the end she had written to say she would come for one term only, pleading poor health. At the end of the first term Emily noticed that she seemed well and happy but she did not ask to have her appointment confirmed, seeming content to let matters stay as they were. This charade went on for two years, until Emily, feeling it more prudent to have matters cut and dried, asked Louisa if she had made up her mind to stay. Emily kindly gave her time to think in case she was uncertain, but Louisa was in no hurry to make up her mind. Barbara's advice to Emily was to go on as before, since Louisa was so good with the girls, and that whether she was permanent or not did not matter.

Then something happened that made Emily change her mind. She had always taken people at their face value and never probed beneath the surface to find hidden depths or indeed hidden vices. These would reveal themselves in time. So it was with Louisa. Quite suddenly Emily realised that Louisa was becoming too intimate with her pupils. This was something she was against since it inevitably led to favourites and that was not to be encouraged. She decided to keep an eye on Louisa and instantly began to notice things that had passed her by before, notably that Louisa encouraged the girls to think themselves ill when they had their monthly periods, made them stay in bed with drawn blinds and no visitors – except Louisa herself who seemed quite willing to run up and down with trays of food, which the domestics flatly refused to do. Emily and Lizzie Garrett had been fighting this kind of behaviour for years. They had fought and flattened someone as well known as Dr Maudsley, yet Emily only now realised what had been going on under her nose in her own college all the time.

This natural function was responsible for much ignorant behaviour, which Lizzie and Emily had long been determined to eliminate. Lizzie had been to Girton and had delivered a short lecture to the girls, telling them that it was perfectly safe to bath and wash their hair when in this condition. Nevertheless Louisa was rapidly turning the girls into invalids: weeks of a woman's working life were lost in this way, and only a few daring women like Emily and Lizzie were trying to repair the damage done by years of superstition and mystery.

At this point it seems that Emily had no intention of asking Louisa to leave, only to ask her not to give young girls the impression that they were naturally delicate, and to stop pampering them. She reminded Louisa how sensibly she had behaved over the Maudsley affair and inquired why she had changed her mind since.

Louisa's reply is not at all clear, but one thing emerged quite plainly: she indicated that the girls found Emily hard and umsympathetic, that they did not dare come to her when anything was wrong because she would not listen. Emily replied briskly that Girton was not a hospital, the girls were not invalids, and the fussing must stop. Louisa paid no heed. Two days later when Emily wished to talk to Louisa about work, she was told that she had gone to bed with a headache. 'It is hard enough to have delicate students,' she wrote to Barbara in a fit of irritation, 'but we need not add to our anxieties by having teachers who are subject to disabling attacks of serious illness.'

A new uneasiness crept into Emily's relationship with Louisa. Hitherto she had been blind to Louisa's faults. Now she had to stop herself from seeing something wrong in Louisa's most innocent actions. It made her very unhappy.

She had reason to believe that complaining letters about her own behaviour to the students were going regularly to Scalands. The contents of Barbara's letters make this plain: there are at least two long ones on health, in Barbara's hand, in the Girton archives. One of them particularly irritated Emily: '. . . they are babies and ought to be treated as babies.' Barbara wrote as though she were a parent and Emily a school matron. There is much more on this theme, both repetitive and boring, but the real interest lies in Emily's reply, which is full of common sense and tolerance towards Barbara's lack of understanding: '. . . I should like to tell you how I look at it,' Emily wrote, 'and then perhaps we shall see better where and how much we differ. I do not think I underestimate the importance of taking care of health, only it seems to me that quite young people can do it better for themselves and the thing to aim at is not continually to be looking after them . . . but to have a generally healthy system going on and only to put in a word now and then, and to be ready of course to advise and help and even to nurse when any special need arises. I think that if girls of eighteen have been trained either at home or at school, this will be enough. We have found it so here as a rule. But of course exceptions may come and we must deal with them in an exceptional way, taking care that they do not suffer seriously but not altering our whole system on their account . . . no doubt college life has made demands on their self-control but that they have not felt it too much of a strain has been shown . . . by their extreme unwillingness to go away even when they have been quite ill. Whenever sending them home was talked of their countenances fell and they seemed ready to do anything if only they might stay . . .'

That year there had been a special case of a girl called Wallis, a bright and clever student whom Louisa was fast turning into an invalid. Shortly before she took Little-go Louisa came to see Emily to say that Wallis was not fit to sit the examination, although the girl herself had just assured Emily that she felt well enough to have a shot.

Emily agreed to her taking the papers if she stopped work the moment her headache returned, at the same time offering her a free consultation with Lizzie Garrett Anderson when the examination was over. Wallis sat Little-go, did well and her health improved, but Louisa shook her head – 'Miss Davies was taking risks'.

It was inevitable that Emily and Louisa should part company sooner or later. It was better so, for Emily with her brisk attitude to young girls and their problems could never put up with Louisa's suffocating ideas of coddling and petting that kept girls immature and bred those school 'crushes' that Emily found so unhealthy. From the beginning Emily had disapproved of Louisa's *tête à têtes* with a current favourite in her sitting room of an afternoon. She was quite sure that they were not discussing work. The hitherto unpublished letters in the Girton archives make the outlines of Louisa's folly perfectly clear. During the whole of her time both at Benslow House and Girton, when she was in a position of trust, Louisa deliberately undermined Emily's authority with the girls. She knew Emily's feelings on the evils of the sole influence of one person on the students but she felt (quite sincerely) that the girls lacked guidance, and saw this as the consequence of Emily's objection to single-person influence. After the move to Girton she decided that Emily was neglectful and that she must assume the leadership herself, since Emily was too weak and wrong-headed to take on the responsibility.

Louisa's reasoning was exceedingly muddled. Some girls were shy and lonely at first, that was natural. But Louisa's attempts to keep them immature by petting and pampering, to make them think themselves ill when they were not, and to extract 'confidences' from them, was to put a wrong emphasis on their emotions. Suddenly Emily noticed what had passed her by before, that some of the girls – Constance Maynard in particular – followed Louisa about everywhere 'like puppies', as she told Adelaide Manning ruefully. Shortly afterwards Emily decided that things had gone too far and she must get rid of her.

Did Emily suspect lesbian tendencies? Or was Louisa's behaviour simply thwarted maternal feelings? Perversions were familiar to Emily, her life at Gateshead had stripped her of illusions, but she never made quick cut-and-dried judgements. She had come to know that what looked suspiciously like lesbianism was sometimes nothing more than a lonely woman's longing for affection and companionship, and she respected such friendships and never mocked or made fun of them. There is no real evidence to make an answer to these questions possible. It seems therefore wiser to conclude that Louisa's actions proceeded simply from self-importance and a longing for admiration, and that there is nothing but today's changed outlook to suggest anything else.

Not once did Louisa openly object to anything that Emily did or said, but was always ready to fall in with the Mistress's ideas and plans, which was strange, since it was well-known that Emily always tolerated contradictions and opposition to her schemes if they led to something better. James Bryce had noticed this and so had John Seeley, and it strengthened their good opinion of her. Like many confident people she never minded owning that she had been wrong in a quarrel or an argument; that was part of her charm.

At the beginning of the academic year 1874 Emily had written to Barbara to ask her opinion of Louisa as a future Mistress of Girton. She admitted that she could see faults in her, in some ways glaring faults, but she went on: 'authority might be the making of her. I think she might carry out our ideas . . . which I am clearer about than I am about anyone else's. When I talk things over with her more and more she almost invariably agrees but that may be partly because she is so much influenced by anyone she happens to be with . . .' In another letter to Barbara written that same month, Emily says that she looks forward to the 'larger staff, each using her own gifts, all working together. My idea of a college is that of a society, not a family. The students have their family life already without us. I think that we ought to supply something different from a home, not an inferior imitation of it, as a family composed of women must be. I should not like the college to be a sort of widow with a great many daughters all about the same age. I think that the society is shaping itself all in the process of growth.'

19

A Traitor in the Camp

Not long after the New Year 1875 matters between Emily and Louisa came to a head. Christmas and New Year had been better than usual. Mrs Davies was now very frail but she cheered up at the sight of Llewelyn's children, their arms full of parcels and flowers. Emily had decorated a Christmas tree and arranged all the presents at the foot, books and toys for the children and something pretty and suitable for everyone else. All too soon the holiday was over and she was seated in a cold train bound for Cambridge and all the problems awaiting her at Girton.

The day before she left London she had received a rebuking letter from Barbara which had made her very angry. It appeared that shortly before Christmas Barbara herself had received a letter from Louisa and another from one of her friends (whom Barbara did not name), full of complaints of Emily's indifferent attitude to the students and the life at Girton. Her 'friend' (whoever he or she was) had been to the college and was very shocked at Emily's apparent lack of concern for the students. Barbara's letter is either lost or destroyed, for it is not in the archives at Girton, where Emily's reply is preserved. Because of her affection for this old friend (who was herself always ready to believe the worst of Emily and give strangers' stories credence), Emily controlled her temper and sent a very moderate reply, for which she deserves great credit: 'I think the people who just look in on us for a little while may be in some danger of both giving and receiving wrong impressions. Do you know that you have given an impression that you have a dislike for some of the students? That you like eccentric ones . . . and do not care for those who are steady-going and like other people. I know this is not true and have said so, but it just shows how easily mistakes can be made.'

When her anger had cooled Emily was full of contrition that she had blamed poor deluded Barbara, but she hardened her heart against Louisa. She was a mischiefmaker, and if left where she was her slyness would taint the college, making life unbearable, so that they would all be at each others' throats and all Emily's work would be ruined. There could be no peace so long as there was a traitor in the camp.

A few days after her return Emily went one evening to Louisa's room, praying as she did so that the conversation that they were about to have would pass off in as pleasant a manner as possible. It was unfortunate that Louisa was not alone; one of her pupils was sitting with her warming herself by the fire in the dimly lit room. Perhaps somewhat too abruptly Emily asked the younger woman to leave, and when she and Louisa were alone she came at once to the point: 'I told her quietly that it had been quite understood that she had accepted her appointment for one term only and since it was more than two years since her arrival it was time to terminate her appointment.'

Emily here implies but does not state 'so you have overstayed your welcome'. She continued her story in a letter to Barbara: 'Louisa got hot and angry and said in a truculent voice that she had never intended to leave: she wants to stay, which is natural enough as the post is about the easiest and pleasantest that could be invented. But I believe more and more to let the old ones go to make room for the younger and later ones who are in some respects so much more satisfactory.'

Louisa showed every sign that she was going to fight to keep her job and not offer to resign, as Emily had expected. Then suddenly she brought about her own downfall. She asked to be put on the Executive Committee to represent the students' point of view, but the Committee rejected her request without one dissenting voice – it was out of the question, but what did Emily want? Her reply was short and to the point: 'I have the strongest objection to the movement for putting the Mistress under the control of the students . . . for that is what it comes to.'

The Rev. John Sedley Taylor, who happened to be absent on that day, wrote to express his shock at Miss Lumsden's interference. '. . . it is only a step from the students themselves attending and sitting in the chairman's place. No, certainly not.'

As yet, not even the Mistress herself sat on the Executive Committee: Emily, as foundress, was the exception to that rule. The Committee would have been chaotic without her firm handling and everything would have taken twice as long; so her presence was essential. In time, when the Executive Committee had become the Governing Body, there were to be many changes and not only the Mistress but all the Girton dons were to be on it as a matter of course. But Louisa was making a silly bid for power which such a conservative body could not possibly have accepted.

Emily's reputation for kindness, good sense and fair play has suffered from Louisa's bitter feelings and jealousy. Whatever the rights and wrongs of the case it is certain now that Louisa did Emily very great harm, and that the affair had later repercussions. It was unfortunate in every sense that the only young woman whom Emily could possibly choose as her first resident tutor was over-sensitive and touchy, seeing slights where none existed and whose own self-esteem mattered more to her than a good relationship with others. Her lack of confidence needed frequent boosting; such natures are awkward to deal with and do not fit easily into community life. Emily had seen the awkwardness years ago but not the slyness that was the cause of much of Louisa's success in the early days; she was able to drop hints and half-truths against Emily without her suspecting a thing. Now that Emily understood the full extent of Louisa's perfidy she could hardly bear to be in her company for a minute. What if ruffled feelings made Louisa suddenly leave in a huff? In that way she could be left in the lurch when work for Little-go or the Tripos was at its most frenzied, but that would not matter to Louisa even though the effect of her going would be catastrophic: nothing might hold her back if departure suddenly seemed the best way of avenging herself on Emily, however chaotic the effect of her departure on others.

As tutor in classics Louisa played an important part in the working lives of the girls, since a greater proportion of them read Latin and Greek than any other subject, partly no doubt because Emily thought no one properly educated without a good grounding in the classics. Louisa well knew that her teaching was essential to success in the Tripos. Yet much as Emily needed her, there were limits to what she could put up with; it was intolerable not to know what was going on behind her back. Barbara was quite wrong to say that the Executive Committee would have given in to her pleas to make the tutor a member because of her excellent influence on the girls but for Emily's opposition; there was never any question of that body agreeing to such an arrangement. Nor did Emily 'get rid of poor Lumsden' to save money. She had already decided some time before that it was cheaper in the long run to have more residential tutors, not fewer. Furthermore, once the numbers had increased, residential tutors were essential to the smooth running of the college. From this point of view Louisa's defection would be an act of treason.

At the end of the Lent Term Louisa resigned and left Girton for ever. But she went without giving her pupils the true reason for her departure. She wanted and succeeded in giving them the impression that she had been 'kicked out' as Constance Maynard put it: 'poor Miss Lumsden, kicked out of the tutorship before she resigned without a chance to say that she would go on. We students can none of us understand that after serving the college so ably for two years she can so easily be pushed out . . .'

Emily saw Louisa go with mixed feelings: anger with herself that she had made a bad error of judgement in appointing her, and perplexity that she could be so deceived. She had worked for two years with a woman who hid her fierce antagonism under a cloak of amiability and a subservient desire to please. It was very puzzling. Hitherto she had always been confident in her dealings with other people, especially those younger than herself; in Louisa's case her instinct had played her false, and she began to wonder if she was becoming insensitive to what was going on around her. Was she so close to the daily life of the college that she could no longer see the wood for the trees? If this was true it was time for her to go as well.

Impulsively she wrote to the Executive Committee warning them that they should begin to think of appointing a new Mistress in the near future. 'Family circumstances' made it imperative that she should resign at the end of the academic year, she said, telling them that it would be better for the college to choose a Mistress with no home ties. She went on to remind them that money was urgently needed and that she would be more use as a fund-raiser outside than cloistered between four walls, her voice silent and ineffective. Memories were short and people must not think that because Girton was flourishing it was also rich.

Now her period as Mistress was coming to an end, she realised that she had gained a great deal from the experience; it had been salutary in a number of ways. She had learned that it was not possible to think rationally when living in the centre of a world consisting of only one sex, all youthful, all with turbulent emotions which were not easy to control; violent friendships made overnight and just as quickly broken, tantrums and quarrels galore, none of them going very deep but serious while they lasted. Great care had to be taken not to seem either too unconcerned or too perturbed by the curious things that happened; a false step could blow up antagonisms to outsize proportions, so the responsibility to remain sympathetic but detached at all times was important. While the college was still small it was the Mistress's role to cool overheated situations and not to judge too quickly.

In her role as defender of the students, Louisa had complained that the rules Emily had imposed were irksome, and that was why they were often broken. Emily disagreed: it was natural for the young to break rules and regulations in their desire to be independent and mature, but when they became independent and mature themselves they would never dream of doing such a thing. From the beginning she had made a point of telling the students why such and such a rule had to be obeyed, and there was then no further trouble. She had answered every direct question quite truthfully, so that the girls understood that certain restraints were necessary for their own good. Even if they did not agree the explanation had always been accepted with a good grace in the end until recently, when she had begun to notice a certain petulance in the girls' manner towards her which she did not like and which she felt sure was the result of Louisa's influence. Louisa had forgotten that she was in a position of trust and was not now one of the students herself.

Emily had been Mistress long enough not only for her own good but for that of the girls too. As she told Adelaide, there was danger in not distancing herself from her work: only by doing so could she look at life in college objectively and discover if things were working out as they ought. It had taken her disagreement with Louisa to make her realise how important this was. She had both liked and respected Louisa, so her failure to live up to Emily's principles had been a shock, more indeed than Emily cared to admit even to herself. It had cast a shadow over her last months as Mistress; but, more serious, it had shaken her self-confidence.

There were other things, too, that she had only seen from the inside. In her first few weeks as Mistress she had come to wonder with some awe how her predecessors had coped so uncomplainingly with the domestic side of the college. Many of the duties were so mundane that a person of much less intelligence could have done them just as well. She herself had wasted much valuable time doing chores which bored her to distraction; she had soon found a capable woman to take over, surrendering a portion of her £100 salary to make this possible.

Here was a state of affairs that must be changed, otherwise the position would never attract the kind of prominent figure so essential to tempt parents to send their daughters to Girton; but how long would they have to wait for such a person to materialise? She had had Louisa so long in mind for this that perhaps she had overlooked others.

The last time Emily had been at Scalands, Barbara's health had deteriorated still further; she was very peevish and tiresome, and nothing seemed to please her. She took Emily to task for not making the most of her position as Mistress; why did she not exploit it more to the college's advantage? This could be done if Emily cultivated Cambridge society. It could not be wise to clash, as she had done, with influential people like Professor Sidgwick and Dr Whewell. Fortunately she could not remember any more names, giving Emily a chance to explain yet again that there was no university society in the sense that Barbara meant; she wished there was, but college functions were closed to women and they were never invited to anything. She was very happy with London society, which was much more civilized.

Emily's dismissal of Louisa was a festering sore with Barbara: what would the students do without this excellent woman? Of all the foolish things that Emily had done in her time this was the worst. The first time from home was always the most painful, homesickness and loneliness could be overwhelming, and there was no one to turn to now that Louisa had gone. Emily thought it best not to explain her views on this point until after she had left Scalands: 'As to their sometimes feeling lonely,' she wrote, 'I am afraid it cannot be helped. I am only surprised that they feel it so little. It is surely inevitable that human beings should in the course of their lives feel very lonely. Don't you know how terribly young wives suffer and even those who are not so young, when first taken away from their mothers and their homes? We must remember that the young women who come here are considered old enough not only to take care of themselves but of husbands, households and children, with very little help from anybody . . .'

There had recently been another short sharp disagreement between Emily and Barbara after Barbara had tried to rush Emily into accepting two of her nieces, aged eighteen and twenty, for Girton. Emily interviewed them but found them ill-informed and immature: she could not see them coping with Tripos work, which they would have to aim for if they entered the college, and she believed firmly that to make them attempt work beyond their mental capacity would be cruel. She refused them, and Barbara was angry, so that Emily had to remind her that Girton 'was not for young girls any more than for young boys. It is a place for young women . . . who can look after themselves . . .'

But Barbara had given her food for thought. Did she handle the students badly? Did she ride roughshod over their feelings, as Barbara had hinted? And was she lonely because she saw members of the university only on academic business? Solemnly she examined her feelings, but had to conclude that she was not in the least lonely or at a loose end. A few loose ends might be very welcome. Besides she had the most delightful of men in Henry Tomkinson for company. He was often in Girton 'keeping an eye on my property,' he explained laughingly. Emily guarded jealously the time she could spare for him, telling herself (quite untruthfully) that since they always spent part of the time together discussing college business, even the long walks in the flat country round Girton could be counted as work.

As the summer term of 1875 drew to a close, Emily began to feel a pleasurable sense of release; in a few weeks she would be free, able to come and go as she pleased, never staying in college longer than she liked. Freedom was very precious to her. She was more concerned about the college than ever, if it were possible, but how much more use she could be outside, for she had kindred interests with a bearing on Girton to keep an eye on too, of which higher education in general was one and the women's cause another. Women as a whole had not changed, although momentous changes were going on around them. Apathy was endemic. Perhaps the malaise could not be erased until a new generation had come and gone, but that Emily did not want to believe.

The isolation of the Girton of those days lowered her spirits so that her work was not so effective. It brought back too vividly the early days of Gateshead, where monotony was her daily companion and she could see no escape anywhere. Yet she could now look back at those years as fruitful and not wasted. They had taught her so much that was invaluable to her now and she had reason to be thankful. How changed life had become.

One thing was not changed – the duties of the Mistress. Now that another was to be chosen, the Committee were forcing Emily to discuss her position and think again.

During her period as Mistress Emily had all the privileges because of her special position, but this would now change. Would another Mistress accept the brutal fact that she was neither on the Executive Committee nor able to direct studies?

Emily's voice on the Committee was a very powerful one. In the early days she had got the reins into her hands and had no intention of letting go. Some on the Executive Committee thought it unfair not to give the Mistress the dignity of a seat among them in order to let her know of their plans for the college of which she was the head. Emily was most anxious to do what was right and had often pondered on the advantages to college and students if the Mistress were a member of the Committee. Then she had thought better of it and said she would do it 'next time'. She consulted Frances Buss. From the beginning she had been on her own governing body; Emily then asked whether her successor as headmistress would also be a member. Frances said she had never thought about it and she did not intend to now: she would let Emily know when the time came: '. . . being on the Committee does not secure the decided effect of making things easier and pleasanter for the Mistress,' Emily wrote. 'I do not consider this a vital question but I should like to do what experience says and is likely to work well . . .'

Suppose the Mistress was not satisfactory? What then? Could the Committee discuss the question of dismissal when she was sitting among them? So far they had accepted her ruling, but now she was to be up against heavy opposition. There was another point too: if the Mistress was not put on the Committee it would be only fair to allow her to nominate the resident teachers, since she alone would be responsible for them. Emily had done this as Mistress, accepting that she was also responsible for her own mistakes. She had had to get rid of Louisa because she could not work with her; surely that was the right of any Mistress? Frances Buss had told her that to choose their own staff was a right that heads of schools were willing to die for. The Committee agreed, so Emily won on both counts when she should only have won on one. The Mistress was still not a member of the Executive Committee, and as Girton grew the omission was to be increasingly an obstacle to progress.

20

'No harm in a little fun'

Emily had no intention of leaving Girton like a mouse suddenly released from a trap and only too thankful to scuttle away. Her departure must be remembered after she was forgotten and the best way to do this was to give a party. Everyone who had a hand in creating Girton, however humble, must be invited to taste the joys of feminine conversation in festive mood, a treat many of the men she had in mind had never experienced. The Executive Committee, the students and trusted friends whom she consulted, were enthusiastic and overwhelmed her with offers of help. Thus encouraged she fixed a date, drew up a list of guests, calculated costs and ordered cards to be engraved.

The interior of the building was still unfinished, the main part of what one day was to be a beautiful garden still untouched, except for a small patch at the front where it was beginning to take shape, but Emily was certain that flaws could be disguised by lanterns hung close to the building to distract the eye. Something of the same sort of thing could be done inside with soft lights, hired palms, sofas and chairs from other rooms placed in strategic positions. Of course there were some who disapproved, calling it a waste of time and money, the sort of thing that happened when one opened one's doors to women; but when the replies to her invitations came in there were hardly any refusals.

The party was to fulfil two purposes, one private, the other public: first to celebrate her return to the world, after three years; second, and more important, to give thanks that the college had been safely launched and now looked as though it was here to stay and grow stronger and more popular with the years. 'Miss Davies's pluck is contagious,' the first-year student Jane Dove wrote to her parents, describing the preparations. Pluck Emily certainly possessed, but on this occasion it was combined with great daring, for her guest-list included names of some of the best-known anti-feminists whose displeasure never failed to make young dons tremble. Dr Whewell was now no more (although his memory lingered on) but if he had been alive Emily would certainly have included him, without a thought for the consequences. Already on her list were men known to be notoriously awkward and difficult in the presence of women. Some had been known to leave functions at which royalty was present because the wine was not good enough or a hated enemy had

176

been spotted amongst the guests. Emily would have to remember that many of these dons had never attended a mixed party before: one don was heard to say severely that 'frivolity with ladies present was never intended to form a part of university life'. Punting down to Grantchester on a summer's day with a maiden aunt was considered daring enough.

All the students lent a hand, even the shyest entering into the spirit with gusto. The largest room in college – the lecture hall – which in daylight looked stark and unprepossessing, was to be turned into a drawing room with an orchestra in one corner and chairs taken from other rooms scattered about in orderly disarray. The girls draped their own Indian shawls over sofas to hide shabby patches, and Emily hired palms and pots of flowering shrubs to brighten dark corners and give an effect of warmth and welcome.

Llewelyn and his wife, who happened to be staying in Trinity Lodge, came to help, charming everyone with their easy conversation and sense of fun. Mary Llewelyn Davies had planned the menu for supper, while Llewelyn had advised on wine, for Emily had no intention of making the mistake of serving poor food and cheap wine. Everything was to be plentiful and of the very best quality.

When drawing up her list of guests Emily had been surprised to find that she knew so many Fellows of colleges well enough to invite them, and for one moment she had misgivings – would there be overcrowding? To be on the safe side she hired more chairs and glasses and ordered more wine. She knew how easy it was to be accused of meanness in that critical society.

There had been one bad scare; influenza was rampant in the town and many public places, including two hotels, had had to close because of lack of staff. But Emily's luck held, very few of her guests fell ill and in no time at all Emily, in pale blue taffeta and lace, was 'receiving' at the top of the stairs with the female members of the Executive Committee.

At first nothing went well, many of the dons did not find it easy to enter into the spirit of the evening and it was quite clear that they had come to scoff, spurn the wine and leave in a body, their duty done. But the guests Emily had imported from London looked so merry and appeared to be enjoying themselves so much that they decided to stay a little longer in case they might miss something of interest. So they accepted just one more glass of wine (which was better than they expected) and then another, so that the evening passed in a flash. Then the supper was so delicious, better than Hall in Trinity where the chef was renowned. Emily was quite prepared for stiffness in some quarters, and she quickly singled out those who were standing alone rocking on their heels and looking out of place, or those who were talking shop to a colleague, quite oblivious of their surroundings. With a few pleasant words she introduced them to special female friends from London, who had been well primed.

Henry Tomkinson worked hard. He talked to all the prettiest girls and broke up many an all-male conversation in just the right jocular way, reminding them lightly that they were not now in their college rooms. He seemed to know everybody and was popular with them all. For the first time Emily was seeing him in a new light; his gaiety and brightness in society surprised and delighted her.

When the last of the carriages rolled away – much later than anyone expected – Emily sank exhausted into a chair. She was very happy. 'The party went splendidly,' she wrote modestly to Barbara, who was in Algiers and could not be present. Lady Stanley gave her opinion in no uncertain terms: 'It went off brilliantly,' she told Emily as she kissed her goodbye. From such a well-known hostess this was praise indeed.

Two days later, as she packed her last trunk, Emily felt light-hearted and optimistic. The college was flourishing and would continue to do so; she was surprised and touched at the nice things most dons said about it. Her time as Mistress was over, but she knew that despite some setbacks she had not acquitted herself too badly.

Frances Bernard was to succeed Emily as Mistress. Well-read and travelled, she possessed many qualifications that would enhance the reputation of a growing college. She was the choice of Lady Stanley, who knew her family intimately and assured the Committee that in every way she was the 'distinguished person' needed to appeal to parents.

After a long talk with her, Emily pronounced her ideal. The Mistress-elect liked the young but was not 'motherly' in any way, and although quiet and dignified, was not afraid of authority or of speaking out when the occasion arose.

Before the Executive Committee had even seen Miss Bernard, Emily had thought it prudent to give them a description of what they must look for in a Mistress of a college: 'She should be conversant with the usages of society in our class and one who will give a refined and cultured tone to college society. This particular thing can only be done by the resident lady and it will of course depend more on what she is than on anything that she does.'

When Lady Stanley produced Miss Bernard, the entire Committee sensed at once that she was much better than they dared hope for. Tall and thin, quiet and dignified, she dressed well but unostentatiously. She talked well too but not incessantly, and was an excellent listener: Emily compared her to Charlotte Manning, who had been such a success with everybody. 'No-one could have managed the pioneers better than Mrs Manning,' Emily was fond of saying, and the pioneers had needed some handling. Miss Bernard had that same air of quiet confidence.

It soon became clear to Emily that while Frances Bernard possessed confidence in one sense, that is in dealing with people, she lacked it when it came to quite small things. This Emily put down to the fact that for all her life in India she had never been asked to settle trivia. Nothing of the sort had come to her attention; amongst the multitude of servants there was always someone whose job it was to see that such matters never reached her. At Girton she leaned heavily on Emily, whom she greatly admired – indeed it was soon plain to everyone that she whole-heartedly approved of her and all she had done for women: the head of Girton was now a loyal supporter. To those who knew about it, her constant references to 'the foundress' and the way she deferred to her were looked on as a bit of a joke, but no one dared say so openly. The letters exchanged between the two women were many and long and often contained nothing but trivialities that need not have been discussed at all. Because of her admiration for Emily she never questioned any decision of hers: 'I am immensely interested in your plans' was typical of one of her warm letters: 'I am full of admiration for the largeness of your views,' she wrote in another. 'We feel here that we march under a stout-hearted general.'

Although Emily was far from vain, she would not have been human if she had not been flattered by so much respect from such a sophisticated woman. And it was perfectly genuine. Indeed it is possible that if Emily had been different, Frances Bernard would not have accepted the post. All her adult life she had been surrounded by women, many of them so artificial and untrustworthy that to meet with simple honesty and true endeavour employed so unselfishly was a refreshing change. She found Emily's wit enlivening and soon discovered that she shared many of her opinions which were too advanced for some people. For all the glamour of her position Frances Bernard had always been lonely, knowing few people intimately enough to talk to them openly of her frustrations, but she enjoyed unburdening herself to Emily. Without being consulted, Frances Bernard had been shipped off to India to look after her eldest brother Charles, his wife having died in childbirth; and when he retired early through ill-health, she was transferred to Viceregal Lodge to do the same job for her uncle the Viceroy, Lord Lawrence. No one had asked her opinion, she had been sacrificed as an unmarried girl to her brother's and uncle's needs. When neither wanted her any more, she had come home – to nothing. Lady Stanley had given her Emily's paper 'Some Account of a Proposed College for Women' to read. Emily had delivered it before the Social Science Congress in 1868, its theme that something was needed to meet the wants of the two thousand sisters of the two thousand undergraduates at Cambridge. Frances had been one of the two thousand and she eagerly read what Emily had to say: 'These sisters will be found for the most part scattered about in country houses and parsonages and in the families of professional men and retired merchants and manufacturers . . . their abundant leisure and many opportunities of influence have hitherto been turned to small account. Yet how much might be made of them. The Hall and the Rectory are the centre of light for a whole parish. If their light be darkness, how great is that darkness . . .'

In many ways it was difficult for Frances Bernard to believe that now she found herself Mistress of the very college she had read about so enviously. The moment she met Emily, small, compact, bristling with energy, she knew that here was a leader she could follow, here was a force to reckon with, whose ideas she would enjoy carrying out.

At last Girton had at its head that 'distinguished personage' whom Emily had always longed for and whom parents could respect and trust. Since the numbers were increasing steadily, it was just in time, as well as a piece of good fortune Emily never expected. In 1875 when Emily resigned as Mistress there were sixteen pupils and more on the books for the coming academic year. Extra staff was needed, and Emily invited Elizabeth Welsh, an old student, to take over Louisa Lumsden's job as resident tutor in classics. Here again good fortune smiled on her choice; Elizabeth proved judicious, good-humoured and an excellent teacher, with none of those strange quirks of character that made Louisa so trying to work with. The following year she was followed by Constance Herschel, also home-bred, who came to teach mathematics. No longer was good taste offended by the sight of girls walking in the grounds with arms entwined or acting as acolyte to one or other of the two young women now at Girton as part of the staff. Suddenly the atmosphere had changed; it was now just what it should be in an all-women's college – healthy, friendly, and brisk.

Although no longer Mistress, Emily was frequently at Girton. These were not mere idle visits to see how things were shaping, but hard working days on college business. She was still Secretary, a key post she could not possibly relinquish even had she wanted to, because she had never had time to train another woman to understand the complex issues connected with Girton. In this capacity she attended to all the correspondence about the meetings of the Governing Body (as the Executive Committee was now called), the admission of students and the entrance and scholarship examinations.

For some unexplained reason the Committee had no permanent chairman, and Emily as a woman could not act (if men were present it was considered unseemly for a woman to take the chair, such were the conventions of the time); yet she summoned the meetings and arranged the agenda. She was careful to keep control tightly in her own hands, and she was stern when it came to discussion: 'short and sweet you must be,' she admonished a female friend who had had to be stopped from delivering a pointless and rambling speech. When one don newly put on the Committee called her 'the permanent, unofficial chairman', she was shocked.

Because of her all-powerful position she was still able to keep the Mistress off the Governing Body, although even she could see that such an anomaly could not continue indefinitely. She had been surprised when Miss Bernard accepted the omission meekly, only asking Emily to keep her informed of anything that might be useful to her. The trouble lay with the Committee – no one felt strong enough to fight the foundress.

When Barbara returned to England in April 1876, Emily arranged to take Frances Bernard to Scalands to meet the woman Emily erroneously called her co-foundress, a title Barbara did not altogether like, since it put on her shoulders an onus she would rather do without. To Emily's joy Frances Bernard found Scalands and its surroundings delightful, but it was a disappointment that she did not feel the same enthusiasm for her hostess; she and Barbara did not take to each other. When Barbara apologised that one of Miss Bernard's social position ('used to something so much better') had to live in a building still unfinished, Frances was openly annoyed – she was too busy to notice her surroundings, she said, and asked 'Cannot Madame Bodichon see that Miss Davies has worked miracles?' When, to make amends, Barbara offered to have the Mistress's rooms painted and papered at her own expense, Frances Bernard consulted Emily: 'surely there is something more urgent needed? Could not Madame Bodichon allow the money to be used on something else?' Emily wrote to Barbara to find out: 'I am much inclined to postpone the work . . . of course the place looks unfinished but this is not altogether a disadvantage, it brings home to people that we have not money . . . and for the students it is not amiss, I think, to have a reminder that the place did not grow up all by itself without any troubles.'

Emily planned to save enough from the fees to do some painting and papering, perhaps on a large scale if the students increased as rapidly as they had been doing lately, but Henry Tomkinson dashed these hopes when he told her (a little brutally) that if the decoration of the rooms cost £300 there would be only £70 left for emergencies. Emily was disappointed: it was unfortunate that England looked on education as a nebulous thing that did not need money. It certainly did not attract it.

Frances Bernard was keen on acting. The English colony in India had performed several short plays among themselves and she had always taken part. Since Emily saw no harm in the performance of a Greek play, she unbent enough to allow the girls to put on the *Electra* of Sophocles; it was certainly not a waste of time, she assured Emily, thus dispelling her last doubts. Frances Bernard took charge, helping the girls to make their own costumes and paint their own scenery, showing as much ingenuity in directing as they did skill in acting. The whole affair was a huge success, and Emily and the rest of the audience enjoyed a pleasant evening. It was a big step forward. Acting was still not considered quite respectable in Cambridge, but undergraduates were now bolder and dons more reasonable and, after all, as Emily remarked, 'the Greek play was an institution in all the best schools . . .'

Emily could not resist telling Barbara all about it. She suspected that she would be pleased that some conventions were being knocked down: '. . . I am glad to find that the inroad on the students' time was less than might have been feared . . . there was no extravagant expense on the dresses . . . the play was given on three nights . . . and was a great success . . .'

It so happened that at the end of Frances Bernard's first year there was so much work connected with the college (including schemes for raising money) that Emily could not get to Cambridge as often as she would have liked. Weekly letters to the Mistress had to take the place of visits, but these were so clear and concise, and Frances Bernard understood Emily's wishes so well, that everything was attended to as though she was on the spot: 'I seem to have always so much to ask you,' Frances wrote disarmingly, but it was never too much for Emily, who employed all her ingenuity in instructing from a distance. Only Henry Tomkinson was critical.

One day while waiting to take her to the theatre, with the freedom of an old friend he picked up a bulky letter lying on Emily's desk addressed to the Mistress of Girton and, weighing it in his hand, said a little severely: 'Is it rather too much telling Miss Bernard what to do and how to do it?'

Later he teased her, half seriously, of running Girton by remote control. He spoke quite good-humouredly, but Emily knew him too well to miss the edge to his voice. In cold tones she demolished the idea that she should throw aside all responsibility because she was no longer Mistress. She would turn her back on the college when it no longer needed her, but not before.

21

Patience and Tact bring Results

Lady Rich, a cousin of Henry Tomkinson and an admirer of Emily's, had died suddenly in 1874 when just on the point of giving the college a new gymnasium. This was to take the place of the makeshift one Emily had devised that first terrible winter at Girton when the whole college had difficulty in keeping warm. She had taken Lady Rich to watch the girls in action in the room at the top of the house, and Julia Rich had been delighted and amazed to see the girls leaping over the old leather horse and manipulating dumb-bells so skilfully that she had offered then and there to have a proper gymnasium built in the grounds. She had not had time to make arrangements about the bequest, for the following week she was dead and the whole college mourned her; the plans would have to be postponed until better days. But Henry Tomkinson stepped into the breach and offered to give the gymnasium to the college in memory of his cousin.

The building of the gymnasium was a heartening sign that Girton was growing apace and expansion was necessary. Another old girl, Constance Maynard, had joined the staff in 1875. In Emily's eyes she had not been entirely satisfactory as a student: too much temperament which she had difficulty in controlling, weak nerves, and a tendency to see slights where none existed. When she applied for the post Emily had grave doubts, but at her interview she seemed to have improved and the Governing Body were pleased with her. Emily gave in, but still with reservations.

Emily knew that there were always a few Constance Maynards and Louisa Lumsdens in every institution, restless, dissatisfied, always grumbling, difficult to deal with, but clever enough to be recommendable. She recognised that there was a grain of truth, but only a grain, in the accusations which they hurled at her. Louisa said bitterly that the students were mere cogs in the wheel of Emily's great scheme: 'It was plain that we counted for little or nothing except as we furthered her plans'; Constance Maynard called Emily 'heartless' and compared her to the steam engine of a ship – 'very kindly but with no more influence on our thoughts and aims than the chimneys or the front door'.

But Emily also knew that, absorbed in themselves and their own feelings, and suffering from repressions of one sort or another, they missed the essential purpose of what she was doing and took her occasional moods of anxiety for intolerance, her open dislike of exuberant affection and over-emotionalism for cold indifference. Of course Emily found some girls more agreeable than others, but she managed wonderfully well not to show preferences or to have favourites.

It is clear, moreover, that unknowingly they both profited a great deal from Emily's example, even from her strictures. Neuroses of the kind that assailed them as young women, emotions of the kind that had marred their judgement and exhausted them physically, would have hampered or halted their later careers, and it was Emily's training that gave them self-control. Louisa Lumsden was for eight years Headmistress of St Leonard's school for girls, and for another five Warden of a university hall for women at St Andrew's, being created DBE in old age; Constance Maynard was the first Mistress of Westfield College, now part of London University, in 1882, and remained in office until 1913. The fact that they were able to achieve this degree of success was entirely due to Emily's unremitting work on behalf of all women over the years. Did they remember this?

Constance showed herself in her true light shortly after her appointment in 1875. She disapproved of Emily even more than Louisa did and constantly went over her head (and Miss Bernard's also) to complain to Barbara, who she seemed to think was the arbiter of discipline for the college. One day she came to Emily, who happened to be at Girton, with what she called a serious complaint: the students thought she had no authority because she was not a member of the Governing Body. This was a great drawback to her teaching. 'As though the Governing Body were a secret society,' Emily explained to the Mistress, half angry and half laughing. But she really did burst out when she wrote to Lizzie Garrett Anderson 'I think Madame Bodichon is too ready to interfere . . .' It was exhausting to have these squabbles with young women who wanted to be treated as adults and yet were very childish.

Good things happened, too. It was a sign of progress that another bastion fell in 1877. Twenty-three dons opened their lectures to women, and Emily instantly decided that her girls should take advantage of this good fortune. The lectures proved very popular, and one waggonette to take the girls to their lectures in Cambridge soon became two. To see that all was as it should be, at first Emily went as well, travelling up from London specially to do so. She warned the girls to be sure to attend regularly and to listen attentively, for the eyes of Cambridge would be on them. In all the discussions which had gone on beforehand Emily had taken the place of Miss Bernard, who felt she was too new. These conferences with different Fellows of colleges were something Emily enjoyed too much to give up, and most of her frequent letters to Barbara contain a sentence beginning 'a visit to Cambridge on college business', which shows clearly the pure enjoyment she experienced when discussing scholarly subjects with learned men. She had her favourites: 'I went to Cambridge yesterday and had a long talk with Professor Liveing about the Natural Science subjects which ended in our deciding that our three new students (Kingsland, Dove and Gamble) had better attend his lectures on chemistry and Professor Humphreys' on anatomy and physiology . . . I don't think Professor H. has had any women in his class before.' Another letter answers an anxious one from Barbara: '. . . Professor Liveing has heard them [the lecturers] and thinks . . . there is no reasonable objection to a mixed class. I should go with them at first and occasionally . . .The students attending the lectures will come in for other privileges such as the use of university skeletons. I have written to Professor Humphreys about his lectures. He has always been a friend of the college and is sure to be pleasant. Professor Liveing went into the matter in the kindest way, taking it up as though it was quite his business to do the best he could for our students. It is certainly a great thing to come within range of these nice friendly people.' Professor Liveing, Professor Humphreys, the names rolled off Emily's tongue with some relish. To have such men listening to her views and talking to her without the least suggestion of patronage was a pleasure to be lingered over and savoured. There is no doubt that they found her company enjoyable and her views full of common sense, while their letters show a respect that was lacking at first. When they argued with her she never took offence, sulked or lost her temper, and she could do what a great many women found difficult – listen.

It was a great achievement to be told that her girls could attend medical lectures and Emily was jubilant, but Barbara's reaction was a surprise. Once the most outspoken of women, not in the least afraid of *risqué* conversation that made Emily blush, she had become sensitive in old age to such talk and had even reproved Emily for picking up some medical expressions from Lizzie Garrett Anderson, whom she now thought very crude. The idea of a mixed class in anatomy filled her with disgust – the study of medical matters would ruin many a well-brought-up girl – and she advised Emily not to allow it: 'One had only to look at Lizzie to see that all her finer feelings had been blunted since she became a doctor.'

Naturally the idea of girls attending a mixed medical class was a bit nerve-racking at first, but the girls as well as Emily felt it a great step forward and were determined to show that they were not shy. Although their hearts may have fluttered with panic, outwardly they looked cool and self-possessed as Emily led her little procession into the lecture hall in good time; looking neither to right nor to left, they took their seats in the back row as quietly as though they were in church. All heads were turned to watch this historic moment, the girls appearing to be unaware that they were doing something totally unprecedented. When the lecture began they stared straight ahead, intent on every word. One don described them in the local press as 'looking uncomfortable', but another, more kindly disposed, called them 'an eager and intelligent bunch of girls'. Emily was in her element. She sat at the end of the row, notebook in hand, pencil poised so that the lecturer could not fail to see that he was appreciated. Of course medical lectures brought their trials. When a specimen of the human brain was passed round for inspection there was an instant hush and all eyes were turned towards the girls, but they did not flinch as they examined it with care, Emily as composed and curious as the rest.

As soon as it leaked out that Girton's young ladies had attended anatomy lectures, all sorts of stories went the rounds of Cambridge High Tables: one, more ridiculous than the rest, was of live lobsters arriving in sackloads at Girton for the girls to use in practice sessions. Emily warned them to take no notice of such nonsense. When girls became a part of daily life in Cambridge, which they would be soon enough, all such silly stories would be forgotten.

Emily was beginning to wish that the college was closer to the university than two-and-a-half miles. It was important that contact with the men's colleges (and especially with dons) should be frequent, so that they could learn to take women for granted and not look on them as strange creatures from another world. Things were slowly improving. Already Emily felt that she was being accepted and that the talks she had with dons were becoming easier and more common. Instead of long-winded academic-style letters there were now informal meetings when difficulties were thrashed out and new ideas discussed, all with a great saving of time. Many misunderstandings were cleared up quickly in this way and a better feeling was generated towards women.

When in May 1875 it had become known that Emily was resigning as Mistress of Girton, she had received a letter from Thomas Holloway, founder and head of Holloway College, which greatly surprised her. He very much wanted her to succeed him as Principal: 'there is hardly anyone in the land whose experience and ability to advise is equal to yours. My brother-in-law returned from New York last week, but before leaving he visited Vassar College where he said he found eight resident women professors. How I wish if it were practical that the whole management of my college should be in the hands of ladies. May I ask your opinion on this subject?'

Her first reaction was typical – how could anyone as wise and experienced as Thomas Holloway think so highly of her, especially when she had none of the qualifications for such an important post? Her second, a feeling of envy for those American women who had the luck to be accepted as the equal of men, without a struggle. There was none of that male superiority in America which was such a hindrance to progress here in England. In a young country women pioneers had had to work shoulder to shoulder with their husbands from the beginning and had never let go. In England there were too many precedents for treating women as second-class citizens. How Emily longed to go to America and investigate everything to do with education herself!

As for Thomas Holloway's offer, she knew at once what she must say. Nevertheless she waited some days to reply, for experience had taught her that a quick answer to a serious question gave the impression that she had not considered it properly. Courteously, but very definitely, she declined: she did not feel that she could accept a post that called for scholarly qualifications. Since she had none, she would not be able to carry out those duties that required an academic training. That she possessed a great many other qualities that Holloway College needed, and that a man as astute as its founder recognised this, did not weigh with her at all. It was not a question of an inferiority complex, but a practical fact that could not be changed so late in life. She was not so self-effacing that she did not realise how much she had done without education. She fully understood since her association with Cambridge dons that perhaps if she had had an academic training she might not have had the courage to do the many distasteful things that had to be done in order to help women to break out of the prisons into which men had so securely locked them.

From her experience of the last few years she now knew that it was not part of the scholarly mind to take speedily to action, if that action might be awkward, and above all Emily was a woman of action. She enjoyed a good fight in a worthy cause and she always fought to win. She had other advantages over the professional scholar too; she had nothing to lose in saying what she thought and defying authority, since she had none of those ambitions that often make the scholar wary of uttering an immoderate word and so perhaps losing some honour he covets. In her long battle with authority she never once considered how her words might sometimes rebound on her.

At the time she received the letter, Emily was becoming very powerful, but she did not fully realise this, otherwise she might have exploited it more. She very much approved of Holloway College and admired its founder, but Girton still needed her and she could not yet leave it to others. She knew where Girton was going, her ambitions for it were clear-cut: she hoped that at first all college-trained girls (Girtonians especially) would want to teach, for only in this way could the standard of girls' education be raised. Schools needed them, colleges needed them, later other careers would be open to them, but for these they would have to fight. Sooner than she had expected (by 1881 in fact) five old-girls had returned to Girton to teach: Lumsden, Welsh, Maynard, Herschel and Scott. That Scott should want to return was a great triumph. The sensation that she had caused in 1880 when she had been placed equal to the eighth Wrangler was well deserved, for it was a remarkable achievement for a young woman who had never done any serious mathematics before entering Girton. Her success – quite unheard-of at the time – proved that a woman with a gift for mathematics and properly taught could be as good as any man, and Emily was proud that Girton had proved this point.

More and more dons were letting it be known that women were welcome at their lectures. Some far-seeing dons had done this long ago, others were following suit because attendance at their lectures was becoming very thin indeed, and no one likes to talk to empty air, however rigid their prejudices. Emily heard this good news at a dinner party in London and returned to Cambridge next day to find out if the lectures were on subjects useful to her students: 'One must show that this offer is appreciated,' she wrote to Adelaide. 'If only the university had been so kind as this from the beginning, how much anguish would have been saved.'

She could not know it, but dons were saying much the same about her: 'How much more reasonable Miss Davies is these days, how much less obstructive and so on.' Some of those who had always been kindly disposed towards women pointed out that struggling alone was not conducive to good temper, that there were still some things about university procedure that she did not understand, and that of course she must be helped.

22

'No better than a slave'

The year 1876 marked a crisis in Emily's life which is still something of a mystery, for the silence that she had learned so effectively as a child had returned to lock the secret away even from those who were close to her.

She had enjoyed Frances Bernard's first six months. The two women got on well together, and Emily knew that she was always welcome at Girton whenever she turned up. All those horrid whisperings and undercurrents of disapproval of which Emily had been conscious and which had made her so unhappy were now quite gone.

On 22 April 1875 Emily was forty-five, a birthday that passed off in somewhat melancholy fashion. She was getting old and feeling her years; she told Barbara a few days later: 'Forty-five is a good age for retiring into private life.' She did not of course retire but she became pessimistic and gloomy, an unusual state of mind with her, indeed so unusual that her friends looked at each other meaningly and put her moods down to the menopause.

She took a short holiday abroad in August 1875 with Jane Crow, but returned looking pale and complaining of aches and pains: she had been too unwell to enjoy herself and only hoped that she had not dampened Jane's enthusiasm, for she too had needed a holiday. Soon she was talking of 'nerves' (this was something her friends had been forbidden to mention in her presence hitherto) and said that she was thinking of giving up parties: 'You will wonder why I am giving up society,' she told Barbara. 'I do not care to undergo the fatigue.' She talked too in a melancholy way about her work; there was little more she could do and she only hoped that all that she had done had not been wasted.

Some days she made efforts and seemed her old self; she even took her nephew and niece skating on an indoor rink and afterwards wrote to Barbara, quite in the usual style: 'I only had one tumble . . .' Then suddenly she took to her bed and stayed there for a month, refusing to see her friends or to give her relations any explanation for such conduct. Mrs Davies's doctor examined her and shook his head: it was quite clear that he did not know what was wrong, but he warned her that Emily was gravely ill. On the day she decided to get up she wrote Adelaide a letter of the kind that would have driven her frantic with impatience in the old days: 'any extra fatigue or worry tends to increase the nervous weakness and irritability which already . . . interferes with what could be called "my usefulness" . . .'

For the first time she talked of her 'very small income' and how she felt a drag on her mother. She chose to forget that she had paid half the fees of more than one Girton student who was clever but impoverished, and that when Mistress of Girton she had never taken a proper salary. She had forgotten that before this mysterious collapse she had travelled on college business to Birmingham, Bradford, Manchester and wherever the Social Science Association happened to be holding a congress, and always at her own expense. She hardly ever missed a Headmistresses' Association meeting, for it was the one certain way of keeping in touch with old friends. There had been no mention of poverty then.

Emily and her mother had started life in London very comfortably off; there had been no question of living in one of the poorer quarters, which would have been the lot of most clergymen's widows, and there had been no crisis since then. Financially England was very stable; there had been little change economically since the Crimean War, and Emily's grandfather had shown his business acumen by investing his money wisely, so that it was nonsense for Emily to write to Adelaide: 'If I feel equal to more work I should wish not to take up public agitation but something I should be paid for so that I could contribute more to the household expenses.' She does not mention what sort of job she had in mind. From Mistress of Girton to governess – hardly! In her self-flagellating mood it gave her masochistic pleasure to dwell on the horrors of life as a governess – she who could not bear to be tied down even by the institution she loved and had created. Matters had gone very far when she announced to her family that she was going to give up the secretary-ship of Girton as well, a powerful position which only she could do properly and which was hers by right. At this, Adelaide rushed round to Cunningham Place, dashed straight upstairs to Emily's room and ferociously attacked her friend as she lay inert on her sofa. A short sharp quarrel ensued. Adelaide called Emily 'a traitor' before rushing out of the room, banging the door behind her.

Adelaide was not the only one who was shaken. The Llewelyn Davieses were seriously worried; her sister-in-law Mary refused to believe she was having a nervous breakdown or suffering from nervous prostration. There must be some other explanation, but what? Mary's liking for Emily and her knowledge of her character gave the first clue as to the real cause of the curious collapse. Oddly enough she was the only one to notice that Henry Tomkinson had neither written nor come round to Cunningham Place to see Emily, and that Emily had not mentioned him once. He had always been so assiduous, so attentive to her needs, so protective (some said so possessive), so helpful and kind. She knew they got on well together and that Emily consulted him about every important issue. It seems strange that Mary, who was close to her and one of her staunchest admirers, did not ask her what had happened to keep Henry Tomkinson away. Or perhaps Emily did confide in her but swore her to secrecy? Since the death of his mother, 17 Cunningham Place had been his second home, for Henry enjoyed female society, and Emily and her mother felt comfortable with a man about the house. It is strange, too, that there are no letters from him after the winter of 1875/6: not a word for Emily's forty-sixth birthday and nothing showing concern for her illness. The omission does not mean that he had not written, since Emily probably destroyed all his letters after that date. But why?

Unfortunately, the solution to this puzzle can only be guesswork, for there is not a single clue in the Girton archives; the evidence has completely vanished. It would have been unnatural for such a woman to destroy all the letters from an old friend unless she had had a severe shock. In recent months she and Henry had clearly been drawing closer together and their relationship had become more intimate. It seems conceivable – even probable – that Henry proposed marriage some time late in 1875, after her retirement party, and that Emily turned him down. It would have been a most suitable marriage in every way, since Henry had everything to recommend him: he was rich, charming, clever and home-loving, with a ready wit and exactly the right sense of humour to appeal to one of Emily's temperament. He was the right age (a year younger than Emily), understood her work and had shared in it for some years and – most important of all – they got on well together. He must have had reason to believe that Emily returned his affection, otherwise he would scarcely have risked a rebuff. Nothing could have been more suitable than that, after so long and so close a friendship, they should decide to marry. He had become such an important part of Emily's life, he understood her well, had helped in her work and was prepared to go on doing so, yet she now cast him off. There is no evidence of any contact between them after 1875.

It looks very much as if Emily's completely uncharacteristic retreat from life in the spring of 1876 was nature taking revenge after an overwhelming emotional crisis. While this must, in the present scanty state of the evidence, remain pure speculation, it can nevertheless be confidently asserted that it fits such evidence as there is better than any other explanation.

So why did she refuse him, if to do so caused her so much suffering? Was it because she felt that she could not continue to do her work for the 'cause' – much of it as yet untouched – with a husband whose feelings she had to consider? Henry Tomkinson had once tried to stop her standing for the School Board; his reasons were of course entirely laudable, nevertheless he had worked against her, and it must have crossed her mind that if she were his wife he might do so again and that the conflict might be painful, even the cause of a serious rift between them. It must not be forgotten that if she married she would lose her freedom in law. Much had been done for married women by 1875 but not enough to suit women like Emily, and she knew that to carry on with her work she must be free and unfettered.

The decision cost her dear: the agony of losing him for ever cut deep into her heart, although she knew that it was the only decision, and in the end she made it bravely. Once long ago she had said that marriage made a woman 'no better than a slave' and that was as true in 1876 as when she first uttered the words.

Did Emily tell Adelaide Manning the truth about her collapse? That it had been caused by her heart and her mind pulling in opposite directions, and that she longed to follow her heart but that her conscience would not let her? Adelaide's change of attitude – from cross incredulity to warm sympathy – indicates that Emily did confide in this friend whom she trusted. It was a relief to do so, but Adelaide believed, like Emily herself, that some fits of depression must be treated a little roughly. When Emily wailed 'I shall never start anything else', Adelaide's answer was a severe: 'I don't believe a word of this.' Without consulting Emily she went to see Lizzie Garrett Anderson to ask her advice, only to find her distracted with worry about her baby daughter, who was desperately ill with meningitis.

Adelaide did not interfere when Emily resigned from the secretaryship of Girton without consulting anyone first, a foolhardy thing to do and unworthy of Emily, beyond saying gravely 'you will regret this'. Not long before, Emily had told Adelaide that the secretaryship was the one job that she would keep in her hands as long as possible. Now, as though in a fit of low spirits, she seemed to relinquish it without a struggle and think nothing of it. She saw that Adelaide was appalled and tried to explain her feelings in a letter: 'The specific work of Secretary to the College . . . I feel bound to do ill or well so long as I hold the office . . . I don't occupy even this limited field so fully or so efficiently as I might if I were stronger . . .' Fortunately, Mary Llewelyn Davies was able to persuade her sister, Mrs Croom Robertson, to take over at short notice. This set tongues wagging, and everyone thought that Emily must be seriously ill. They wagged even more when Henry Tomkinson resigned as college Treasurer and gave up his seat on the Governing Body as well. Emily said it did not matter, as she would take over as Treasurer in his place. Adelaide thought this a piece of bravado, as she knew that Emily was useless at finance and would mess things up in a week.

By August 1876 Emily was out and about again, paler, thinner, more subdued but working in a modified way, and attending Governing

Body meetings in her own right but not as Secretary. When Mrs Croom Robertson offered to hand the post back, Emily declared she was not strong enough. It was not long, however, before she began to assert herself again, and when it was suggested that someone else should interview the new lecturers and arrange the girls' studies, she would not hear of it. Except for not acting as Secretary she would do her duty as usual, even taking charge of the entrance examinations next year. It would be less effort than teaching someone else how it should be done.

Before the new term started at Girton she travelled to Scalands to see Barbara, now partially paralysed after yet another severe stroke: she could no longer walk or paint but relied on her friends for amusement. The shock of seeing her in this pitiable condition made Emily take a long hard look at herself and give thanks that she was still all in one piece with no permanent physical damage.

This brief holiday was worthwhile since at Scalands Emily met a young Girton student who helped to look after Barbara in the vacations in return for some financial help. Hertha Marks was devoted to Barbara, knew all about Emily and was ready to give her impressions of Girton, which Emily had not seen for some weeks, the longest period that she had ever been away from the college. She questioned Hertha eagerly about her work as a scientist, the Tripos results, the increase in student numbers and the new Mistress (with whom Emily had carried on a correspondence despite her doctor forbidding exertion of any kind). Hertha's enthusiasm was infectious: she always loved returning to Girton after the vacations, she said, it was 'such fun scrambling for breakfast, quizzing lecturers and talking shop with the other students from morning till night. Work does not seem like work but a delightful form of amusement.' Emily enquired eagerly for news of the Royal Society Congress where Hertha had been asked to demonstrate the electric arc, thereby creating a sensation, since working with electricity was thought to be dangerous for a woman.

A curious side-effect of Emily's illness or nervous collapse was her inability to see how much she had achieved in fifteen years. It maddened Adelaide to hear her say that she had wasted her time far too much and that if she could have her life over again she would use it not only more usefully but differently. When Adelaide rebuked her, saying that she was fishing for compliments, she was indignant and in turn accused Adelaide of being hard and unsympathetic.

The two friends were out walking together in the spring of 1877 when the conversation turned on a small book that had recently been published called *Useful Lives*, written by a female missionary to induce other females to enter the mission field as a vocation. Emily was rather taken with the idea, but Adelaide smartly retorted that she never thought anyone as sensible and level-headed as Emily could possibly be taken in by a cynical trap set to persuade some poor lonely widow or dissatisfied spinster to go to an unknown, possibly unhealthy, country, to do work for which she was unfitted and probably for a mere pittance, too. With a sigh Emily confessed that she had been so taken with the advertisement for the book that only the thought of her aged mother had prevented her writing for particulars. After all, she was good for little else. Adelaide replied that although her imagination was acute she could not quite picture Emily moving in saintly fashion among a lot of savages, only pausing to read snippets of the Bible in a language the natives did not understand.

Soon after this Emily began to get well rapidly. She realised at some stage that unless she took herself in hand she might become a permanent invalid like her father. As soon as she was well enough to travel she went to Girton, where the warmth of her welcome overwhelmed her: everyone said that she had been missed. Over a leisurely chat in the Mistress's rooms, she was brought up to date with all that had been happening during her absence. As Henry Tomkinson had long ago predicted, Frances Bernard had coped very well indeed and Emily saw how greatly she had increased in confidence. They talked of Barbara's cruel illness and of Emily's fear that she too might be going the same way.

A surprise was the portrait by Rudolf Lehmann for which she had given only three sittings before she fell ill. Hanging in the dining hall it looked very striking against the stark white walls. Her reaction was just as Frances Bernard expected; it flattered her, she said. Laughingly, she remarked that she hoped that it would not spoil her appetite next time she dined in Girton. The visit did her good, for it brought back an urge to start work again: it did more, since it made her realise how important trifles became when one was ill and confined to bed. In future she would be more kindly towards the sick. At once she proved this when she wrote to Barbara: '. . . I hope that you may be able to find some good in this and to look upon the forced idleness . . . as the rest which you have earned by years of assiduous exertion . . .'

Quickly she plunged into work; half measures had never been her style. A sign that she was rapidly becoming herself again was the way she totally disregarded her doctor's orders to 'take things gradually', as she cheerfully told Barbara in a letter she tried to make light-hearted. She let the Local Examination Board know that she was ready to invigilate again. When going through the lists she was struck by the way Latin was being neglected by girls: out of 129 candidates only five offered Latin, 'the rest scatter themselves over German, Zoology, Botany and other trumpery.' This is what happened when she did not attend a School Mistresses Association meeting for over eighteen months. She made a note to have a word with Frances Buss and others who had fallen in with the modern habit of neglecting the classics 'because they thought them useless'.

Again ignoring doctor's advice, she made a quick visit to Dublin where an entrance examination for Girton was to be held for the first time. She found the Dubliners delightfully hospitable and generous, and returned with two £50 scholarships in her pocket for girls from Derry and Coleraine. Her visit to Edinburgh for the same purpose was ruined by rain. Nevertheless to prove to herself that she was now sound in mind and limb she put on stout boots and a waterproof cloak and doggedly went sight-seeing: 'One must always behave in a strange city as though one may never visit it again, and see everything,' she wrote to Barbara by way of excuse.

Before long she was so perfectly recovered that she gave herself a long promised treat, an Italian holiday. Elizabeth Welsh went with her. To go in December was deliberate – colder weather, but fewer tourists, and cheaper. Elizabeth Welsh had never been abroad before. She had been a delicate child and her parents had felt that they did not dare risk foreign food and foreign doctors, although travel was becoming more common and large continental towns catered for the fastidious English. Emily had not travelled extensively, but she had visited France and Belgium for quite long periods, had lived for some weeks in Algiers and Switzerland, and this gave her the right to be considered 'travelled'. Elizabeth was only too glad to leave all the arrangements in Emily's hands. She did not demur when (in the nicest possible way) Emily decided what towns or beauty spots they were to visit and how long they were to stay at each.

They made straight for Florence without lingering on the way and nothing could have been better, for Elizabeth was gratifyingly ecstatic: why had she not been here before? Every day they went sightseeing, Emily with *Baedeker* in hand. Whenever they entered a church Elizabeth noticed that Emily prayed briefly and without self-consciousness, never making a parade of her devotions but treating such behaviour as quite natural. Privately she thought that Emily must possess a remarkable constitution: here she was, spending long hours sightseeing after a severe illness that had left her weak for months and that made her declare she was long past exertion of any kind. She never flagged in Florence or suggested that she was in the least tired, and since she was the elder of the two Elizabeth thought it ill became her to complain. It was the first of many holidays the two women took together. Indeed Emily became so addicted to travel that she vowed to stop frittering her money away but to save it for holidays abroad.

When Mrs Davies died in 1886 Emily sold 17 Cunningham Place, which had been their home since 1861, and bought a small maisonette close to Barbara's London home in Blandford Square, a house now owned by Llewelyn Davies and his family. In 1887 Adelaide Manning was persuaded to buy a flat on the other side of the square, a mere stone's throw from Emily's new home. It had only just become vacant but Emily made her snap it up with all speed; small flats were at a premium in London and such another might never come on the market again. Besides it solved the problem of loneliness in old age for them both.

23

'There is no going back'

Girton in the 1880s was acquiring a reputation for comfort that was not strictly justified: Emily knew that it was merely because each girl was allowed the luxury of a bedroom and sitting room to herself, an arrangement that was not always possible in the new women's colleges that were springing up in Oxford and the provinces, because of lack of space. From the day that the college was conceived Emily had planned it so, because of her belief that every young girl needed at times to be alone in order to develop emotionally, intellectually and spiritually; if results were anything to go by, she was right. Many did not agree with her – it was 'teaching the young to be self-indulgent' and a 'stupid waste of space' – but she fought hard for her beliefs and in the end silenced her critics. A visiting American academic, who had asked to be shown round Girton, was so pleasantly surprised by the girls' sets, their practicality and their tasteful decorations, that they quite effaced from his mind the bad impression that the first sight of Girton made on him – it was among the ugliest buildings he had ever seen.

It did not do Girton any harm when a national newspaper published the American's impressions of women's colleges in England and showed that he rated Girton as exceptionally comfortable and well-designed, much better than American colleges, which could be accused of overcrowding. The women's colleges were very much in the news at this time because of the Girton agitation for degrees, so the *Cambridge Chronicle* sent a reporter to London to interview the traveller. Never before had they taken the slightest interest in this women's college built on their door-step, nor in its foundress whom many had never heard of. Fortunately the visitor was of an expansive nature and gave the *Chronicle* facts and figures which opened their eyes. He had heard that a new building was about to be added to this already spacious college and was to cost about 40,000 dollars, a large enough sum by American standards for forty or fifty small bed-sittingrooms; no college authorities in the States would dream of allowing a young student to have two rooms all to herself. Yet despite this luxury the college was run on strict economical lines; for instance when compared with the excellent library at Vassar, the Girton library was meagre indeed.

Emily was quick to seize on this piece of publicity and turned it to her college's advantage: she wrote to the *Chronicle* explaining that the library was small because the college was poor but that this fact did not deter the students in any way: they begged, borrowed or bought books themselves, and their Tripos results were excellent despite this disadvantage. In 1884 patience had its rewards: a new library was built through the generosity of Lady Stanley; it was big enough to hold all the books the girls needed, collected together through an ingenious scheme of Miss Bernard's, who wrote to leading authors, asking them to present books to Girton College library.

There was no doubt about Girton's poverty: the fact could not be hidden, although the grounds facing the main road were slowly improving as shrubs and bushes grew and more were added, thus bit by bit eradicating the air of neglect that had so offended some members of the Governing Body. Emily always refused to budge from her original plan to build more and more student sets as money became available. Numbers meant power: she had no wish that her college should be a pigmy among giants. Perhaps Girton could never be as large as Trinity, but it might become as big as Magdalene or Peterhouse. She realised of course that other things were urgently needed: scholarships, fellowships, money for research, a chapel, but student rooms must remain her first priority.

She regretted, she told the Governing Body over and over again, that she was forced to refuse the alternative plan of bed-sitting-rooms or two girls sharing one bedroom, because it would not suit the Girton image. She intended to continue as she had started: 'This great boon, the power of being alone, is perhaps the most precious distinctive feature of college life as compared to that of an ordinary family.' She had set a high standard for her college, and one day she hoped that Girton would no longer be the poor relation; but there were times when she wondered if she were the only far-sighted one on the Governing Body. There were occasions when everyone of them seemed obstructionist.

In 1879 the college was left a substantial legacy of £19,000 in the will of Jane Catharine Gamble. At once Emily said she hoped it would be agreed that it must be spent on more buildings, but there was strong opposition. Had she forgotten that Girton was in debt? In the end Emily had her way: seventeen acres of land close to the college were bought at once and work commenced on more rooms where Emily hoped to house twenty-seven new students. She had plans for a new large dining hall and better kitchens, but the opposition dug their heels in: 'Miss Davies is forgetting the debt.' Some were deeply shocked that Emily could contemplate new buildings while Girton owed so much money. But she had not watched Henry Tomkinson handling college finances for nothing: she explained that to pay off the whole of the debt at a stroke was uneconomical and short-sighted. Only some of the money must be used to decrease the debt, and the rest must be spent on student rooms. It would be over-cautious to leave the money untouched in the bank for a rainy day. True, it was mainly the older members who felt this, but it was the one scheme Emily had no patience with, and in 1880 she wrote in despair to Adelaide Manning: 'We are in a state of stagnation, not able to move or increase our numbers and no one is likely to leave or give us money while we are doing nothing with what we have.' When Barbara died in 1891, leaving the college £10,000 free of conditions, even the use of this legacy was subject to endless argument.

It was all very well for the Governing Body to congratulate Emily when more and more girls applied for places at Girton, and then to look astonished when she said that she had nowhere to put them. She was well aware, too, that behind her back it was said that she had 'a mania for building'. Such talk left her cold, while it did upset her to have to tell intelligent eager girls that she had no room for them. Schools had improved beyond recognition by the 1880s, and there were now few candidates who were not well grounded in the right subjects.

Shortly after Barbara's legacy, Girton had another smaller windfall when a Madame Pfeiffer left the college £5,000. By the terms of the will it was to be used on something that could bear her name, so scholarships were chosen, without any quibbling, and Emily showed that she was by no means so blinded by building-mania as they thought, for she agreed at once.

When in 1895 Lady Stanley died – the fiercest opponent of any building schemes and, as an atheist, to any place of worship – it was at last agreed to build a chapel by subscription: no longer should Girton be called 'that infidel place'. It was completed in 1902 and inaugurated by Emily's brother the Rev. John Llewelyn Davies, who had always been and still was a staunch supporter of his sister's schemes. The ceremony was at first intended to be a quiet one, but so great was the interest shown that Girton was packed to the doors with past and present pupils, dons from every college and well-wishers from far and wide.

In his address Llewelyn Davies referred to the bad old days when women were left out of everything that was worthwhile, when no one (certainly no man) thought it necessary to educate a person who had no rights under the sun and whose role in life was too low to be worth considering: 'there is no thought now,' he said, 'in any considerable part of the community, of going back upon what has been done.' In many ways Emily had cause for satisfaction, but with her temperament it was unthinkable that she should not be formulating more and better ideas to improve the lot of women. The new chapel, though very much appreciated, was not one of these. She had done without it for years because there were other places where girls could worship; extra student rooms would benefit them more, but the sanctimonious had criticised sharply and unkindly. 'Fancy! and Miss Davies a clergyman's daughter . . .'

Girton and Newnham students did not fraternise in any way, which was strange since there were so few women in Cambridge. It was not that they refused to do so, it was more subtle than that. Girtonians simply did not admit that Newnham existed, and when on occasion they were forced into the admission, they made it plain that Miss Clough's hostel (which was the way they referred to it) was some kind of poor relation they had vaguely heard spoken of. This snobbish lack of friendliness was noticed, of course, as everything to do with Girton always was, and the students quickly acquired the reputation of showing that they were superior; and when they were accused of pride they disarmingly agreed – they were proud of being at Girton.

A certain hidden rivalry went on at the same time. In the summer of 1881 Jemima Clough and the Sidgwicks gave a garden party to which neither Emily nor the Mistress of Girton were invited. It was a very lavish affair, with the local press very much in evidence (two long columns were filled with the list of distinguished guests). Emily (who did not in the least mind being left out) read the account with interest, wondering how they could afford to spend so much on something pleasant but worthless. She was even more surprised when she was told that it was merely a dress rehearsal for a bigger affair planned for the summer of 1883, when Newnham hoped to be honoured by royalty.

After such a snub from Newnham it was all the more surprising to receive a letter from Jemima Clough about six months later, asking Girton to join with Newnham in buying a disused chapel almost next door to the Fitzwilliam Museum, that looked as though it could be converted into a laboratory. The price was high, but it could make the purchase possible if Girton would buy a half share; then students from both colleges could use it. At first Emily thought it a good idea, but on reflection changed her mind: she got the feeling that Newnham wanted her help for one reason only, '. . . that we should take the major part in providing the money.'

Pondering on the matter a little longer, Emily began to realise that there was no advantage in such a purchase for Girton. When she went to inspect the building she found it in poor condition and in need of heavy repairs. Besides, it was some distance away from Girton, although almost next door to Newnham. That would inevitably be a cause of constant friction, especially in winter when Girtonians would have a long cold bicycle ride against the wind. She had only just given permission for her girls to ride bicycles into the town (hitherto they had been allowed only for a country spin) and some people had criticised her for it as both dangerous and unbecoming. Then there was the question of standards: Girton girls were doing more advanced work in all subjects than Newnhamites, and that might make it impossible to share the teaching; yet not to do so would be uneconomical. No! It would not do after all. Emily sent a polite refusal.

In the course of the negotiations Emily learned a great deal about how Newnham was run from Charlotte Scott who had a great friend there. It made Emily feel a little guilty listening to Charlotte prattling away, but curiosity won over discretion. After all, she had always wanted to know but felt she ought not to ask, and here was Charlotte talking freely (and most amusingly too) about Miss Clough holding a kind of reception (behaving like a high priestess) every night at eight and the girls bored to tears. She was not displeased to discover that Newnham was run more for the convenience of the servants than of the students, whose work timetable was very curtailed as a result. It was a source of satisfaction, too, to have the myth of Jemima Clough's scholarly mind exploded: she was a very simple kindly woman with a somewhat timid nature, who shied away from controversial and revolutionary ideas but possessed a real bent for running a large household economically. Like so many women of her generation, she had been thrown by circumstances into the teaching profession, for which she was inadequately prepared; fortunately in the schools of her day very little teaching talent was required. She was much influenced by her brother Arthur, who had been Arnold's favourite pupil at Rugby, and it was he who had spurred her on to greater and greater heights, for which she was ill-equipped. The hostel at Cambridge had come as a blessing, it might almost be said as a blessed relief, for at last she could do something she did well and was happy doing, while the Sidgwicks attended to the academic side.

Now Emily understood why, when she and Jemima had met at a headmistresses' conference some years before, she had found the head of Newnham singularly ill-informed on higher education and discovered that she had not even bothered to read Emily's little book on the subject. But she was a kindly soul and wanted every woman to be educated, although her ideas for doing this were ineffective, so Emily had dismissed her as a possible ally; no vigorous controversial speeches would be expected from that quarter. 'Since she is nothing, people get fond of her and that is how she gets on.' It was sad to learn that the reasons Newnham was so popular were cheapness and the lower entry standard. It only proved again how eager girls were to be educated and how they would be willing to put up with a lot to get the chance.

Emily would have liked Girton to be cheaper but it was pared down to the bone as it was, and with the cost of living rising there was no hope of this. From the beginning she had tried to set certain standards; she had always employed excellent teachers so that learning should be a pleasure and not a chore. The new tennis-courts had cost a fortune, levelling the ground had taken months, but Emily could not keep a note of complacency from creeping into her voice when she took friends to watch the girls play. Before long, they would catch up on numbers, of this she had never a doubt, and contrarily she tried to remind herself that it was quality not quantity that counted. Nevertheless the fact that Newnham was larger awoke a fiercely competitive streak in her of which she was a little ashamed but could not suppress. From time to time she reminded herself that Girton girls were better educated and certainly secured better jobs than girls from other colleges.

Lately she had heard that Miss Clough wanted to give up the special examination that she had once been so happy to embrace and have her girls prepared for the Tripos. As if it was possible to take such a leap overnight as though there was nothing to it! It was also being said that 'Newnham has some really good mathematicians this year'; but what standard were they using, Emily wondered. 'I do not think they have one candidate to send this year, two-thirds of the girls only take the higher local which hundreds do at home . . . while ours take the real and complete thing.' Such sharp criticisms of another college were not usual with Emily. She had of course long ago forgiven the Sidgwicks and Miss Clough for making her endure months of anxiety; but that did not mean that she could forget.

The University of London had opened its doors to women in 1878. Remembering Lizzie Garrett's struggles, Emily could not help shedding a few tears for her and those who came after her whose cries for admission had fallen on deaf ears. Notwithstanding the toughness and unreasonableness of the opposition to her entering the medical profession, Lizzie had made a huge success of her chosen career and was still going from strength to strength. Oxford, too, encouraged by the growth of Girton, was casting aside the cautious streak so common in academics and beginning to turn the hostels (bought to accommodate those who were attending the Ladies' Lectures) into women's colleges: Somerville and Lady Margaret Hall started in 1879 and, as Lady Brodie had predicted all those years ago, they had only dared go so far because of Emily's enterprise and courage. The provinces, too, were becoming more daring, and colleges in Manchester and Liverpool were already filling up and had waiting lists. 'Women long to be educated,' Emily had told a somewhat cynical male audience in Cambridge in 1869: how quickly she had been proved right! Women only needed the chance. Looking back, Emily marvelled at the change in girls coming to Girton in the late 1880s; they were so much better equipped than the first famous five, although the five had shown the greater courage.

Human nature was very strange. Emily never expected praise, but it was irritating to be asked so often why Girton cost more than Newnham.

When told that individual teaching (among other things) cost money, she was asked it if was really necessary. 'People at a distance are not aware of our superiority,' Emily told Barbara, 'I think we must give more scholarships.' That Girton's superiority was better known than she thought was proved ten days later, when a relation of Miss Clough's wrote wishing to enter her daughter for Girton. Emily had to read the letter twice to make sure. What a triumph! 'If coming to Girton gets into the family it might go further . . .,' Emily wrote gleefully to Adelaide. How much easier life became when one was successful.

During the past year Emily had done her best to advertise the college, travelling again to Scotland and Wales to visit schools in her self-appointed task of talent-spotting. So successful were these tours that the following year she went again to Dublin to interview some candidates who sounded promising, but the moment she set foot in the first school she could see that the pupils (not to mention those who taught them) had little idea what higher education meant. One young girl, anxious to improve herself, asked where Girton was: was it in England? 'Great ignorance prevails here.' Recently Emily had taken to spending some part of the Long Vacation term at Girton. This was a period of permitted, but not compulsory, residence of six or seven weeks in July and August. She found this quiet time in Cambridge in some ways the jolliest; everyone seemed in such a good mood and the weather so much better. It gave her great pleasure to see the girls go off for picnics on the river or long walks, and to come across others having tea in the garden with friends, looking pretty in their summer dresses and straw hats. It was all relaxed and happy, a far cry from those horrific predictions that learning would make women masculine and unfit to be wives and mothers.

Visitors were always impressed by the easy congenial atmosphere and the friendly attitude of the students to those who taught them. Americans especially never failed to mention it. Sometimes Emily thought that Girton was a name more honoured in the United States than in England. Every summer tourists from America came in large numbers to see the college and ask questions about the standard of work in order to compare it with women's colleges in their country. If she was on the spot Emily enjoyed showing them round herself, and she never failed to marvel at the genuine interest (amounting almost to reverence) that they had for education. Emily had in mind at some time, perhaps not too far distant, to create studentships for American girls; it all depended on money, and that was as difficult as ever to find: a little more of it would mean that they could go forward at a greater speed, for there was still much to be done. People so often wished to help, and then with the best will in the world acted unwisely and without consulting the college, proving over and over again that good intentions were not enough.

Such a case occurred in 1881 after 'Scott of Girton' had been bracketed

Eighth Wrangler in the Tripos. A Mr and Mrs Steadman Aldis of New-castle, on their own initiative and without consulting Girton, collected names for a petition and sent it off to the Cambridge Senate asking for women students to be given degrees. Of course nothing whatever came of it. Later Mrs Aldis wrote to Emily to explain that at first they had intended to collect local names and send them to Girton, but support had grown to such an extent that they thought it might help Girton in the fight for degrees if they sent them direct to the Cambridge Senate. She had not the heart to tell them that they had acted without knowing the Cambridge Senate, which resented outside interference in its affairs and of course thought Emily behind the whole business. Indeed they had nearly upset the applecart by acting too soon and without due prepara-tion. For some time now Emily had been waiting for a moment to ask for degrees at a moment when to refuse would embarrass the Senate; a false move might lead to a suggestion that in place of degrees university certificates – which would carry very little weight with prospective employers – might be introduced, and that this might put off the admission of women to degrees for years.

Indeed, this is exactly what happened. A Grace was passed the following year (June 1882), authorising the issue of certificates to women, stating the class they had obtained in the Tripos. As Emily had feared, the issue of certificates proved no temporary measure; it endured for more than sixty years. Emily had only recently asked for and been granted three representative members from the university to sit on the Governing Body in order that Girton College's views could be put before the Senate in an unbiased way. So far the new members had attended just one meeting and Emily did not wish them to think that they had only been appointed for a single purpose – to help in the fight for degrees.

Nevertheless, there were repercussions which affected Emily most unfairly. Sidgwick wrote to tell her that it was all her fault and that to ask for degrees at this stage was 'harmful and merely harmful: I am anxious that the new colleges should act in harmony.'

To act in harmony with Newnham was something that she had hitherto refused to do, since this would seem to put the two colleges on a level. Furthermore, she would not join with any institution that did not fulfil proper university rules, as Girton had always done. To sit for the Tripos under irregular conditions was mischievous, and she often said so in public.

Since the Senate had refused to grant the Aldis petition Emily felt that perhaps now was the time to ask for something else in its place; so she promptly wrote for formal sanction to be granted to women in order to allow them to sit for Little-go and the Triposes 'as of right' in future and to put an end to all informal arrangements. Some months later the request was granted without the slightest fuss. Thus Emily was relieved of an annual burden at examination time that was as troublesome as it was tedious. It was a victory but only a small one, as she told Barbara: 'What we gain is that what we have been doing all along as a favour will now be secured as a right.'

Lizzie telegraphed her delight: 'Heartiest Congratulations even in spite of its limitations which probably won't last long.' Lizzie understood the situation perfectly, but many others greatly exaggerated its importance, as Emily told her in her reply: 'the fuss certain members of the university make about "this triumph" is too silly.' Meeting Dr Stuart casually in the street she was taken aback when he stopped, shook her cordially by the hand as he similarly congratulated her on her 'victory', saying 'I think it would be difficult to estimate the value it will have on women's education.'

24

Not Rights but Justice

At the end of the Michaelmas Term 1885, Frances Bernard resigned as Mistress of Girton to become the second wife of Dr Latham of Trinity. Under her sensible guidance Girton had flourished, quickly settling down into a peaceful routine that did everyone credit. The students had found her approachable and sympathetic to their problems and could talk to her easily, and although she was very shy it never seemed a barrier. The Committee liked her, too, and her loyalty to the foundress could not be faulted. Her complete lack of personal ambition meant that she made no demands for herself and was anxious only to further the good of the college, for which she worked hard and conscientiously. Although Emily rejoiced in her happiness, she saw her go with a sinking heart: 'there will never be such another'.

Unlike the bad old days when hardly a single woman could be persuaded to take on the job, there were more applicants than the Committee expected and the standard was high. To Emily's surprise Louisa Lumsden applied, an act of folly after all that had taken place; Emily sensed that she was relying on the Committee to outvote the foundress and for one moment thought so, too, for several members were very keen to have her back – 'such a good influence on the girls'. The Committee's attitude does great credit to Emily, who had not taken them into her complete confidence and had kept to herself all that she had suffered from Louisa's spite and antagonism. If she were to be given a second chance, now, the college would lose all it had gained under Frances Bernard and once more would become a place of jealousies, restlessness and dissension. It was unfortunate that Barbara strongly backed Louisa. She was in one of her periods of remission and feeling much better; she took up the fight on Louisa's behalf, having forgotten all that had gone before. She wrote heatedly to the Committee complaining of Emily's folly in letting such a prize escape her, but in the end Emily's calm refusal to be bullied won the day. It would be no use having Louisa back (and this time in a much more important position) because she had not changed.

Victory had its price. At the next Governing Body meeting Emily was defeated when she tried to keep the new Mistress from becoming a member. Part of her had the sense to see that times had changed and that she must change with them, but the other part was still doubtful that it was wise. The fact that Elizabeth Welsh, whom she much liked and respected, had been chosen as Mistress helped very much to still her unease. She had been told severely that the omission was awkward, and that now that the position was filled by educated women the whole role of the Mistress had changed. But stubborn though Emily was on this point, she had realised already that women like Elizabeth could not be allowed to waste themselves on trifles and that sooner or later she would be forced to give way, which would not be at all dignified.

In view of this it is a surprise to find Emily writing to Adelaide to say that in future the Mistress must not take it for granted that she would be a member of the Governing Body. 'What has happened must not create a precedent.' Ten years earlier she had written to Barbara, 'being on the committee does not secure the desired effect of making things easier and pleasanter for the Mistress . . .'

When the college was first founded Emily's views were more liberal. 'As the college grows it will tend to be governed more and more by the resident staff,' she had told Barbara. Was it a growing love of power that made her change her mind? When Constance Jones (another old-girl) was appointed Mistress in 1903, Emily fought again to keep the Mistress off the Governing Body. Hers was the only dissenting voice. Her defence was surprisingly weak for one of her nimble mind: there were moments when she was Mistress, she said, when she had felt very awkward at committee meetings, yet at the time she had neither mentioned the fact nor shown any signs of it. She was a little shocked when she was told that she was becoming as old-fashioned and conservative as the dons who had stood in her way all those years ago and were still withholding degrees from her girls, and that if she did not revise her views she would be left behind.

Changes were coming thick and fast to Girton. Because of better discipline in schools, rules were respected and taken for granted, and because the college was so much larger there were none of those tiresome cliques whose one object was to outface authority. It had been necessary to take on more staff, and yet again other old-girls were drawn into the fold. Emily could feel satisfied. She liked familiar faces round her, to see how Girton had influenced old pupils and whether her predictions for this or that girl had been fulfilled. It never ceased to surprise her how many-sided young women were these days; when Frances Kensington (whom Emily knew well as Secretary of Bedford College) took over the secretaryship of Girton from Alice Croom-Johnson, she was quite willing to take on the management of the finances as well: she found no difficulty with mathematics, she told Emily. Women were becoming used to taking on a big responsible job and thinking nothing of it. Emily remained on the Governing Body as Honorary Secretary, although the really hard work was done by somebody else. Thus she was left free to continue her important work of seeking full membership of the university and admission to degrees for women, which she was beginning to suspect might take a very long time.

Girton was now never without a waiting-list, and it gave Emily much satisfaction to know that this justified her adherence to her original plan to see that as many girls as possible received higher education; steadily and surely she was helping women out of darkness into light. At this stage an academically élitist society was not a good idea. That is why she would not yet spend money on research which only a few could pursue.

By the end of 1889 Emily had two objectives left that she felt were worth striving for – degrees and votes for women, in that order. She could not rest, she said, until she had both in her grasp.

She was now nearly sixty but looked years younger, and was as full of energy, ideas and plans as ever. Success had not come to her easily. She had had to fight hard for everything and the struggle had cost her both despair and tears, but it had never seriously occurred to her to give up. These days she had many trusted followers, a very different position from that of 1862 when, as an untried young woman, she had joined hands with Lizzie Garrett, both with little in their favour except courage, determination and their affection for each other. From such small beginnings a revolution in the lives of other young women had been born and was still going on.

Success never failed to surprise her, but it had come and had not made her arrogant or blind to the stupidities of her fellow men. She saw how false the arguments against degrees had become, but she could sympathise too, for she knew that they had arisen from the 'fierceness of fear' by which she herself had been attacked so often. Women had shown themselves to be cleverer, tougher and more determined than men had ever believed possible, and with proper education had shown their brain power to be equal. To the average male, careers for women meant rivalry, and no one could predict where that would end. To stop women having degrees slowed down the process of equality which worried them so much; it was a case of self-preservation and they seized it with both hands.

By the late 1880s Emily was not a lone voice demanding more privileges from the university. Girton students, confident and proud young women who were determined to make their mark in the world, were adding their voices to hers and had begun agitating for justice. They canvassed names for a petition, men as well as women. They painted posters and organised a march through Cambridge holding banners aloft. Residents were scandalised and dons speechless with rage; here on their own doorstep was revolution. Although she made no attempt to help them, Emily travelled to Cambridge to wish them well at the start of their march and thought how bright and lively they looked: it augured well for the future. They were confident, they told her, because they knew that they were the equal of men intellectually, having proved it in open competition, and now were determined to be given the same privileges.

Young women on the march with banners held high were a shocking sight to Dr Perowne, the Vice-Chancellor. When he heard of the march he ordered university regulations to be scrutinised in order to have the young demonstrators apprehended for acting illegally, but no such edict existed. The police were no help either, for the march was properly conducted, the young women peaceful and orderly, many smiling cheerfully. It seemed on that first day in May 1888 that Dr Perowne was the only one who was holding on to what he called 'the old values'. That women should so disgrace themselves was a thing he did not care to think about, he told Emily, to which she replied, 'Well, Vice-Chancellor, if you grant them degrees, I am sure they will promise never to march again.'

Perowne was in a very irritable mood on the day that he went to the Arts School to deliver a speech condemning education for women. He was a man who very much liked to make strong speeches in public and this time he surpassed himself, for he spoke harshly about the folly of giving women a university education, the first time for years that such a thing had been said in public. There were many against it still, of course, but the women's movement had become so strong that few dared voice such an opinion, except in a whisper. That women in Cambridge had become a part of life and must be accepted with a good grace was advice Dr Perowne spurned. He cherished a fond hope that if ignored and treated like pariahs they would fade away and hide their heads in shame. Instead no such thing was happening, and wherever he went they were there, behaving as though they owned the place. But one thing he hoped and prayed he would never do – bestow degrees on women in his sacred Senate House.

On that day in the Arts School when Dr Perowne rose to speak, Emily was in the audience; and as she listened to his speech she felt as though she had travelled backwards in time. But how convincing he made these stupid old-fashioned sentiments sound, although every word he uttered was totally wrong and, what is more, had already been proved so. He was contemptuous, he said, in a voice filled with passion, 'at the way some ladies imagined that no woman had been educated before. What of the mothers and sisters of distinguished men? Their education might have been of a different kind but it was the only one that mattered . . . it must not be assumed that sound education for women was limited to the new movement . . .' Much applause greeted this speech, but Emily seethed with anger and only just managed to remain in her seat until the end. 'The old humbug,' she wrote to Adelaide. 'When I consulted him about representative members of the Senate to sit on our committee he was very gracious, but of course to admit Girton students to be a regular part of the university was a very different thing.'

In her fight to give women the degrees that they so much deserved Emily believed that anything that could further the cause was legitimate. So far the controversy had been mainly a Cambridge one, and except for the young women themselves – who were refused the best jobs although they had received the best education – the outside world took little interest. But by 1888 the row became more public and the national newspapers took up the question, very much on the side of the university. Emily surmised that *The Times*, then the most influential newspaper, had been 'got at' and that the unnamed writer of its first article ('to give women degrees would restrict their present freedom to choose what is best in education and examinations') was a Cambridge don from whom she had heard the same arguments before; there was not a criticism with which she was not familiar. What was the meaning of this? It was surely meaningless, since the university could not even offer such freedom to men, let alone to women. The *Daily Telegraph* was next in the field but not much more enlightening: 'Degrees for women would injuriously affect girls' schools', while the *Morning Post* warned solemnly that all should oppose degrees for women who did not want to see co-education in England. Emily could have laughed had not the matter been so serious.

Over the years Emily had built up a good relationship with the newspapers, which many times had published her letters, giving them a prominent position and sometimes even adding a short article reinforcing her argument. The time had now come for another letter, short and to the point as was her habit, stating exactly and clearly what was wrong. *The Times* was her favourite medium and she addressed her few words to its editor: '. . . since several students are now taking the complete degree course, reside the full three years, are taught by the same teachers, are subjected to the same educational privileges, examined by the same examiners, achieve the same honours, why should they not have the same degrees as men?'

In the course of the next twenty-four years plenty of arguments were produced, all purporting to prove why women should not be allowed a proper degree. Such stupidity was intolerable, and Emily told herself she must have patience, but she knew very well that such nonsense drove her frantic and that she was always deaf to advice if it meant she must stand still. Up to now she had gone forward steadily and slowly but always onward, overcoming setbacks as they arose and never giving way completely to despair. But now wherever she looked she was blocked by implacable enemies who put her into a torment of misery, and against whom she had no weapons. Then, as so often in the past, she took herself in hand, decided that the battle was going to be long and tedious and that she had better reserve her energies instead of wasting them in fruitless opposition. Quite deliberately she began to reserve her strength, only occasionally writing to a newspaper correcting some point that was wrong and putting a new one forward, for it was important to keep the controversy in the public eye. The world at large must never think that women did not care.

Girton's new secretary, Frances Kensington, kept Emily up to date with what was happening in Cambridge. One term when the mere mention of degrees caused ructions, she made a list of reasons given by dons as an excuse for not granting degrees. She told Emily that they were all pathetically similar and would not hold water for a moment if it came to a fight: degrees were 'inexpedient' – a word beloved by dons – 'a mixed university would not suit Cambridge' and it was their intention to keep it unmixed. This recalcitrant attitude affected the undergraduates and many an ugly scene took place. An effigy of a woman was burnt outside the Senate House while voting on the 'woman question' was going on, and it became common practice to riot and let off fireworks and throw rotten eggs whenever it looked as though the university might give way. Letters to *The Times* abounded, pushing out many more important matters. To Emily, watching in London, hysteria was the order of the day. Perhaps the letter that really angered her was one from Professor Gardner, a man she liked, but who could not bear to see his beloved university changed: 'women are better off as they are – it is a good thing educationally to be unfettered by degrees,' and so on.

At a Social Science Congress in 1887 Emily had directly attacked Henry Sidgwick for sitting on the fence, but got little response. Had the public given up taking an interest? A week later she was interviewed by a reporter from the local paper who wanted her views. 'Of course they do not want to give us degrees,' Emily said. 'I heard only yesterday that if the university were rash enough to give way it would not be long before women were ruling the roost everywhere and doing good men out of a job.'

Then suddenly it looked as though everything could be changed. In 1887 a Girton student, Agnata Ramsay, was the only candidate to be placed in the first division of the First Class in the Classical Tripos. When the news broke, the papers made much of it. *Punch* showed a cartoon by Du Maurier of Mr Punch himself bowing Agnata into a first-class carriage marked 'Ladies only'. Here at last was the outstanding achievement Emily had been waiting for and she rejoiced with all her heart. 'They cannot refuse us now,' she cried – but they could and did.

The university's refusal to recognise Girton's triumph angered Emily, and she wrote to Henry Sidgwick warning him that Girton students would renew the fight: 'Agnata Ramsay's success makes it all the more imperative to give degrees to women,' she wrote. 'We have heard of more support in Cambridge than we dared count upon and are by no means hopeless of success.' Brave words that even to her own ears had a hollow sound. Nevertheless she next wrote to Dr Jackson to hear what he had to say: 'Girton students have been asking whether something could not be done but there seemed no special occasion for moving, our idea was to wait for some striking success such as would arouse public sympathy and then to act . . .' This of course was exactly what the Steadman Aldises had done at Newcastle when 'Scott of Girton' was bracketed Eighth Wrangler, and that had led nowhere. This led nowhere too: Dr Jackson replied shortly that the 'time was inopportune'.

Slowly Emily was beginning to learn that there were many among the older generation of dons who still believed that the Local Examination for girls (from which Girton had sprung) was merely to improve the education of girls who wished to become governesses or schoolmistresses. Dr Perowne, the Vice-Chancellor, must have believed this; he saw no connection between higher education and Local Examinations and had never read Emily's pamphlet. She saw a ray of hope in this ignorant denial of her achievements; her opponents would one day be caught off guard and give more than they meant to give. Their case was weak, their arguments spurious. It was now a question of patience. The students were solidly behind her; they would never give up. Dr Jackson, once so genial and friendly, had become openly hostile and accused Emily of infecting her students with her unique iron will. With some satisfaction she knew that he had never spoken a truer word. She wondered what he would have thought had he read, as she had, some anonymous doggerel verses composed at Girton, making all the dons who had spoken against them figures of fun:

> No fear have we of competition
> On equal terms and like tuition
> To keep us from the fellows' table
> Yours but to vote for Thursday's graces
> Assigning us our rightful places,
> Then honour, fellowship and riches
> Will give us all we want – the breeches.

The last few lines were what every don feared.

25

'We'll take care the world shall know it'

The late 1880s and early 1890s were a period of growth and consolidation. Girton was admitting 35 or 40 students a year by 1895, and 755 girls had passed through the college by the turn of the century. But expansion brought its natural consequence in renewed demands for full membership of the university and participation in its government, the denial of which seemed more irksome and more absurd with every passing year. By now, a dozen other universities in Great Britain were admitting women on equal terms with men; only Oxford, two in Ireland, and Cambridge – where it had all begun – still excluded them.

In 1896 Emily published a new pamphlet, 'Women in the Universities of England and Scotland', in which she retold – though with excessive modesty – the story of her achievements and set out her further demands; but at the age of almost seventy she was now taking a less active part in the daily life of Girton. The students in residence now formed the vanguard of what soon came to be called 'the Girton agitation'; to draw attention to their grievances, they organised a series of public meetings which were well attended and peaceful until one evening male undergraduates reacted so violently that a march by the girls was broken up, stones were thrown, and the police were called in to put down the disturbance. They treated the girls gently and arrested none of them. Emily was furious, caught the first train to Cambridge, assembled those whom she believed were to blame in the dining hall and (perhaps unfairly) admonished them severely, pointing out that they had risked prison sentences which would have ruined their careers.

However, the pressure thus generated had an effect on the university, which in the autumn of 1896 appointed a syndicate (the Cambridge word for committee) to seek a solution acceptable to both sides. Two scholastic agencies gave evidence before the syndicate in support of the Mistress of Girton's claim that girls who could produce only a certificate to show that they had fulfilled all the requirements for a university degree were disadvantaged when seeking employment in comparison with those who possessed degree certificates issued by a university. Evidence given on the other side included the extraordinary

213

and quite unsupported assertions that the presence of women at lectures 'limits the freedom of speech of lecturers' (unfortunately no examples were given!) and that 'any serious increase in the number or influence of women would tend to prevent men from coming to Cambridge.' In February 1897 the syndicate recommended that the university should grant women titles of degrees but should still deny them membership of the university. The formal discussion of the syndicate's recommendation in the Senate House in March 1897 (and an earlier discussion of the same subject) produced some splendid examples of masculine prejudice and academic hair-splitting. One speaker combined them both with an appeal to his hearers' deep-rooted hatred of innovation, misrepresenting the proposal as an invitation to the university to adopt a tiger cub on the specious ground that 'it is a such a little one, and can't do any harm, and won't be in the way, and will please the children very much'. By far the wittiest and most enlightened speech was made by the eminent legal and constitutional historian F.W. Maitland. He first demolished the notion that an intelligible distinction could be drawn between a degree and the title of a degree – 'Bachelor of Arts' was itself a title, he remarked. To Emily's delight, he then proceeded, in a subsequently famous phrase, to ridicule the suggestion that the women's colleges at Oxford, Cambridge and elsewhere should join together to form a federal university for women. The most suitable place for such a thing, he said, would be the waiting room at Bletchley station; it should be called the 'Bletchley Junction Academy': 'you wait there, but you do not wait there always. You change for Oxford and Cambridge.' (Bletchley is halfway between Oxford and Cambridge, which were at that time linked by railway.) But the proposal to give women the title of BA was rejected by a three-to-one majority of the Senate in May 1897. Cambridge women had to wait until 1922 for even this crumb of comfort, and until 1948 for full membership of the university.

The suggestion that a separate women's university should be established had been put forward on several earlier occasions. Emily had always vigorously opposed it: nothing could be wholly satisfactory, she insisted, except complete equality with men, and that necessarily implied equal membership of the same existing institutions. It came up again, briefly, a little later the same year, when Holloway College (of which Emily had become a governor when she declined the invitation to be its head) called a conference to discuss its own future. Three possibilities were open to it: to seek a licence to confer its own degrees, to promote a women's university, or to join the University of London. Emily spoke strongly against the idea of a women's university, stressing that it would not bring any of the advantages claimed for it; almost everyone at the meeting agreed with her, and there was loud applause when one of the last speakers said, 'I think we may say as the result of this morning's discussion that the idea of a separate women's university is dead.' Royal Holloway joined London University, and no more was heard of the separatist plan. Once more, Emily's good sense had pointed the true way forward.

26

'A treasure not lightly to be thrown away'

When Barbara Bodichon died in June 1891 after suffering a series of strokes that turned her into a permanent invalid, Emily felt that she had lost not only a true and loyal friend but also a colleague who understood her difficulties and (Emily persuaded herself) backed her up in everything to do with the college. It is impossible to discover whether Emily knew in her heart that this was not the case, but it scarcely mattered if she did, for the important thing to remember about this curious relationship is the fact that it was a friendship that made Emily happy, and that if she wished to credit Barbara with feelings that she did not possess it did no harm.

Barbara never influenced Emily deeply; she did not possess the ability to shake her resolve when her heart and mind were set on something she knew to be right. In fact all in all her influence over Emily was very slight. In the early days of their friendship Emily knew that Barbara's values were not and never could be hers, nor would she want them to be, but she loved Barbara for what she was and did not wish to see her changed. Her statuesque beauty, her thick golden hair, her slow measured walk (George Eliot based the character of 'Romola', in her book of the same name, on Barbara and called her walk 'queenly'), her ability to paint with such ease, the charm which drew people to her and bent them to her will, even her self-absorption which irritated others (though not Emily) – all these qualities Emily found most appealing. Beauty always attracted her, and because she had no vanity and knew she had no looks herself, she never envied Barbara in the least. She never forgot (as she tells us in her Family Chronicle) that Barbara and her sister, Nannie, were the first people she ever met who sympathised with her feeling of resentment at the subjection of women.

Two other major influences on Emily's early public life had already disappeared long ago, with the deaths of Frederick Denison Maurice and John Stuart Mill in 1872 and 1873, respectively. She wished she could have got to know Mill better, for he was a man from whom one could learn, but he allowed so few people to get close to him that although she regretted his passing for his step-daughter's sake, she could not say she missed him.

Frederick Denison Maurice was another matter, although there was much in his Christian Socialism that Emily did not agree with: it made him look too harshly on the shortcomings of the world. For instance his attitude to journalists who only did their job irritated her by its childishness. She very much believed in the power of the press for propaganda purposes; that was the reason she went to work on the *English Woman's Journal*. She had so wanted it to further the cause of feminism, and that it had not done so was no fault of the *Journal* but of those who wrote for it: they were too highbrow for their readers. She had been very disappointed in this venture, and this had made her sympathetic to Maurice's bewilderment that Christian Socialism did not catch on as he expected. Emily knew why: it was too theoretical, too slow and too lacking in drive as expounded by Maurice. But she knew Maurice to be a really good man whose ideals, though often mistaken, were utterly sincere. His influence on her had been real and important, for it was during the long conversations they had together in her brother's rectory drawing room in 1862-3 that Emily began to see clearly some definite purpose to her life. Their friendship was neither warm nor close, but it endured, for, curiously, they had much in common. Both were optimists, and both believed that people were on the whole more good than bad and that everybody had a better side and could be redeemed. Both derived much pleasure from their fellow human beings and both longed to improve the quality of life for those who could not do it for themselves.

When Henry Sidgwick died in 1900 at the early age of sixty-two, Emily mourned him sincerely. They had often disagreed, sometimes bitterly, and because of her dedication to the Cause Emily would have had to fight him whatever her private feelings, for there had been nothing personal in her dislike of all he stood for and for what he believed – through ignorance – to be good for women. She bore him no malice and had long ago forgiven the cruel way he had deceived her. Shortly before his death he had been active in trying to expunge compulsory Greek from the Previous examination because he wished to replace it by the 'more modern side of schools'. To Emily's surprise the proposal was lost by a large majority, and afterwards Sidgwick prophesied 'a long period of slow decline', using as his example the case of the Chinese mandarin who clung to worn-out forms of literary examinations with disastrous results.

Emily sympathised with his disappointment; she had had so many in her long and fierce fights with university authorities that she understood how low his failure had brought him. Shortly after hearing of his defeat she came across him gazing into a shop window and impulsively

217

went up to him, took his hand and said how very sorry she was that his efforts at reform had failed. To her surprise he seemed hardly bothered, but started to talk of a psychical research congress he and his wife were about to attend. Unknown to Emily he had taken up spiritualism.

When Jemima Clough had died suddenly twelve months earlier in 1899, Emily had written at once to the Sidgwicks, who were said to be 'bowed down with grief' at this calamity for Newnham. Such consternation caused Emily to reflect with some complacency on the smooth running of Girton. If she were to die tomorrow the college would continue on its way quite undisturbed.

Girton students were becoming insistent that funds must be set aside for research: the Governing Body backed them, but Emily still resisted. She understood that research was essential if the college was to hold its own in Cambridge and be able to compete on equal terms with the men's colleges, but she continued to think that other things should still have priority: more student rooms, an increased endowment for the library, new kitchens – and even perhaps more trees in the garden.

A legend has grown up that Emily never understood the importance of post-graduate work, and therefore did not see the necessity for money to be set aside for it. This was not true at all; she recognised the importance of research as clearly as any trained scholar could, but she also felt that very few Girtonians were yet qualified to undertake it, and that therefore for the present money might be better spent on other things. Above all, she remained firmly convinced that student numbers were the first priority, for size meant power, and until Girton was larger it could not exercise its full influence as the pioneer of higher education for women. Barbara Stephen says that the need for research was felt as early as 1883, a mere ten years after the move to Girton. This may have been so, but as long as money was scarce and there were not enough rooms to accommodate girls still on the waiting-list, it was undeniable that more rooms were urgently needed. However, Emily was not so stubborn that she could not make exceptions. Constance Jones was considered so brilliant that directly after her last Tripos examination Emily made arrangements for her to return at once for research. When there were grumbles at Constance's good fortune, she pointed out that after two Firsts in the Tripos she was outstandingly well qualified.

Was Emily wrong about all this? It was plainly very difficult to balance two well-justified but competing claims when the money to finance both was lacking, but in the circumstances Emily's policy of delay was probably right. She had always said that the trouble with women was their eagerness to run before they could walk: 'At first you can't wake them up, they are so indolent, and then when you do make them interested they must do everything all at once.'

27

A Touch of Heartbreak

The turn of the century found Emily still at Girton consulted about everything to do with the college, yet talking seriously about the necessity of cutting the knot and doing it soon.

She had become a part of the college to such an extent that new students sometimes became confused as to which of the two women was Mistress: was it Miss Davies or Miss Welsh? When informed, they were still confused about Miss Davies's real position: she was authoritative, knowledgeable and very much in charge, while Miss Welsh was often heard to say that she must 'consult Miss Davies' when a decision had to be made about work, so they christened Emily 'the little instigator' to distinguish the two. Of course Emily's possessiveness about college matters caused gossip in the university behind her back, and someone or other was always asking 'how can Elizabeth Welsh stand it?' It surprised everyone that the 'two heads' (as they were often facetiously called) never quarrelled or even disagreed; indeed it was obvious to everyone that they got on splendidly and that the atmosphere in college was calm and unruffled even when, as occasionally happened, there was a crisis.

Of course Emily was not in residence every day of every term, since she had frequently to be in London for meetings, or collecting data from libraries for a speech or a pamphlet, or attending a social gathering; but whichever it was it was almost always college business, for Emily had come to look on her London jaunts as furthering the good of the college, otherwise she would be wasting her time.

During one bad winter when Emily suffered a severe bout of influenza which was slow to leave her, Elizabeth Welsh missed Emily's lively company, longed for her to return, and was uncertain whether she was taking the right decisions. She would only breathe easily again when Emily came back.

It was a way of life that suited Emily perfectly at that period. She did not want it to go on for ever, yet she continued with her excuses for delaying the break; this time next year perhaps would be time enough, she needed just a few more months to clear up her complicated affairs, although everyone knew that her papers were in perfect order. She could not be untidy if she tried, but that did not prevent her referring to her affairs as though they were in a muddle, much to everyone's amusement.

Now that there was money enough for more than one resident tutor there were times when both women could be absent together. Though Elizabeth was fond of music, she could never be bothered to make arrangements for an opera or a concert herself but relied on Emily to decide when both deserved a relaxing evening. It was fortunate that Emily preserved that happy knack of creating fun out of very little; almost without warning she would whisk Elizabeth off to London by the afternoon train to attend an opera or a concert. Lizzie was always glad to put them up for the night, and next day they would be back in Girton before they were missed.

The first and last time Emily saw Queen Victoria was on one of these occasions. She had taken Lizzie and Elizabeth to a concert of Mendelssohn's music when, just before the curtain rose, the Queen appeared in the royal box. It was almost a shock to see the small plump figure dressed in black with wonderful diamonds, a white lace cap on her head. No one had expected her until a message from the Palace announced that she was on her way. Mendelssohn had been a friend of hers and of the Prince Consort's, and both had sung duets to his accompaniment. Mendelssohn's music reminded her of 'former happy days', and for this reason she was making one of her rare public appearances that night. At the end she was applauded again and again, the three women clapping as vigorously as the rest.

It was the death of the Queen in 1901 that prompted Emily to take an active interest in the suffrage question once again. As she put on her mourning dress on the day of the funeral she was reminded that she too was mortal and must not delay her departure from Girton much longer or it might be too late to take up other work. She was struck by the way all the obituaries praised the Queen for the admirable way she had handled her dual role: 'Her wisdom, courage and fidelity in no way interfered with the duties of her domestic life.' Emily had been preaching similar sentiments for years; her whole adult life had been spent showing that an educated woman could work at something that interested her intellectually all the better for having a home and family, and vice versa. Such work enhanced a woman's personality and made her more efficient and interesting, but almost every man she knew had disagreed. Yet here at last were male journalists admitting publicly that this was not only possible but desirable, and that the Queen had proved it.

As early as 1887, when fully occupied with college affairs and before Emily had thought seriously of retirement, with an eye to the future she had joined the 'National Society for Women's Suffrage'. But she did so only on one condition: that for the moment she was allowed to be a non-active member. How could they refuse? They were proud and delighted to have her name on their list on any terms, as it would be certain to encourage others to join. A year later an attempt was made to persuade her to accept office in the society but she declined – she had no time, although she would try to attend meetings occasionally. So matters remained for another fifteen years. She kept her promise, but found the meetings so ill-managed as to be almost out of hand: everyone talked at once, interrupting with irrelevancies until she longed to crack the whip and cry 'Order'.

In the end Elizabeth Welsh resigned first, in June 1903. She had never been strong and would not have stayed on as long as she did without Emily to share responsibility. The fear that Emily might leave her on her own hastened her decision to go. She convinced Emily that someone younger and stronger was needed, and that with increasing numbers the job was becoming too exacting for her. Her delicate constitution and her fear of too much decision-making give a clue to her pleasure and relief that a stronger personality than her own had always been near to settle difficulties and relieve her of worry. Another old pupil, the Vice-Mistress, Constance Jones, was chosen to take her place. A better choice could not have been made: she was young, strong-minded, a great academic success and mildly eccentric. As a student she had sailed through her examinations with an ease that astonished everybody, since she was one of the dwindling number of girls who had never been to school and knew nothing of institutional routine and discipline. Her response to rules and regulations and the regimentation of college life surprised those in authority: when asked if she found this difficult after the ease of life at home, she said she welcomed order and tried to practise method because it gave her more time for study. She had read moral science, a new subject that did not as a rule appeal to girls, but there had been the difficult question of the right supervisor. Fortunately Emily managed to persuade 'clever Mr Keynes' (the father of John Maynard Keynes) to take her on, a coup that many other colleges envied.

With Constance Jones's appointment the ridiculous uncertainty as to whether the Mistress should or should not have a seat on the Governing Body came to an end. Shortly after taking up her post Constance was elected to the Governing Body, with Emily's the only dissenting voice; but by now Emily voted only out of principle. When the result was announced she was the first to take the new Mistress by the hand and kiss her on both cheeks. Elizabeth Welsh, who witnessed this scene, could see that Emily was quite relieved to have the matter decided for her. At the same time Emily told the Governing Body that it was time that there were more Cambridge figures among them and that when there was a vacancy she would see that this happened.

The following year Emily herself resigned. Some thought that she had resigned out of pique, after being forced against her will to allow the

Mistress to be a member of the Governing Body. There was no truth in this whatsoever. Her close friends knew that the real reason why she was going was boredom: there was nothing left for her to do now that she had dropped the fight for degrees, which she felt would not come in her lifetime. Girton was running smoothly, there was no longer any worry about numbers – the waiting-list was getting longer and longer as results got better and better – and most important of all, Girton was taken for granted in the university.

There was another reason she thought it time to go: she hated opposing the college on research. Fighting the university was one thing, fighting the college quite another. It was not that she was against research, as posterity has come to believe; all she asked was for a further postponement. There would be time enough for research when the college was big enough to stand on its own feet and thus powerful enough not to be crushed by the men's colleges. Of course she would not have resigned on this issue alone, but now that her usefulness to the college had virtually ceased she felt idle, and feared that soon she would be running to seed.

It was a comforting thought that she was not leaving the college in the lurch. So many old girls had bitterly complained to her of the cruel way the lack of a degree hampered their careers, that the last time she was in Ireland she had spoken to the governors of Trinity College, Dublin, who thereupon generously offered students educated at the older universities their own degree without further examination – an offer that the graduates of Oxford and Cambridge gratefully accepted. By 1904 (the year of Emily's resignation) two hundred Girtonians had taken the Dublin degree.

At her own request Emily left Girton without any special celebrations in her honour: she hated fuss and had a 'perfect horror' of long eulogistic speeches that were more like obituaries than encouragement to enjoy a happy and useful retirement. She asked that there should be no collection among the students for a present – most of them found it hard enough to make ends meet as it was – and no special dinner with sentimental reminiscences. Public occasions of this sort were bad enough. She had had to listen, inwardly embarrassed, to such a speech when in 1901 on its ninth jubilee Glasgow University conferred honorary doctorates on a few distinguished women of whom Emily was one. Constance Jones had gone with her to Scotland and had laughingly rebuked her for looking cross when the Chancellor praised her achievements with much warmth. Afterwards Emily had said that he went too far, as men were apt to do when speaking in public; they never knew when to stop.

In the end she agreed to a dinner with only staff and students present, and her health was drunk in champagne. No one dared defy her and make a speech. Because of her unwillingness to accept praise, Emily is herself partly responsible for the obscurity into which she and her achievements have since fallen. Most historians of the nineteenth century, including even those specifically dealing with education, hardly mention her name, but instead attribute her achievements either to Cambridge University as a corporate whole or to other people. They must bear their share of blame for this omission, but there is no doubt that Emily, too, was at fault. She deliberately left no complete or descriptive record of what she had done except the Family Chronicle which she reluctantly began to compose under pressure from her nephew and neither corrected nor finished. It has, of course, never been published. The consequent gaps can be filled only from her voluminous correspondence, which until now has never been properly exploited as a source of her life and work.

Emily planned to soften the break from Girton by spending a month in the autumn of 1904 in Kirby Lonsdale with her brother Llewelyn. The visit was arranged for October, just at the time when Girton was reassembling for the Michaelmas Term, and Emily would have been full of bustle and plans, meeting the new students and greeting the old; and without anything being said Llewelyn understood this. This beloved brother was now an old man, somewhat bent and grey after the hard years in one of London's toughest parishes. The career of a merely fashionable clergyman had not appealed to him (society had flocked to his sermons) and if his life had been hard, it had also been satisfying. Now, with his wife dead and his children grown up, he had been living for some years in semi-retirement in this quiet Yorkshire living. Brother and sister planned some long walks together if the weather was good, and to Emily this was an important part of getting fit for the new work to which she much looked forward.

She had dreaded the break with Girton: it had taken her four years to make up her mind to go, but to outsiders her departure seemed sudden. She expected gossip and wanted to dispel it as far as possible, in case in some way the college should be harmed. She worked out a plan to do this which pleased her, although it was far from ideal. She wrote Adelaide a letter which she thought would make further explanations unnecessary. 'There will be no talk about my resignation until some such thing happens as the issue of an appeal without my name . . . if this happens I should like my friends to say somewhat vaguely that of late years since college business has been transferred to Cambridge it was thought suitable that Cambridge names should appear. It could be thrown in if necessary that I have not withdrawn from membership of the college and my name will appear on the annual report as heretofore . . .'

Adelaide saw at once that the letter hinted at some row or at disagreement between Emily and the Governing Body, and that she

223

must show it to no one, especially since it had already leaked out that Emily had had to give way on the question of allowing the Mistress a permanent seat on the Governing Body. Since nothing like a difference of opinion had happened nothing must be said or done that could be wrongly construed. Adelaide put the letter on one side and pretended to forget it. But she saw something else in this uncharacteristic explanation – signs of deep, suppressed emotion which for once made Emily lose a grip on herself and not see the possible consequences of her action.

Two days after the end of the summer term Emily left Cambridge for the last time as 'Miss Davies of Girton', the name she had come to be known by in university circles. She decided on an early train and bought herself a first-class single ticket, for she wanted to be alone. Over and over again she had rehearsed the moment and the way she would look – brisk and unconcerned – if she met someone she knew, for only Adelaide guessed that she could not leave without pain. However many times she stayed at Girton in future, nothing could ever be the same; that part of her life was over. Crying had never come easily to her, and this had earned her a reputation for hard-heartedness that she did not deserve. She sometimes had tears in her eyes from frustration and anger, but with real pain such relief was impossible.

The daily papers that she had bought 'to catch up with the news' as she told Adelaide, lay unread on her lap; instead she gazed out at the scenery, eyes half closed, her mind travelling faster than the train over the past fifty years of her life.

How girls had changed since the days when she and Henry Tomkinson had gone to Girton village to find a site that would be suitable for a women's college. They had discussed the limitations imposed by custom and etiquette on the Victorian girl and Emily's plans to change them. She had particularly hated the convention that one girl in a large family (usually the most capable) was chosen to be 'the daughter at home', the subservience to the male sex and obedience to parents inculcated by the books of Charlotte Yonge and Mrs Ellis. Timid and gauche, their emotions suppressed, of no consequence in the world, women were then unrecognised even by the law.

So many of her friends in those early days had been unhappy and hopeless, longing to leave home but too afraid to say so even to their mothers, consumed with guilt, with nothing to do and no way of developing their talents. They could not break loose because the Victorian girl had no money, so was tied to her home and her mother's apron-strings. Many girls married in order to gain a little independence, only to be disillusioned because they had married for the wrong reasons. In the 1860s and 1870s, the English spinster was offered religion as a solace; Emily herself was expected to embrace it after thirty when it looked as though marriage had passed her by; instead she had set out to change the lives of these girls and had succeeded.

When Emily first decided to found a college, she had in mind women like Florence Nightingale, who had been on the verge of a breakdown until the Crimean War, and Lizzie Garrett, who had had the greatest difficulty in fighting her way out of the cocoon that hemmed her in (her mother called her ungrateful and said that for a daughter to want to be independent was shameful). But Lizzie had been too strong-minded to collapse and had in the end succeeded in getting her own way and retaining the love of her family as well. Many had not shown such strength of purpose, although they had the ability. Anna Lloyd, the intelligent Quaker who longed to do something useful in the world, had not been able to stand up to the hostility of her sisters but had to leave Hitchin and tear herself away from a contentment she had never known before to return to a life of emptiness.

How different things were after fifty years of one woman's struggle and strife! Parents now encouraged girls to go to university, and schools saw to it that they were taught the right subjects. Even poor girls like Hertha Marks were enabled to win scholarships by proper teaching, with enormous benefit to themselves and the country. This young Jewish girl was a scientist of remarkable ability and was one of the first women members of the Royal Society, thus bringing honour and glory to Girton.

Although she no longer had any formal connection with the college after 1904, Emily had been pressed to retain a room in Girton and to pay occasional visits to the college. Characteristically, she had insisted on having only a small room (in the early days she had complained that members of the Executive Committee had looked on the college as a free hotel where they could stay whenever they wished, and did not want to lay herself open to the same charge). She kept away from Girton for the first two years after her retirement, but thereafter usually spent two or three weeks there every summer. It became a common sight to see her of a morning, clad in a blue dressing-gown, her hair in two plaits, sponge-bag and towel in hand, going down for her bath.

On the occasion of her visit in 1906 she was full of excitement and eager to hear of all that had happened in her absence. She went at once to see the new swimming-pool, to the building of which she and many others had contributed. Compared with the tiny town baths at Hitchin where she and the first five students had learned to swim, it looked frighteningly deep and forbidding. She felt she would be too scared after forty years to remember even how to float. In the spring of the previous year she had been taken by Frances Buss to the magnificent new swimming-pool and gymnasium recently built by the North London Collegiate School. Because the school authorities had not arranged for instructors, the pool was used only by a daring few, and most of the equipment in the gymnasium was lying idle. She could not help feeling proud when she saw how far more regularly the Girton pool was used. Poor Frances Buss! She was too suspicious of innovation and too slow to accept anything that looked at all dangerous. Dorothea Beale at Cheltenham Ladies' College was no better.

Looking at the dresses the Girton girls wore now for exercises and games, Emily could not help remembering the fuss in the early days at Hitchin when legs were supposed to be indecent. Although nowadays their loose dresses were exceedingly short, the girls walked back to their rooms without a wrap and quite without embarrassment. How different from the time when the length of a dress had been a matter of deep concern and when she herself had attempted to design something which would put a stop to the grumbling. (She had come up with an eastern-style garment, baggy trousers and a high-necked blouse: she had shown it to Lizzie and both women had dissolved into peals of laughter, so ridiculous did it seem.) The contrast prompted her to reflect on the changes wrought by the passing years: without regular visits she would soon become a stranger in what had once been her second home.

Another way of keeping contact was the annual Old Girls' dinner at the Hotel Cecil in London. The first took place in 1905, and Emily had made a speech about the early struggles and her ignorance of university rules and the ways of dons. One day in a rage, she had told a bunch of them how unkind they were and had been surprised when they looked amazed and even distressed. This had taught her, she said, that men had no idea how brutal and cruel they sometimes were without intending it; they were so unused to women that they honestly believed that their anti-female rules had been evolved primarily for women's protections.

At these dinners Emily mingled freely with the students and kept in touch with their opinions. Thus she learned, to her dismay, that the Prayer Meeting Society, which had been started long ago by Constance Maynard, had grown out of all proportion. She had always disapproved of the way in which first-year girls were dragooned into joining as soon as they came up, because she disliked the unhealthy emotional atmosphere generated at the meetings. Invited to hear a paper on Christianity and Socialism (she found it very muddled) at one of the Long Vacation meetings, she was upset to see that as they left the room afterwards the girls linked arms and held hands. Still worse was the guilt induced by the confession of trivial misdeeds, for it led to uncontrollable sobbing and left the subject shaken and spent. She was uncomfortably reminded of the trouble Louisa Lumsden and Constance Maynard had given her thirty years ago.

Nevertheless the changes were on the whole for the better, although a constant vigilance had to be kept. The fire brigade (to which all girls belonged) took their duties seriously; the bicycling club was very popular, and recently after passing a police test they were allowed to ride their machines into Cambridge for lectures and tea parties. What resentment she had caused in the early days when she forbade them to ride in the highway but to stick to the lanes round Girton.

In the summer of 1908 she stayed rather longer in Girton because the heat of London that year was stifling. It was long enough to get to know the students quite well, and Emily was invited to picnics in the garden, trips on the river and Shakespeare readings, all of them accepted. She returned their hospitality with a dinner in the town. Thus she had a chance to study the girls at close quarters. Their frank open manners pleased her: they were unselfconscious and confident, and took higher education as something every girl must have. They talked to her freely of what they intended to do, amazing her by their ambitions: 'it is so pleasant to be at the college' was a simple enough phrase but it made Emily's heart glow. 'After each lesson I feel as if a spur had been thrust into my mind,' Anna Lloyd had said to her many years ago – and here it was still, but much more low-key because taken for granted.

The way the modern girl dressed quite delighted Emily; it was simple and unaffected; a coat and skirt in serge or tweed with a blouse. Dressing for dinner merely meant a fresh blouse. At the Saturday night dances in the library, there was also little dressing up; still the girls looked young and fresh and very attractive, with their hair piled on top of their heads in charming loose curls. Emily was enchanted. She was astonished, too, because no one had told her that undergraduates were now allowed to be invited to these little hops. Even in the old days, Emily had thought segregation absurd. During her period as Mistress she had gone to Trinity to ask Professor Thompson, then Master of the college, if he would allow some of his young men to be invited to these informal dances; but he had looked at her with such an incredulous expression on his face that she had dropped the subject hastily.

Segregation of the sexes was so unnatural. It made girls self-conscious and awkward in the presence of men and caused much unhappiness. Emily was thankful that she had been brought up freely with her brothers: her knowledge of how the male mind worked helped her to deal with difficult dons, since she understood that fear stood in the way of proper communication. What could be expected of men who, once enrolled in a college, hardly uttered a word to a woman so long as they remained under its roof. Dr Venn had told her that during the whole of his time as an undergraduate he had met ladies on only three or four occasions; 'and these were not exactly lively functions!' Sir Leslie Stephen's case was even worse, for during the whole of his three years at Cambridge, he never spoke to any woman but his bedmaker. This, it seems, was quite usual.

One thing made Emily very happy – chaperonage had been dropped completely. She had always thought it the most ridiculous duty ever allotted to middle-aged mamas and aunts, and nothing less than an outward show of gentility, which, thanks to education, was fast disappearing.

28

Fear as a Deterrent

When Emily retired from Girton she was seventy-four years old, an age when few men or women think of starting new and arduous work. But Emily still thought of herself as young. She remained brisk, her head bursting with new ideas about the suffrage, schools, and reforms of all kinds. She was beginning, too, to have a vision of women in Parliament, a vision as remote then as a college for women had once been. In spite of the pain of parting, she was looking forward to a new and exciting life. The admission of women to Cambridge degrees, which would have set the seal on her tremendous achievements, had eluded her, and this public failure was infuriating. She knew that the university's refusal might prove to have imposed more than a temporary delay, yet she was supremely confident that nothing could stop women now that they had gained in self-confidence. Degrees would not be withheld for ever, but they might be many years coming. Meanwhile, it was time for her to find new fields of endeavour.

As she had foreshadowed when she rejoined the National Society for Women's Suffrage in 1887, the suffrage question was now to become her main concern. It was a logical step; she was returning to the public issue which had first engaged her interest forty years earlier.

Pressure on the Government from the suffrage societies had never completely died down since that memorable day in 1867 when Emily and Lizzie had driven to Westminster and handed their monster petition to John Stuart Mill in order that he could use it when he moved the amendment to the Reform Bill. There were thirty of these societies scattered round the country, but they had degenerated into little more than women's clubs, torn by dissension and jealousy, paradoxically almost completely disengaged from the franchise movement and – what was more damaging – from each other. When a matter of common concern arose they acted independently and thus failed to further the interests of the movement. This attitude endangered what support they had once gained in Parliament, support which was vital to their interests, could they but have seen it. They needed taking in hand; and this Emily proposed to do by completely reorganising the lot, a stupendous task that would have daunted a younger and stronger woman but for which she was very well fitted by experience and temperament. Within a matter of weeks she had put them under one central control, got rid of inefficient workers and installed a system of communication by messenger that was both easy and cheap – reforms without which no progress could be made. Apart from lending her name – now known throughout the land – this reorganization was to be the one great contribution which Emily was able to make to the suffrage cause, despite her age.

In 1867 at the time of the Mill fiasco there had been considerable although diffuse support in the Commons for women, led by the important figure of Disraeli, whom Emily had reason to know would have backed Mill's amendment if the latter had not mistakenly asked for the enfranchisement of all women irrespective of age or standing, despite Emily's repeated warnings. But there was still fragmentary sympathy for the cause among politicians of all parties, although not one had the slightest intention of doing anything practical to advance the cause. Emily's duty, as she saw it, was to awaken in these lukewarm sympathisers a real desire to see that women got justice, and in women a willingness to demand it.

Some progress had been made over the last forty years. For instance, women could now vote in municipal elections, although married women were excluded because their property still belonged to their husbands, until the Married Women's Property Act of 1887, which for the first time allowed women to hold property independently. On the other hand Gladstone's Reform Bill two years later, of which women had such high hopes, did not mention them at all, although it gave the vote to farm-labourers whether or not they could even read or write. Gladstone defended this shocking discrimination with the lame excuse that the 'extension of male suffrage was a cargo as large as the country could carry'.

Indignation was not universal: many women said that they were willing to wait for better times but could not foresee that Gladstone's blunder was to have disastrous repercussions. Rebuffed once more, some women felt that the only way forward was through violence; the eventual rise of the militant suffragettes was the outcome.

Before she could do anything, Emily had to find somewhere to live. Because she had spent so much time at Girton before her retirement, she had been living in lodgings while in London but now she needed a home of her own. By Christmas she had found a suitable small place in Montague Square, got her furniture out of store and started a series of afternoon tea meetings on the lines of the old Kensington Society which had been so popular in the 1860s. Ever since her return to London she had been collecting names of middle-class women with time on their hands who might be directed into useful voluntary work, very much like those who had been of such help when she was founding Girton. She did not realise that in the course of the intervening thirty years prosperity had made that sort of woman lazier and less enterprising. Nevertheless her idea was liked and she did not receive a single refusal to her invitation. Wisely she disguised her real object, which she intended to reveal in a series of informal talks. 'Women's suffrage is the entertainment. The hostess invites her friends . . . often without knowing if they are for or against it or simply very much in the dark about it . . . tea and cake induce talk, it is then that the informal talk begins . . .' The first meeting was not a success. The women had come to enjoy themselves and showed little sign of wishing to be serious: they believed that they had gained so much without the vote that they were content with things as they were. Discouraged, Emily wrote 'unenthusiastic' across the list for that day. Next time she explained how matters stood more carefully and in greater detail, pointing out the part they could all play in their own destinies if they so wished.

Over the years she had come to see the suffrage question rather differently. She had dropped it in the 1860s because the indispensable educational background was lacking. Now she felt that Parliament would be bound to grant the franchise as more and more women became educated and developed minds of their own. She said this to Millie, who at once gave a sharp rejoinder: 'women can't wait that long!' Yet the first tea meeting had shown her that women were willing to wait until doomsday. Married women did not want the vote, single women had no use for it, and whether married or single they had no wish to meddle in politics; all were agreed that the foundations of society would be undermined if married women were given the vote. She began her next tea meeting with a warning: indifference and lassitude were not the same as opposition, but did not exonerate them from responsibility if by doing nothing they kept the vote from women who did want it. 'You say you do not want to see your own sex in Parliament, but such a contingency is not for the moment practical politics,' she told them, explaining that at first not all women would get the vote, only one vote to each household was proposed, and if the householder was a man the vote would fall to him. Even if only a million women were qualified to vote, enough women would be added to the electorate to raise the status of all women, though not enough to exert undue influence. If her guests wanted to help, they could begin by writing letters to newspapers, articles for magazines, pamphlets and leaflets, and by talking about their wish to be given the vote. She told them how she herself had written a plainly-worded article in the *Girton Review*, explaining the few simple ways in which women could help in the movement. Indifference might come from preoccupation with other interests but 'indifference to the movement, though it may be explained, is not really justified'. Suffrage societies were not as popular as they should be, otherwise they would not suffer from such an alarming lack of funds. Paid help was desperately needed, so was larger accommodation, money for paper and printing. The organisation was calling out for help from every woman in the country. She tried to awaken a sense of shame by telling them that in 1893 women had been granted the vote in New Zealand and in Australia in 1904, yet England had the audacity to call these countries backward.

One morning in November 1906, just a year after she had settled into her new home, Emily was reading *The Times* in her sitting room when she was struck by an item about a Mrs Pankhurst – described as a 'militant suffragette' (a term Emily had never met before) – who had been arrested for breaking windows in Downing Street and was now serving a short prison sentence in company with one of her daughters. At once Emily sensed danger: violence alarmed her, for she knew that it would put an obstacle in the way of the suffrage movement and might delay it for years. Disconsolately she told Adelaide 'the general public are alienated by proceedings in which we are by no means implicated.' Her first action was to beg all peaceable workers for the franchise to keep aloof from the militants and to make it known in every possible way that they strongly disapproved of Mrs Pankhurst's tactics. But not everyone felt as she did, for it soon leaked out that Millie Fawcett and some members of the hitherto peaceable suffrage societies had joined together to give a dinner for Mrs Cobden-Sanderson, a strong adherent of Mrs Pankhurst, on her release from prison. Emily sent Millie a sharp rebuke: 'You are wrong and misguided . . .'

The Pankhurst faction had in fact been working away since 1902, using only a moderate amount of lawlessness at first, and so small in numbers that the press had scarcely noticed them, until they suddenly became more violent. All Emily could do for the moment was to redouble her efforts to show that they were a minority and that her societies were as much against them as the general public. But all in vain: few seemed to believe her, and acquaintances who used to smile and nod now cut her dead in an insulting fashion. One day, walking through Hyde Park on her way to a committee meeting, she was suddenly pushed from behind, fell and hurt her ankle. Another time rude names were shouted at her as she entered a theatre with her niece Margaret. It made Emily furious not to be able to retaliate: a letter to *The Times* was a feeble retort and did nothing except to let people know what was happening. Nevertheless all avenues must be tried: 'It is alleged that of late women have been showing their unfitness for the suffrage. Is this reasonable? During the last half-century thousands of women have been showing their fitness by well-considered and efficient service to the community in various departments of life. The value of their work is not disputed . . . Recently some women have taken to more violent methods and have attracted much attention in the press

. . . but have been rejected and repudiated by the earlier leaders of the movement.'

In February 1907 the peaceable franchise workers in London organised a big demonstration, planned to coincide with a similar one in Manchester to show the public that they strongly objected to the militants. Emily marched at the head clad in her doctor's cap and gown; fortunately the route chosen – from Hyde Park to Exeter Hall – was not too long for her. It had been pouring with rain all night, and the streets were awash, but those taking part in the 'mud march' went steadily on. Although much the oldest there, Emily kept up with the rest and showed no signs of flagging. Next day she wrote jubilantly to Adelaide 'what about too old now?'

In June the following year she joined in a much bigger demonstration when fifteen thousand women gathered on the Embankment to march to the Albert Hall. It was a glorious summer's day and everyone was in excellent spirits. Again Emily marched in the centre of the front row, standard bearers walking a little ahead. An attack by militants had been threatened, but Emily felt well protected by a posse of police walking casually on either side. The same month Emily was chosen to be one of a small delegation to Mr 'Bookstall' Smith, the First Lord of the Treasury, to ask for his support for women's suffrage in Parliament. Millie Fawcett led the deputation and did all the talking, but nothing came of it except frustration and fatigue. A little later a second deputation was reluctantly granted an interview with the Chancellor of the Exchequer, Asquith, but with equally negative results. After a talk with the Prime Minister, Campbell-Bannerman, the little group were scarcely more hopeful: he told them that they had made out a 'conclusive and irrefutable case' but that he was a sick man and about to retire so could do nothing for them.

In the following year, Emily and Millie went to see the new Prime Minister, Asquith, whom they found as nervous as a kitten. Recently the militants had taken to arson and attempted assassination; Asquith thought that his visitors might have a bomb or a knife hidden in their skirts and could not get rid of them quickly enough. Later that week they went to Exeter Hall to hear him speak at a public meeting, because they had been told that he was to make a statement about the enfranchisement of women. They arrived early and sat in the front row, a formidable pair, stiff with disapproval. When Asquith rose to speak they did not clap and hoped that he had noticed this gesture of disrespect. Asquith had put on weight, moved heavily and spoke ponderously, and they guessed at once that what he was about to say would not please them. He compared himself to Orpheus and the suffragettes to the old women of Thrace: 'they were the sort that made the hideous way'. His complete failure to understand the nature of his audience and the temper of their demands is a sign of the total incomprehension with which masculine authority viewed female suffrage once the militants were taken to represent it.

Recently, an Anti-Suffrage League had been formed, headed by Mrs Asquith, Mrs Creighton and Mrs Humphry Ward. 'Here is a group of supposedly intelligent women,' Emily told Adelaide, 'who cannot tell the difference between militants and non-militants, although we have made it perfectly clear.' But as Emily pointed out to Millie, these were not distinguished women, only women who happened to be married to distinguished men. Their opposition meant nothing.

Fear was the great deterrent which prevented an all-male parliament from granting women the vote, especially as women were now fighting their way more and more into public life. For years Emily had been familiar with this distrust. She had first met it in Cambridge, where it had culminated in furious anger when women asked to be given degrees, a natural request that was treated as a threat of open warfare. Most men took this line, but there were exceptions: Keir Hardie, for instance, who had left the Liberal Party and founded the Independent Labour Party in 1893, had always been an ardent supporter of the feminist cause and spoke frequently in favour of votes for women in and out of Parliament, until he inadvertently went too far when in 1902 he strengthened the opposition by declaring that he looked forward to the day when women would be treated as they deserved: 'Women will then play the part of the equal not only in wages but in all other matters appertaining to industrial life. The possession of the franchise itself would give women a new standing of power and would enable them to win for themselves concessions which today are withheld.'

Emily read the speech and her heart sank: 'equals' – 'new standing of power' – 'winning concessions'. These were words to strike terror into the hearts of men who saw the future in terms of competition with women, men who were determined to keep them out of positions that they regarded as their own by right. Of course in time every conscientious woman would want to climb to the top of whatever career she had chosen, and why not? But Emily, who had spent the best years of her life struggling for equality for women, knew that men could not swallow too much of the truth all at once. Progress would come only gradually; women on the whole understood this and thought it safer and more lasting that it should be so. Both sexes looked on Keir Hardie's utterances as too extreme, just as in 1867 they had regarded Mill's demands as too much for Parliament to digest in one lump.

Emily advised her own society to say that they understood that Keir Hardie was looking a century ahead. Two weeks later, when talking to a group of textile workers, Emily tactfully explained that she looked on the question of women's advancement as a gradual progress and that men had nothing to fear in their lifetime. To round off her feelings on this subject, Emily sent a short article she had written to the *Girton Review* making her feelings perfectly clear: 'I desire the removal of the disability which in my opinion is unjustly and unwisely inflicted upon women, because I believe that indirectly it would have a deep and far-reaching effect – that of raising the status of women. As such it would tend gradually to remove hindrances to their well-being and increase their self-respect and their sense of responsibility and to favour their development on true and natural lines.'

Emily was not finding it easy to work with Millie; their goal was the same but each took a different route towards it. This would not have mattered if there had been some bond of affection and understanding between them. As a child Emily had been very fond of Millie, as she was of all the Garrett children, but she had particularly encouraged the younger girl to join the conversations between Lizzie and herself when Emily visited the family in the holidays. On one of these occasions Millie heard Emily say: 'It is clear what has to be done; I must devote myself to higher education while you, Lizzie, open the medical profession to women. After these things are done we must see about getting the vote.' She then turned to Millie: 'You are younger than we are, Millie, so you must attend to that.' Emily's words had come true, and instead of being delighted that a woman of Emily's distinction and experience was prepared to work under the direction of a younger woman, Millie could not rid herself of the feeling that Emily coveted the position of President of the National Union of Women's Suffrage Societies for herself. Millie had been attacked by a cold feeling of apprehension when in about 1903 she had heard that the formidable Miss Davies was once again becoming interested in women's suffrage. Even as a child Millie had noticed that Emily possessed a 'strong and masterful character and a logical and far-seeing mind'. Emily's record had proved that she was right. Emily did not know of Millie's fears, and Millie never understood that her fears were groundless.

From the beginning Emily had decided that her energies could best be employed in reorganizing the suffrage societies (a task she had accomplished in the first year after leaving Girton) and believed that she made it plain that in all else she was perfectly willing to serve under Millie, for at her age she could not contemplate holding a position which required a great deal of travelling and public speaking. Furthermore Millie could never forget – although Emily never remembered – that Henry Fawcett had proposed marriage first to Bessie Parkes and then to Lizzie, and that Millie had been his third choice.

Millie's antagonism was of long standing, and had begun to show thirty years earlier when Girton's fortunes were at a critical stage and Millie had deliberately sided with the Sidgwicks in 1869 in the controversy over the 'Ladies' Lectures'. Emily soon sensed that Millie did not welcome her

235

rejoining the movement, although she did not know why, but sensibly she took the line that the work was too important for quarrels and that Millie's moods must be ignored. The antagonism continued but never burst into flames, because however much divided them they were after all both on the same side in the greater matter of peaceful protest versus militancy.

The violence of the militants was increasing steadily, but this was not the most alarming thing about them. By 1906 the Pankhursts and a good many of their followers were manifesting a deep hatred of men, a strong antipathy that coloured all their actions and ran through everything they said and did. It was such a strong emotion that once their passions were aroused they were capable of committing any misdeed, perhaps even killing in cold blood. Winston Churchill had been pushed onto a railway line in front of an oncoming train and hauled back onto the platform only just in time, Asquith had been attacked with a whip as he stepped out of a carriage. Other lives were threatened and no one, certainly no politician, was safe from attack of some kind.

This ruthless activity flew in the face of everything Emily believed in and had inveighed against. For years she had preached in and out of Girton that no true feminist should ever be fanatical, however keenly she felt the injustices she had to endure. She had taken good care that her own Central London Society was free from this prejudice by giving them an informal talk on the destructive potential of such unnatural emotions. They must remember that once they got the vote they would have to accept the guidance of a male Parliament on many things they did not understand, that insults flung at politicians at this stage would be remembered long after women had forgotten them, and that this would make it difficult to ask for help: 'Good men are not conscious of unfairness in their dealings with women. They are willing to give ample justice, and an appeal to their sense of justice makes no impression because they feel they are being perfectly just in preserving the present state of affairs.' She warned all those working for the suffrage against acting foolishly in the mistaken belief that they were martyrs in a noble cause.

Emily and Millie, at one on this point, decided that there must be a clear line of demarcation drawn between 'them' and 'us', especially since the militants had shown signs of a dangerous lack of control now they had begun to realise that they had worked for four years and yet were as far from the vote now as they had been in 1902. Emily noted the change of tempo with alarm. The militants were giving way to a recklessness that boded ill for every man and woman in the land, and not least for the peaceful workers. There was so little that she and her supporters could do to combat this, except let as many people as possible know the difference between the two kinds of suffrage workers. With this in mind, Emily wrote to some old friends, including Lord Milner and Lord Robert Cecil, one in the Lords, the other in the Commons, asking them to make the difference between the two parties perfectly clear in both Houses: 'The old law-abiding school of suffragettes', she wrote, 'find it the more necessary for them to be in evidence at the present moment as the actions of the new and noisy sections are apt to monopolise attention and the whole movement is misrepresented and misunderstood.'

In a depressed mood she wondered if a handful of letters made any difference. The present government failed to listen to the truth. Only the other day Lloyd George had refused to see her and Millie 'on account of militancy'. He had done so after Emily had written a polite letter, in which she explained that the older suffrage societies totally condemned the conduct of the militants. 'Men will believe what they want to believe,' she told Adelaide, 'and be quite sincere about it.' Nevertheless, every avenue must be tried to make authority see the difference. She had walked in Hyde Park recently and seen the devastation wrought by a group of hotheads – all the palings pulled up and scattered over the grass. Her attitude was hardening, yet despite everything that the militants did both she and Millie deplored the treatment these women received in prison – it was barbaric.

The fact had to be faced that it was no longer a case of a few miscreants damaging public property because of frustration and mis-understanding, but of misguided human beings who loved violence for its own sake. She wrote a plea for discrimination for her suffrage society to distribute, begging all right-thinking people 'not to desert a cause which is nonetheless worthy because unworthy action has been taken in its name.'

29

'A novel and ambitious sound'

By the summer of 1912 it was fifty years since Emily had come to London and begun her work for women. Girton wanted to celebrate the occasion privately, if Emily was willing.

The reason for inventing such a jubilee was not lost on her: she was getting on in years and might not be alive when Girton's own jubilee came round in 1919. Her first reaction when she received this delightful invitation was one of wonder: was it really fifty years since she had come to London with her mother, set on improving the lives of women and full of confidence that she could do it?

To mark the occasion £700 had been collected among the present students, and Constance Jones herself made the presentation: 'Miss Jones read a short quietly-worded address placing the fund unreservedly at my disposal,' Emily informed Lizzie on her return from two happy days in Cambridge. There and then she had handed the cheque to the secretary of the building fund to be used for more student rooms. Although Lizzie had never been a student at Girton – it was founded too late for her – she so admired all the unselfish work that Emily had achieved for women that she sent her £1,000 together with a letter in which her deep and lasting affection for this true friend shines through: 'I wish it to be applied as you wish,' she wrote, 'personally I should like to see all the buildings completed, but I am quite satisfied that you should decide. It would be nice to call the new wing after you, if you approve. I am sure that all who are old enough to remember you and share in the general advancement of the women's cause would be glad to connect your name with the new wing . . .'

The anniversary fell on a perfect June day, and after tea Constance Jones took Emily on a tour of the garden. The two women sat talking quietly for a time in the honeysuckle walk, described by Constance in her book 'as the most wonderful spot in this wonderful garden'. Looking round at its beauty and the well-kept state of the rest of the grounds, Emily reflected on what had once been the most unpromising state of the land round the early building and how she had almost given up hope that there would be money enough over from more important things to create a garden at all. Faith and hope had prevailed. Long ago she had learned that if one held tight to them both and did not worry overmuch about material things, everything would come right in the end. She wished that Frances Metcalfe, who had worked so hard to improve this garden, had lived to see it now.

During the next two years she visited Cambridge several times to keep an eye on the building of the new wing that was to be named after her and to advise on improvements for the student rooms. Few things had given her so much pleasure. The new wing was completed just in time to be opened before the declaration of war put a stop to all building.

When war broke out Emily was as startled and unprepared as everyone else: she had been told so often that there would be no more war that she had come to believe it and hoped until the last moment that it could be averted. She had never taken a great interest in politics, unless it affected the women's cause. Her eyesight was not as good as it had been, the newsprint was far from perfect, so that she had every excuse for not following events with quite the care that she should. She had not heeded the growing momentum of disasters until she read the declaration 'We are now at war with Germany'.

Later she was a little ashamed that her first reaction had been to bewail the loss of her usual autumn holiday abroad with Elizabeth Welsh. The thought of widespread destruction and carnage in the France she loved distressed her deeply, and made her think that she might never cross the Channel again. All her life war had been going on in faraway places, but this was frighteningly nearer home. Mistrusting the common mood of jingoism and quick victory, she came to the depressing conclusion that all suffrage work would have to be put aside until the end of the war, however distant that might be. She was eighty-four years old already and might be too old when the war ended to be of use any more.

In a few days she had become accustomed to the new situation; her spirits revived; she became brisk and matter-of-fact. What work could she do to help bring about victory? She had not quite the energy she once had, nevertheless she longed to be of use. For a month she called on officials who were running various departments to offer her services in any capacity, but was turned down every time as too old. Sensing her disappointment, Lizzie – now far from well – invited Emily to accompany her to Dover to see her first batch of women doctors and trained nurses off to France, where they were to open a hospital for the wounded. Lizzie had herself gone ahead and found a suitable building that would serve as a hospital, and would have returned to active work herself if she had been well enough. She was five years younger than Emily but her hard battles in the medical world and her work among London's poor had taken their toll.

When she had first heard about the hospital, Emily had written to

Lizzie offering to go out to organise it, a task she could do now as well as ever, but Lizzie felt it would be too much for her, so even that had to be given up. In time she forced the authorities to give her some useful work, so they put her in touch with a bandage-rolling group and a knitting circle: neither of these jobs was ideal but she did what she could cheerfully. Thus the tea meetings started all over again, but now it was Emily who needed instruction. The women whom she had criticised for laziness towards the suffrage were showing themselves to be expert with their knitting needles, and it was Emily who was left to make the tea and butter the scones.

Since she could speak French she interpreted between some of the Belgian refugees and those who were trying desperately to house them. Tension was high, continual quarrels broke out not only among the Belgians but among their English hosts. Emily restored order with a mixture of firmness and sympathy, and quickly calmed the fears of the Belgians by explaining that all the authorities were trying to do was to ease their assimilation into an alien society and to show that they felt sorry for their plight.

She was immensely proud of the work Girton graduates were doing to help the war effort. Many old Girtonians were keeping schools open by replacing male staff on active service. Many others were employed in munitions factories and Emily visited them there. Cheerful and efficient, they worked at tedious jobs with a deftness and speed that Emily attributed to their intellectual training. There seemed to be nothing the educated girl could not do, and at last they were being given a chance to show how many-sided they were. She heard of one girl who had taught herself braille in order to teach soldiers blinded in battle, and for one moment Emily felt that she might do the same herself, but common sense prevailed. Manipulative skills had never been her strong point and there was no possibility that the compensations of old age had miraculously bestowed them on her.

At the outbreak of war Llewelyn Davies relinquished his living in Kirby Lonsdale and returned to London to be near his sister and daughter. He had been a widower for thirty years and began to realise how easy it was to be cut off by war and distance from those he loved. Although almost ninety he very much wanted to be of use: perhaps he could take the place of a curate now in the forces, visiting the sick and bereaved, of which he had had much experience, he wrote to Emily. No sooner said than done: Emily went to see the vicar of a church in Hampstead, who greeted the idea with delight. Despite his great age, Llewelyn's mind was as alert as ever and his compassion boundless.

Llewelyn had chosen Hampstead because it was then a quiet suburb and much patronised by the elderly, as well as being a reasonable distance from the London he loved. Within a short time, Emily had purchased two small houses close to each other and in a month they had both settled in. For two years Llewelyn had a new lease of life; then in 1916, returning home on a bleak December day, he caught a chill and in three days he was dead. He had lived a good and selfless life and Emily tried not to grieve, but she missed his kindly interest in everything she did, his cheerful laugh and his need of her. All through her working life he had been behind every one of her projects, praising, encouraging, and giving advice when asked. The bond between them was very close. It seems probable that Llewelyn alone knew what had happened between Emily and Henry Tomkinson, but if so the secret went with him to the grave.

The following year Lizzie died. Emily had loved her like a sister and because she was five years younger had taken it for granted that she would go first. Eleven years earlier she had been with Lizzie when Skelton Anderson died of a stroke; not all Lizzie's skills could save him. Her simple epitaph for her husband ('he lived a good life') was right for her too. Lizzie's death brought back the pain she had felt ten years earlier when she had opened *The Times* one morning and seen Henry Tomkinson's obituary staring her in the face. Many bitter-sweet memories which had long ago lost their sting were revived and for a short time she gave way to tears. The past was leaving her the sole survivor and she felt her loneliness keenly. Even Adelaide was now out of reach. Bedridden with arthritis, her fingers too crippled to hold a pen, she had suddenly ceased to write letters, although Emily wrote regularly. Mistakenly she had gone to live in the country at the outbreak of war, for peace and quiet, but so far away that it was too difficult for Emily to visit her.

Emily tried not to dwell on the loss of so many who had shared her life, although her feeling of isolation was growing. The hours that she once spent at her desk answering her voluminous correspondence in her neat clear hand had to be put to other uses now: she had plenty to say but few to say it to. She was only too aware that the past was receding from her, but with a self-deception she had never used before, she excused such feelings by convincing herself that she did not have enough to do. Active all her life, time now hung heavily on her hands. If only she had more exacting work – but no one would give it to her. Recently a firm of publishers had written to ask if she had ever thought of writing her autobiography or a book of reminiscences. The suggestion startled her. But remembering her boredom in putting together her 'Family Chronicle' when she was several years younger, she politely declined. Her memory was undimmed, only her eyesight sometimes gave her trouble, but her judgement was still balanced and sound, and this told her that the history of higher education would interest very few. For years now it had been taken so completely for granted that it was no longer news. She was strangely reluctant to admit how large had been her own part in bringing about this change in outlook.

Nevertheless for tidiness sake she ought to put her boxes of letters in order. It is only because she did this that we still have so much original material from which to reconstruct her life and thoughts. To her surprise the work was more pleasurable than she expected. In the winter months every day after tea she would settle down by the fire, a large basket of papers at her feet, sorting and reading the extraordinary record of her long life. We can only be thankful that to make herself anonymous – that curious unexplained instinct that would not allow her to admit to her mighty achievements – she did not make a bonfire of the lot.

Among her letters was a thin packet from the Bishop of Durham: he had been among her fiercest opponents in 1867 and had ever remained so. A formidable woman was outside his experience until he met Emily, and he had no idea how to deal with her, so took refuge in abuse. Her steely blue eyes seemed to him to penetrate his very soul, and that alone was enough to make him uncomfortable. He had heard rumours of her anti-ecclesiastical attitude which left him, he said, with no words. His letter of 1867 was packed with invective against women serving on committees, local examinations, colleges and degrees for women. Another of 1897 was an exact replica of it. Emily could imagine him gnashing his teeth as he condemned higher education while surrounded by its excellent results: 'So much brainwork for girls would be disastrous . . . if a woman is forced to submit to conditions which have been laid down without consideration to her requirements she must suffer.' He refused to admit that women had bloomed and had not suffered nervous breakdowns or gone off their heads, thus denying the evidence of his own eyes and still maintaining that, in the end, long periods of heavy study would take their toll: he had seen such calamities occur before to those who had not heeded his warnings.

Emily longed to share the joke with Lizzie, with Adelaide or her beloved Crow sisters, but perhaps it was just as well that she did not expose the stupid sayings of this crazy old man to the public at large as a figure of fun: there was little enough respect for the Church as it was.

Little more than six months after the end of the war, Girton celebrated the jubilee of its foundation with a very grand garden party that lasted two days. Every living Girtonian seemed to be there but, alas, the foundress was absent. It was not that she was 'too frail to attend', as the *Girton Review* suggests, but that she was suffering from a summer cold and was persuaded that at almost ninety it would be wiser to stay at home. That she had lived to see this day was satisfaction enough, although if she had been present she would have been gratified that one of her much-criticised 'decided views' was at last universally recognised as completely right. How often had she defended herself against the charge that to emulate the men's colleges in every respect and compel her students to take the Tripos examinations was wrong and that one day she would regret her stubbornness. She had however pressed determinedly on, resisting all persuasion and ignoring mounting animosity even from her own students; and now, almost fifty years later, they praised her for doing the right thing and for refusing to listen to contrary advice.

How sweet it would have been on that July day to hear her old students openly acknowledging that the views she had always urged so forcibly had proved in the end to be correct. But she did savour a still greater triumph when she read an article in the next issue of the *Girton Review* by none other than Louisa Lumsden, among the loudest of her critics in those difficult early days: 'Miss Davies was right . . . if we were to deserve university degrees we were bound to obey university regulations and from the first days at Hitchin Miss Davies set before us this difficult task all unprepared. Her view was undoubtedly right. Women who embarked on this great adventure had to be measured by recognised standards and no others . . .'

The justification of another of Emily's controversial opinions was also fully recognised at the jubilee in speeches from the platform; against much opposition she had said that Girton's limited resources should be spent on buildings to house larger numbers of students rather than on research; now after fifty years a full programme of research was being undertaken, none the worse for the delay. Thus another piece of her ancient wisdom was praised as 'quite right' on this memorable day.

Work for the suffrage had ceased on the outbreak of war. Emily was convinced that if the conflict lasted more than two or three years, her chances of seeing women hurrying to the polling stations to cast their first vote would be gone for ever. Even if she survived the war, which was doubtful, she might be bedridden or too infirm to vote herself. Happily she was wrong on both counts. Among her documents in the Girton Archives there is preserved a single sheet of paper headed 'Resolution to Emily Davies from the organisation committee of the London Society for Women's Suffrage, 19 June 1918'. The text reads 'The organisation committee of the London Society for Women's Suffrage, meeting as they believe on the eve of the passing through the House of Commons of the clause in the Reform Bill which ensures the enfranchisement of women, sends its affectionate greetings and congratulations to Miss Emily Davies, to whose zealous and able leadership the advance of women in different fields owes so much.' At last women had been given the vote by the Representation of the People (Amendment) Act of 1918. Now, women over thirty could vote, thereby enlarging the electorate to three times its previous size, from seven million to twenty-one million. (By 1928 the age limit was 21.)

On 14 December 1918, Emily, then eighty-eight years old, walked to the polling station to cast her first and last vote. She went quite alone, a tiny figure dressed in black, her blue eyes sparkling, a smile on her lips as though she was enjoying a secret joke. She used a stick but did not lean on it, and showed no other signs of infirmity. Did she smile because she remembered that long ago Barbara Bodichon had promised that if she died before women got the vote, she would rise from her grave on polling day and, clad only in her winding sheet, accompany Emily all the way and cast her ghostly vote along with hers?

On Emily's ninetieth birthday *The Times* sent a reporter to interview her. Because she disliked publicity, at first she hesitated: what did the press want to know? At the end of the war she had decided that she was too old to be useful and that she must retire from active work. What she had set out to do she had done, and in this she had been luckier than most. Some never lived to see the results of their endeavours but it was her good fortune to see all but one of her dreams (university degrees) fulfilled. In a few years no one would remember her name. Girton was her memorial, and so were the hundreds of women who had passed through its doors to go out into the world well equipped and able to fulfil themselves in satisfying work. Recently she had heard herself spoken of as 'that remarkable Miss Davies' and someone had called her 'famous' to her face, but she was unmoved. Such fulsome praise never lasted; she would not do what the Victorians of her day called 'making a show of herself'; that would be cheap. Nevertheless she gave the interview, thinking it easier to consent than refuse. It passed off very pleasantly. Emily opened the conversation by saying that the only remarkable thing about her was that she had lived to be ninety. Education, she reminded her interviewer, was not a romantic subject, it was rather like medical matters, it should never be mentioned in public. At least that is what she had been expected to feel when she set out to see that women got their fair share of it.

After this promising start the journalist steered her round to talk of 'the old days' and Emily fell into the trap. 'You can hardly imagine what the situation was like then: no high schools for girls, no university courses, no women doctors. So few occupations offered to girls that a society for promoting the employment of women had to be formed. Why, when Queen's College in Harley Street was founded the Reverend F.D. Maurice felt it necessary to apologise for giving the name "college" to this institution. "In this connotation," he said, "it has a novel and ambitious sound . . ." '

On her ninety-first birthday Emily gave another interview to *The Times* and was pleased when her questioner turned out to be a woman, whose courtesy and great interest in all she had done showed that she had come well prepared. When the interview ended there seemed little that she did not know of Emily's life. They had tea together and Emily learned all about a journalist's career – how remarkable it was that women stepped so easily into jobs that once had only been performed by men.

Before she left, and in order to make no mistakes, the interviewer recapitulated the main achievements of Emily's life. Emily listened intently and at the end looked up in amazement: 'Did I really do all that?' she asked.

30

The spirit of her age

Emily died at her home in Belsize Park on 13 July 1921, in her ninety-second year. She had no particular illness, was never in pain and was cheerful and considerate to the last, but she had lost the desire to stay alive. Of recent years she had taken to sitting in her garden when the weather was fine, an open book on her knees, her eyes closed in gentle sleep. It was thus that she drifted away, happy and optimistic to the last.

It was once said of her that she was 'born before her time'; during the last few days of her life she said of herself that she had lived too long. Many years before she had told Lizzie that life could hold little for her once her work was done and all those she loved had gone. In the end her energy diminished suddenly together with her good eyesight and her acute hearing. She still read, although she could no longer walk to the library, and still kept a list of every book that had passed through her hands: a formidable and lengthy one it must have been, but it never reached the safety of the Girton Archives and must now unfortunately be considered lost for ever.

It was a glorious July day when Emily's coffin was committed to the earth. Her funeral was sparsely attended because she had specially requested that it should be for 'family only', so that Girton should not be disturbed if she died in term-time. She had become a national figure, but although her obituaries were many and profuse with praise, and her memorial service in St Martin's-in-the-Fields packed with those whose lives had been transformed by her, not one realised her true importance. Almost single-handedly, she totally transformed the place of women in public life.

For the last few months she had been living more and more in the past, because it was there that she could communicate with her friends. Since Lizzie's death she had got used to her own company and thus loneliness was banished. She told her niece Margaret that providence had been kind to her; there had always been someone close at hand to strengthen and encourage when she needed it most. Now phantom figures more real than flesh and blood were her companions; lifting her spirits when she was down, helping her to overcome the difficulties of old age and keeping her sense of humour alive.

Unlike most of her contemporaries she had learned from childhood to make her own decisions, so that whatever happened she could stand on her own feet: her outward docility and habit of obedience had been a pure facade to cut trouble to the minimum in order to preserve her energy for the things she really cared for. She enjoyed playing schoolmistress to an imaginary class, teaching them Latin from her brother's primer. Her conception of education was strict: the classics were important for the formation of character, which was as necessary as learning; and both should develop equally side by side. As she got older and more infirm, and writing letters became a chore, the philosophical calm that had sustained her in her youth returned to comfort her. To be of some use in the world, however humble her situation, was her great ambition; and as her days shortened, she began at last to believe that perhaps some part of it had been fulfilled.

To the end she kept in touch with Girton: old girls, themselves no longer young, wrote to her in affectionate terms, which were never exaggerated terms, since they knew how much Miss Davies disliked everything that was highly coloured. She had never encouraged them to address her by her first name; such familiarity was alien to the age in which she had been brought up and it never occured to her to drop such conventions. Nevertheless there was real affection on both sides, freely expressed in her own letters until she was too weak to write more than a kind word of thanks 'for your long letter just received'. That Emily was able to do right up to the end.

'Where should we have stood without Emily Davies? Where should we stand without Girton College?' asked H.A.L. Fisher, President of the Board of Trade and chief speaker at Girton's jubilee in July 1919. 'Let us suppose that no such person as Emily Davies existed, that Girton College had never been founded . . . How much worse it would have been for England.' 'Miss Davies's very existence has been the greatest blessing,' echoed her audience as they looked at the material results of over fifty years' battle to give women their due.

Emily herself thought otherwise. The older she became the more convinced she was that if she had not founded Girton someone else would have done so. She did not say this to arouse the immediate response of a paean of praise, quite the contrary, but to show that she was not unique, a person set above others, special in every sense. Her friends called this 'ridiculous humility' and did not share it. Lizzie would burst out in anger against her, longing to shake her to make her see sense. All to no avail. In 1882 Lord Lytton suggested that since it was the jubilee year of a female Queen, he should arrange for Emily's great work to be honoured by a decoration. Emily would not hear of it. Honours she had never sought and never would. Politely she told this old friend that if they were offered, she would refuse to accept them. But why? What was at the root of this dislike of accepting her due? She had made so few mistakes, she had so little to be ashamed of. She was not shy; confidence bubbled out of her so that even the most obtuse could sense it immediately. But there was more to it than that; she had the happy knack of imbuing others with her own confidence. In the Cambridge days, when life was a battle, she had so impressed Mr Archer-Hinde with her adroit generalship that he forgot her sex and abandoned his opposition. Even Lady Stanley had called her 'a true leader', after she had heard her reprimanding a group of recalcitrant lecturers who had blatantly disregarded her wishes: 'I should like it to be understood that I am not ready to carry out any other idea than the ones I have tried to explain.'

She would never compromise, but this did not mean that she would go blindly on without first of all reflecting on the possible consequences of her actions. She thought out every move in advance, thus avoiding mistakes. Early in their friendship Lizzie Garrett noticed this: 'Emily has the kind of logical mind that can see the end from the beginning', a rare quality which enabled her to take the lead in everything she undertook; the responsibility for decision-making was hers by right. Instinctively she knew when to give way; for instance, when Lady Stanley, a confirmed non-believer, threatened to resign from the college committee if Emily built a chapel, she gave way. Lady Stanley's unruffled temper under provocation, reliability, good sense, loyalty and wise counsel in committee was invaluable to her. Her reward came when Lady Stanley endowed the library that Girton so badly needed.

Her indomitable nature and refusal to be outfaced was of great benefit to her students, nor was she ashamed of using feminine wiles to get her own way. It was a cause of wonder to many that she had no difficulty in persuading the most distinguished dons in the university to teach her girls. Keynes was said not to have hesitated when Emily asked him to supervise 'an exceptionally clever girl'. Her knowledge of the way the masculine mind worked came in handy when the committee cavilled at what they called the needless luxury of allotting a complete set of rooms to each girl. Space and privacy, Emily knew from experience, were essential if the students were to concentrate and prove their ability. In her book Constance Jones explains how she benefited from the conditions at Girton: 'They enabled me to combine social intercourse and solitude in a way not often met with. In Hall you are one of a throng, in your own rooms you could be as free from interruption as in a private house . . .' Issues like this made it imperative for her to keep control of the committee to prevent false economies; once these amenities were taken away, they would be difficult to restore.

That she was masterful cannot be denied, but she was not domineering, nor a bully. If she had been either weak or vacillating, she would not have been able to accomplish all that she did. She was aware, too, that she sometimes hurt the feelings of others, but this she accepted as inevitable. When Constance Maynard, with her customary arch smile, denied putting pressure on first-year students to join her Bible class, Emily was not deceived and at once forbade recruitment earlier than the second year. She refused to be outfaced by Louisa Lumsden, whose longing for close friendships and admiration made her molly-coddle the girls in a way Emily found objectionable. In the early years her eyes and ears were everywhere and she never hesitated to be outspoken although it lost her the good will of many. Popularity was something she never sought.

As soon as it became known in the early days at Girton that Emily preferred to spend money on more student rooms than on a chapel, she became the target for criticism as the foundress of that 'infidel place'. The charge was not really justified, but her own habits and many of the practices she permitted at Girton seemed to give substance to it. Lady Stephen has stressed her conventional nature, yet she was not averse to breaking all the Victorian rules about how a woman of her upbringing should conduct herself on the sabbath. She was often seen in the summer sitting in the garden knitting openly on a Sunday; she allowed the girls to use the gymnasium and the tennis courts on a Sunday and permitted them to go on river picnics if the weather was fine. Such goings-on offended the pious who were very much against enjoyment on the sabbath. A non-conformist living near the college waylaid one of the girls and dared to ask her how much time she spent reading 'the Good Book': Emily was 'spoken to' severely on this point: smilingly she assured her critic that the girls had no leisure during the week and 'it is such a shame to spend a glorious day like this indoors'.

Never once did Emily insist on attendance at church, or chapel on the sabbath: students were old enough to decide for themselves. Besides, to be dragooned into praying and singing hymns did harm rather than good, it built up resentment that lingered for years and took away Christian feelings. Free to decide, all the girls at Girton went to some form of religious service on a Sunday and it never occurred to them, whatever their faith, to miss morning prayers read by the Mistress.

The critics drew venom from the fact that as the daughter of one well-known cleric and the sister of another, Emily appeared to be turning her back on the faith in which she was brought up. This was not in fact true; her faith remained strong throughout her life, but she found Evangelicanism, and indeed Victorian religion as a whole, unsatisfactory because too harsh and narrow-minded. She was thought harsh when she drew a distinction between 'frivolity' and 'pleasure', which her contemporaries confused with each other. She identified frivolity with idleness and a vacant mind, while pleasure refreshed body and mind for labours anew. As early as 1860 she wrote '. . . the absence of any definite occupation . . . is in itself calculated to encourage a trifling habit of mind, injurious not only to the women who indulge in it but to everyone with whom they have to do . . .'

The criticisms that pious Victorian society hurled at her behind her back for allowing the college to remain without a chapel for so long were as nothing compared to the horrified whispers that followed the mere mention of her name after she and Lizzie had attacked the great Dr Maudsley for his article in the *Saturday Review*, condemning all they had worked for. Indignation gave way to horror when they learned that two public figures (and ladies too) had most indelicately called a spade a spade in a popular periodical where even young girls could read it.

Lizzie was blamed for teaching Emily not to use euphemisms – refusing to refer to a pregnant women as in a 'delicate state', a woman in labour as 'taken ill' or a menstruating woman as 'unwell'. When one bolder than the rest asked her why she would not use these expressions, she coolly answered 'because they are plainly untrue'. Emily and Lizzie deserve the highest praise for bringing menstruation out into the open, thereby cutting away at what was then regarded as the root of women's inferiority. The consequence was that menstruation no longer hampered a girl's mental development just at the time when education was beginning to show the way to a better and fuller life. This alone was a tremendous advance, and had an effect on books like the *Home Doctor* of which every household possessed a copy. Caution was foreign to Emily's nature. Exercise, open windows, fresh air and fewer heavy clothes were all considered risky, but all were part of the Emily Davies creed. Emily herself had discarded her numerous petticoats years before, although her style of dressing was conventional and hardly ever changed. It was because of her insistence on these things that the college sailed through two dangerous epidemics unscathed. Oddly, the medical manuals took longer to accept them: even in the 1920s exercise was still to be undertaken 'with great caution'. A recently published book points to the remarkably good health record of Girton in contrast with Newnham, which was in the town and had no facilities for exercise. This, together with the overcrowding, produced a steady deterioration in health among the girls each term.

In the space of no more than fifty years Emily transformed the life of Englishwomen. Small, soft-spoken, with a calm manner that disguised her urgent authority, she was in fact a revolutionary. But she has never been properly recognised and has been denied the fame which her work deserves, while others of lesser merit have been accorded a higher and more honourable place in history. While the curious blind-spot of historians of the nineteenth century in overlooking her achievements is irritating, Emily's own stubborn refusal to leave a complete record of her life has made this omission understandable.

The truth, unmistakable once the evidence is displayed, is that Emily Davies conferred a freedom upon women without which they would have been powerless to make all the other advances which have so benefited mankind this century. No feminist in the debased modern sense of the word, she was in this way the greatest feminist of them all.

APPENDIX

Emily Davies and George Eliot

Much has been made of Emily Davies's alleged admiration for George Eliot, which is presumed to have arisen from a genuine love of the famous author's novels. She did indeed admire them, but not until the last of their three meetings, in 1871, did she manage to get George Eliot to talk about them.

At their first meeting, which took place in the autumn of 1867, George Eliot kept the conversation well away from her own work but concentrated embarrassingly on Emily's plans for a woman's college which she gushingly said had always been her dream. This meeting had been arranged by Barbara Bodichon, a close friend and devoted admirer of George Eliot's, who had asked the novelist to invite Emily to tea at the Priory, Richmond, where George Eliot was living at the time with George Lewis, a married man estranged from his wife.

Emily was eager to meet Mrs Lewis (as she tactfully called her), for not only had she read all her books with much pleasure but because she imagined her to be one of those rare novelists who were also passionate feminists. In her novels she displayed a depth of sympathy for the down-trodden female of her day that had shaken Emily and others by its intensity, so that she had come to be known (erroneously) as a great exponent of the women's movement. Because of their apparent sympathy Emily was delighted at the chance of meeting her.

When the invitation arrived it was more condescending than warm and showed Emily clearly that to spend a happy hour discussing her books was not the reason George Eliot welcomed the meeting. 'Mrs Bodichon assures me,' she wrote, 'that you would like to call for some conversation on the desirability of founding a college . . .' Emily had expressed no such wish and could only guess that (as so often) Barbara's pen had run away with her.

Although the college had not yet materialised, plans were well advanced and ways to raise the necessary money were being discussed among Emily and her supporters. It had never occurred to her to ask the advice of a writer who had shown no practical sign beyond her novels that the improvement in the lives of women was a subject she held close to her heart. Moreover the parents Emily had so far consulted were very nervous that education might change their daughters' attitude towards their less fortunate mothers and that they would come to look down upon them. Emily could too well imagine what would happen if it became known that a woman, however famous, who was living in adultery, was a prominent supporter of such a revolutionary idea as a college for young women. She knew, too, that it would give mothers, especially, just the excuse they needed to keep their daughters safely with them at home. If this happened, she might as well throw her plans into the fire. Even as it was, she would have to handle the consequences of her visit to the Priory with the utmost care.

There is no doubt that George Eliot thought she was doing Emily a great favour by inviting her to her house, and Emily sensed that, like many intellectual people, she was perhaps unworldly enough to suppose that because she was so well known her name would carry weight in every quarter. She mixed mostly with advanced women like herself, and in her formative years had been influenced by John Chapman, the publisher, and his set who preached free love and were only happy practising it. This had cut her off from more staid Victorian society where standards of morality were strict.

In comparison with George Eliot, Emily was not famous, though certainly not unknown, and it never occurred to her that George Eliot was shrewd enough to guess that as soon as Emily's college became a reality her situation might be very different indeed. For the present the novelist wished to establish the superiority of her own position. In order to put her visitor at her ease, however (and to emphasise the privilege of meeting a celebrity), she assumed an air of informality by opening the door to Emily herself.

Emily's first impression of George Eliot, the woman, was not favourable. Her sombre clothes did nothing to lessen the pallor of her skin and the jet black hair that tumbled in curls about her shoulders seemed to emphasise the heaviness of her face and added years to her age, for although older than Emily she was still a comparitively young woman. Her unsmiling face was not welcoming either, and struck chill into Emily's heart so that she wondered if her hostess had been taken ill. Impulsively she asked if Mrs Lewis would prefer her to call another day, but she was assured that it would make no difference; she was always more or less in pain.

At first conversation was stilted, but over tea George Eliot relaxed and was soon in ecstasies at the idea of a college for women: she had only refrained from doing anything about it herself because of serious misgivings of the effect of a college education on family life – it might break the bond of family affection and family duties. Did not Miss Davies have similar misgivings? Emily assured her that she did not: it was this false conception of family duties that she was rebelling against. This hypocrisy produced only a narrow and selfish family life which encouraged the separation from men in interests and education. She hoped, she said, to put something better in its place that would strengthen rather than disturb family ties.

George Eliot next touched on the vulgar alarm of men that women might be unsexed by education: 'Did Miss Davies think this possible?' Emily replied emphatically that she did not, to which George Eliot answered that she was glad of that.

The novelist then said that there was one thing that she had much on her mind: she hoped that Miss Davies would not make examinations for girls compulsory, a woman's constitution might not stand the strain. Once again Emily had to tell her that she was wrong; and it was only by taking the same examinations as men that women could prove that they were the equals of men, the 'strain' was the same for both sexes, no greater for women than for men. This rejoinder startled the other and she stared wide-eyed at Emily as though she found the statement hard to believe, murmuring under her breath that surely there must be other ways. As she spoke she rose and walking to her desk she picked up a cheque for fifty pounds which she handed to Emily as a contribution to the new college's building fund, adding rather naively: 'Mr Lewis thinks it a good idea to let it be known that the author of *Adam Bede* and *Romola* supports the plan for a woman's college.'

As she left, Emily was filled with wonder that such an intelligent woman could ever suppose that the society of her day would view the support of an adulterous woman as advancing the higher education of middle-class girls.

References

To avoid distracting numerals throughout the main text, a page number and phrase are used to identify the quotation or statement documented here. References to letters give the initials of each correspondent, date and, where necessary, source. References to publications not by Emily Davies are given in full the first time they are cited and thereafter abbreviated. For example, B. Stephen, *Emily Davies and Girton College*, p.13, would become Stephen 13.

The main *published* writings of Emily Davies are listed on pp.271-2. Those with an accompanying asterisk are reprinted in *Thoughts on Some Questions Relating to Women*.

The *unpublished* material is contained in three collections: the Emily Davies Letters and Papers which includes the Family Chronicle (FC in the reference section), Bodichon Papers, Bradley Papers, Parkes Papers, 'Prelude to Arcadia' – Girton College Archives, Cambridge; the Emily Davies Letters – Fawcett Library, London; and the Constance Maynard Diary – Westfield College Library, London.

The following initials are used in the place of full names:

AA	Annie Austen (formerly Annie Crow)	EHM	E.H. Morgan
AJ	Anna Jameson	EP	E. Perowne
AL-S	Annie Leigh-Smith ('Nannie', also NL-S)	FB	Frances Buss
		FM	Fanny Metcalfe
AM	Adelaide Manning	FT	Frederick Temple
AR	Anna Richardson	GC	G. Charles
BB	Barbara Bodichon (formerly Barbara Leigh-Smith)	GGr	G. Gardner
		GG	George Grote
BRP	Bessie Rayner Parkes	HH	Harold Hutton
CM	Charlotte Manning	HR	Henry Robey
CMay	Constance Maynard	HS	Henry Seeley
CS	Charlotte Scott	HSi	Henry Sidgwick
EB	Elizabeth Blackwell	HTa	Helen Taylor
EC	Edwin Chadwick	HT	Henry Tomkinson
ED	Emily Davies	JB	James Bryce
EG	Elizabeth Garrett ('Lizzie', later EGA: Elizabeth Garrett Anderson)	JC	Jane Crow
		JG	John Griffiths
		JL	J. Liveing
		JP	John Potts
JS	J. Seeley	MP	Mark Pattison
JST	John Sedley Taylor	OH	Octavia Hill
JSt	J. Stuart	TDA	Thomas Dyke Acland
LL	Louisa Lumsden	TH	Thomas Holloway
LlD	Llewelyn Davies	THu	Thomas Hughes
MA	Matthew Arnold	TM	Thomas Markby
MD	Mary Davies	WA	William Allingham
		WMG	W.M. Gunson

LL	Louisa Lumsden
LlD	Llewelyn Davies
MA	Matthew Arnold
MD	Mary Davies

TH	Thomas Holloway
THu	Thomas Hughes
TM	Thomas Markby
WA	William Allingham
WMG	W.M. Gunson

CHAPTER 1
'A difficult child'

Page

7 'phrenologically speaking . . .': Family Chronicle 1840

7 'Our education answered . . .': Evidence given by Emily to the Rev. Mark Pattisson during the hearing of the Royal Commission on Girls' Schools, 1865.

8 'Probably only women . . .': ED to AR, 1868.

9 'dullness is not healthy . . .': Speech before the NAPSS in 1864.

10 'sold widely': FC 1830.

10 'could not be guaranteed': FC 1830.

10 'my beloved husband's health . . .': FC 1828.

10 '. . . for whom their father . . .': FC 1841.

11 In the years since . . .' FC and various letters written much later in life.

12 After dinner Mr and Mrs Davies . . .: FC 1842.

12 'Lister and his wife . . .': FC 1841.

13 'civic and religious belief . . .': FC 1841.

14 'poor women . . .': 'Some Questions Relating to Women', 1862.

15 'as a start': ED to AR, July 1852.

16 She begged . . . Anna Richardson . . .: From the FC and AR letters.

17 Emily Davies had a caustic wit . . .': J. Manton, *Elizabeth Garrett Anderson*, p.40.

17 'Her dainty little figure . . .': MS of E. Townsend, Girton College.

17 'I was a young woman . . .': Manton 44.

CHAPTER 2
'Self-help, not charity'

Page

20 He had astonished . . .: Bodichon Papers, 1858.

21 'Barbara was the first person . . .': FC 1858.

21 although separated, both these women . . .: Parkes Papers, 1857–8.

21 'Women's unwillingness . . .': The *Saturday Review*, June 1854.

22 'self-reliant, intelligent and thrifty . . .': B. Stephen, *Emily Davies and Girton College*, p.35.

22 Long ago she . . .: Barbara Bodichon to BRP, 1854.

22 'one of the cracked people . . .': Bodichon Papers, 1858.

23 'grandly innocent and simple': Stephen 35.

23	classes for servants . . .: FC 1859.
24	'Working class women . . .': FC 1859.
24	'self-help not charity . . .': FC 1859.
24	'We are saving it . . .': FC 1850.
25	donations towards a medical clinic . . .: LlD to MD, 1858.
26	Lizzie had come . . .: Manton 52.
27	'The most important listener . . .': EB to BB, Nov. 1859.
27	'patience and firmness . . .': ED to EG, Nov. 1859.
28	it was splendid for 'reasons of health': Bodichon Papers, Nov. 1859.
29	Emily removed her boots . . .: Bodichon Papers, Nov. 1859.
29	'I think it a more healthy . . .': FC 1860
29	'I feel so much cause . . .': FC, Oct. 1860.
30	. . . he would not take it . . .: FC, Nov. 1860.
30	. . . this quiet part of London: FC 1861–2.
30	'It will be very nice . . .' EG to ED, June 1862
31	'the loneliness is considerable . . .': FC 1862.
31	women messed things up . . .: Collected from Louisa Smith's letters and quoted by ED in her speech on 'Women and Degrees' given before the Social Science Association in Nov. 1863.
31	Emily made a point . . .: EG to ED, Feb. 1863.
31	students might become 'larky': FC, Mar. 1862.
32	'these men are all advanced liberals': FC, April 1862.
32	It was hard to believe: FC, May 1862.
32	'to provide a liberal education . . .': FC, May 1862.
33	there were clear signs . . .: Manton 124.
33	to give up now . . .: ED to EG, June 1862.
33	Next, the College of Surgeons . . .: FC, June 1862.
34	'It is distressing . . .' EG to ED, June 1862.
34	'and after one encounter . . .': Manton 134–5.

CHAPTER 3
'Shut away from the light'

Page

35	She used it . . .: ED to EG, Aug. 1862.
36	'Mr Maurice's face . . .': ED to EG, Oct. 1862.
36	'The matter with the working class . . .': ED to AR, Nov. 1862.
36	When Lizzie urged Emily . . .: FC, July 1862.
37	'Frivolity is not harmless . . .': 'Thoughts on Some Questions Relating to Women', pp. 59–61.
38	'a new beauty to his words': ED to JC and AR, Oct. 1862.
38	'so simple and kind . . .': ED to AR and JC, Oct. and Nov. 1862.
38	'It is rather nice . . .': ED to JC, Dec. 1862.
38	'The talk ran on people . . .': ED to AR, May 1863.
38	Tea with John Stuart Mill . . . unnaturally awed: ED to CM, April 1863.

38   'How London spoils one . . .': ED to JC, Jan. 1864.

40   . . . until her father retired . . .: FC; Parkes Papers, 1860–1.

40   . . . she returned the book unopened: Parkes Papers, 1863.

40   'I can work . . . they are impossible.': Parkes Papers, 1863.

40   . . . she longed for the independence . . .: 'Prelude to Arcadia',
       unpublished manuscript.

41   Matthew Arnold's name . . .: Parkes Papers, 1863.

41   'I would never have written it . . .': ED to EG, 1863.

41   'such an omission . . .': EG to ED, 1863.

42   '. . . as to Emily Davies . . . she is half unconscious': BRP to BB,
       Parkes Papers, 1863.

42   'It is her journal . . .': ED to NL-S, 1863.

42   'a touch of vulgarity . . .': AJ to BRP, Parkes Papers, 1857.

42   'If you unwisely . . .': Parkes Papers, 1860.

42   'It is certainly not easy . . .': 'Letters to a Daily Paper', 1856.

43   Emily said this was impossible: ED to BRP, Parkes Papers, Sept. 1863.

43   'Bessie is evidently . . .': ED to EG, Sept. 1863.

43   'It makes me sorry . . .': ED to BB, April 1863.

43   'I do not think that . . . I knew you.': BRP to BB, Parkes Papers 1859.

CHAPTER 4
A Mission Discovered

Page

46   'I cast about . . . meet the case.': ED to AR, 1863.

46   'We are going to make a try . . .': ED to AR, 1863.

47   'The examinations would be worth having . . .': ED to AR, July
       and Aug. 1863.

48   'I will gather the opinions . . .': JL to ED, July 1863.

48   'If she wants to do this thing . . .': Related in a letter from ED
       to AR, Aug. 1863.

48   . . . it was not in their interests: FC 1863.

48   'With her ability . . . she is bound to succeed.': FT to JG, Oct. 1863.

48   'If publicity . . . knowledge and mental training.': TD–A to ED,
       Oct. 1863.

49   'In conversation with friends . . .' TDA to ED, Oct. 1863.

49   'Girls are different . . .': Taken from several letters received by ED
       in 1862 and 1863.

50   'most had laughed . . .': JP to ED, Jan. 1863.

50   'There is no harm in him . . .': HT to ED, Jan. 1863.

50   'there is nothing so provoking . . .': ED to HT, Oct. 1863.

51   'this has been going on . . .': ED to EG, Oct. 1863.

51   'Our breath was quite taken away . . .': ED to AR, Nov. 1863.

51   'which is so common . . .': ED to HT, Nov. 1863.

51   'After all, they are the lords . . .': ED to GC, Nov. 1863.

51   'faints and hysterics': FC, Dec. 1863.

52   He added insult to injury . . .: Draft letter to HR, Dec. 1863.

53   'We are enjoying ourselves . . .': ED to EG, undated, but evidently 14 Dec. 1863.

53   'Perhaps he was disappointed . . .': ED to EG, undated.

53   'How did these rumours get about . . .': ED to HT, Nov. 1863.

54   'So I asked . . .': ED to HT, Dec. 1863.

54   'Some such plan . . .': OH to ED, Mar. 1864.

54   'We are going to invite . . . dreadfully unsafe.': ED to HT, Mar. and April 1864.

55   'Dr Robey's speech . . .': ED to HT, April 1864.

55   '. . . good sisters, wives, mothers and nurses': Report of the York meeting, 1864.

55   'Unmarried men do not know . . .': ibid.

56   'Women are not healthy . . .': ibid.

57   'The scheme for boys . . .': TM to ED, July 1864.

57   'I do not see at all . . .': TM to ED, Aug. 1864.

57   'I object very much . . .': TM to ED, Feb. 1865.

58   'One scarcely imagines . . .': ED to JP, Aug. 1864.

58   'time and quiet to study . . .': JP to ED, Aug. 1864.

58   'You would think . . .': ED to HT, Jan. 1865.

59   'Bring up everyone . . .': TM to ED, Mar. 1865.

59   'Thingss are very serious . . .': ED to HT, no month, 1865.

59   'If one had only . . .': ED to AR, undated.

59   'It was a note from Miss Buss . . .': ED to AR, Mar. 1865.

59   'This will be the stepping-stone . . .': EG to ED, Mar. 1865.

60   'I know you would have gone . . .' ED to HT, Mar. 1865.

60   'I suppose it is the first payment . . .': ED to CM, April 1865.

CHAPTER 5
Spoiled Children of Fortune

Page

61   '. . . it has become a saying': Opening speech by Lord Brougham at the Social Science Congress, June 1864.

61   'I hardly think . . .': MA to ED, Dec. 1865.

61   'nothing can be done in a hurry': ED to AR, Jan. 1866.

62   'although the Senate . . .': HR to ED, Mar. 1866.

62   '. . . I expect it will be useful . . .': ED to BB, June 1866.

62   'analogous to a clerical meeting': ED to AR, June 1866.

64   'reactionary and a lot of puppets': EG to ED, no date.

64   'I got the feeling . . .': ED to AR, Nov. 1865.

64   'I hope you will not think . . .': ED to GG, June 1866.

64   '. . . I have some doubt . . .': GG to ED, Jan. 1866.

66   'He asked me to tell you . . .': LlD to ED, Mar. 1866.

66   Henry Robey wrote . . .: HR to ED, Mar. 1866.

66   'The Commissioners had decided . . .': HR to ED, Nov. 1866.

67   'I should like to have Huxley . . .': ED to HR, Nov. 1866.

67   'What I have to say . . .': ED to HR, Nov. 1866.

68   'there are two in London . . .': ED transcript, Dec. 1866.

69   'perfect womanliness': Ridley 3–4.

69   . . . such a grasp of the subject: ED Papers.

69   '. . . I feel very hopeful . . .': ED to BB, no month, 1866.

69   After ignoring her: ED to BB, July and Aug. 1866.

CHAPTER 6
For Friendship's Sake

Page

70   'a want of thoroughness . . . the charities concerned': Report of
      the Royal Commission on Schools, 1868.

71   'What society says to them . . .': ED, 'The Higher Education of
      Women' (1866), ed. Janet Howarth (1988), p.61.

72   'I am afraid . . .': ED to HH, Dec. 1866.

73   Why not found . . .: ED to AR, April 1867.

74   'Scalands is not a place . . .': ED to AR, Aug. 1863.

75   'it is absurd of people . . .': BB to WA, in H. Allingham and E.B.
      Williams, *Letters of William Allingham*, p.81.

75   'I felt just a little . . .': BB to HT, 1867.

76   'In your paper there are two . . .': ED to BB, Nov. 1866.

77   'I have tried to stifle it . . .': ED to HT, Nov. 1866.

CHAPTER 7
A Refusal is Sometimes a Blessing

Page

79   'I hope in the future . . .': ED to AR, June 1866.

80   'I can handle this . . .': FC, June 1866.

80   'I should like to see . . .': ED to HT, June 1866.

81   ' "on the same conditions . . ." ': ED to HT, June 1866.

82   'people who have not been brought . . .': Extract from ED, 'Secondary
      Instruction as Relating to Girls' (1864).

83   '. . . it is to be as beautiful . . .': FC and ED to AR, Oct. 1867.

83   'so light with large windows . . .': ED to AR, Nov. 1867.

83   She wished with all her heart . . .: AL to ED, Dec. 1867.

84   'It is not a large sum . . .': ED to HR, Jan. 1868.

84   Everything will depend . . .': ibid.

85   'I expect that': ED to MP, Jan. 1869.

CHAPTER 8
'The trumpet must be blown with no uncertain sound'

Page

86   'The trumpet must be blown . . .': Emily's paraphrase of 1 Corinthians, 14:8.
87   'There has been a question . . .': ED to HT, Dec. 1867.
87   'It was not exactly acrimonious . . .': ED to EG, undated.
87   'insisting that the girls . . .': ED to BB, May 1867.
87   'It frightens me a little . . .': ibid.
88   . . . the college should not seem to be . . .: JB to ED, Nov. 1867.
88   'your suggestion is admirable . . .': ED to AR, Dec. 1867.
88   'I am so much obliged . . .': ED to HT, Dec. 1869.
89   'This will not seem much . . .': ED to AR, Mar. 1868.
89   'a most important and difficult . . .': ED to HR, Mar. 1868.
90   'stick at it . . .': ibid.
90   'There is a frightful coolness . . .': BB to ED, no date.
90   'thank you for your kind words . . .': ED to BB, Mar. 1868.
91   Henry Robey struck the right note . . .: AA to AR, Mar. 1868.
92   'One has to steer clear . . .': ED to AR, Aug. 1868.
92   'There is more interest . . .': ED to BB, Sept. 1868.
93   'It does worry me a little . . .': ED to BB, Nov. 1868.
94   Emily said that . . . determined . . .: ED to BB, Nov. 1868.
94   'I do not feel able to judge . . .': HS to ED, Aug. 1867.
95   'How much money . . .': ED to BB, Aug. 1868.

CHAPTER 9
A Cat and Mouse Game

Page

96   'I think you would not long . . .': ED to BB, Aug. 1868.
97   'The real difficulty . . .': ED to Mrs Bradley, Jan. 1869, Bradley Papers.
98   Five minutes later . . .: Amberley Papers.
98   was not Christianity . . .: Lloyd 96.
98   'too revolutionary to succeed': ED Papers, 1868.
98   'It seems to me . . .': ED to AM, June 1868.
99   '. . . is it because . . .': ED to the editor of *The Times*, 1868.
99   'a girl's proper university . . .': ED ro the editor of the *Manchester Guardian*, 1868.
99   'there are not nearly enough . . .': ED to AR, April 1868.
100   'As to the composition . . .': ED to HT, May 1868.
100   'one of the unfortunate people . . .': ED to HT, Aug. 1868.
100   'nothing is more calculated . . .': ED to HT Aug. 1868.
100   'It seems to me . . .': ED to HT, Aug. 1868.
101   She would play it cunningly . . .: Stephen 196.
101   'Not until the early 1880s . . .': D.A. Winstanley, *Late Victorian Cambridge*, p. 235.

102   'The progress of science . . .': Winstanley 223. See also J. Roach
       in 'Victorian County History of Cambridgeshire', III 260–1.
102   'Stop and reflect . . .': JB to ED, June 1867.
102   'we think it a pity . . .': JB to ED, Nov. 1867.
103   'I shall stand up to you . . .': Stephen 197–8.

                         CHAPTER 10
                 Life Will Never be the Same Again
Page
104   'I am well content . . .': JS to ED, Jan. 1869.
104   'Cambridge is not a healthy . . .': ED to BB, Jan. 1869.
105   'you must see besides . . .': BB to ED, Feb. 1869.
105   '. . . but I think that it may . . .': ED to BB, Mar. 1869.
106   'It is no good putting it off . . .': BB to ED, Mar. 1869.
106   Henry Tomkinson pointed out . . .: HT to ED, June 1869.
106   'They vary widely in attainments . . .': ED to BB, July 1869.
109   'Were they lying awake . . .': Several letters to BB.

                         CHAPTER 11
                 'Everyone needs a purpose in life'
Page
110   Because Emily did not quite trust . . .: ED to AR, Oct. 1869.
111   'her teaching was inspired ': ED to AR, Oct. 1869.
111   'We quietly ignored . . .': LL in Girton Review, 1907.
112   She had noticed . . .: Taken from Emily's pamphlets and
       speeches.
112   'this is college life': ED to BB, Nov. 1869.
113   'I believe I could do that . . .': L. Lumsden, Yellow Leaves, p.26.
113   'there is no harm in it': Lumsden 29.
114   'I have been sorry . . .': ED to HT, Nov. 1869.
114   'The ringleaders . . .': Emily Gibson, ED Papers, 1869.
115   '. . . after the arrangements . . .': Manton 91.
115   'strong words': ED to AR, Dec. 1869.

                         CHAPTER 12
                       No Second Chance
Page
116   In private Clark told Emily . . .: ED to AR, no date.
117   'Her view of coming here . . .': ED to AR, Dec. 1869.
118   'Just at the moment . . .': HS to ED, Mar. 1870.
119   take your troubles . . .: LlD to ED, Dec. 1862.
120   Dr Cartmell responded . . .: ED Papers, Oct. 1870.

120   a letter from the Council: ED Papers, Oct. 1870.
120   'everything has gone quite smoothly . . .': ED to AR, Dec. 1870.
120   'Out of all these flowers of loveliness . . .': *Punch*, 4 Jan. 1871.
121   Emily Sherreff was becoming restless . . .: ED to BB, Mar. 1870.
122   'She evidently thinks . . .': ED to CM, May 1870.
122   '. . . an amiable affectionate woman . . .': ED to CM, Mar. 1870.

CHAPTER 13
'Preposterous things sometimes get done'

Page

123   'I should not consider . . .': ED to BB, April 1870.
123   'It's queer why they want me . . .': EG to ED, Oct. 1870.
123   'I suppose I ought not . . .': EG to ED, Oct. 1870.
124   'we have not any . . .': ED to HT, Nov. 1870.
124   'your name has been proposed . . .': EC to ED, Nov. 1870.
125   'I believe that . . .': Part of Emily's address to the electors to the Greenwich School Board, Nov. 1870.
125   'It cannot be worse . . .':ED to HT, Nov. 1870.
125   'I am sorry you . . .': ED to HT, Dec. 1870.
126   'I have had some experience . . .': ED to School Board Managers, Nov. 1870.
126   'The way to good health . . .': BB to ED, Nov. 1870.
126   'Lizzie Garrett does not believe . . .': ED to BB, Dec. 1870.
126   'I felt myself nervously hurrying . . .': ED to HT, Dec. 1870.
127   'I am glad the Board . . .': ED Papers 1870.
127   She defended compulsory school . . .: ED Papers 1870.
128   All sorts of people . . .: TH to ED, Nov. 1870.
128   'Speaking does not get easier . . .': ED to AM, Nov. 1870.
129   'moved forward a century . . .': ED to AR, Dec. 1870.
129   'I should be sorry . . .': Manton 207.
129   'You have lost yourself . . .': Manton 206.

CHAPTER 14
'A prey to all sorts of fears'

Page

131   'I think you may . . .': ED to Mrs Bradley, Jan. 1871.
132   'without actually seeing something . . .': ED to AR, Feb. 1871.
132   '. . . I should like to be . . .': ED to HT, undated.
132   '. . . as soon as the sum of £7,000 . . .': ED to AR, Sept. 1871.
132   '. . . three miles from Cambridge . . .': ED to HT, Sept. 1871.
135   'it is working against the college . . .': ED to AR, Dec. 1868.
135   It was therefore plain . . .: ML to ED, Jan. 1869.
136   'I am longing for . . .': Amberley Papers, vol. II, p.302.

136   'You will see . . .': JST to BB, Jan. 1871.
137   'I am sure it is generous . . .': ED to HS, May 1871.
137   'unjust and incomprehensible conduct': and 'into a state of antagonism':
       A.S. and M.S. Sidgwick, *A Memoir of Henry Sidgwick*, p.242.
138   She had always taken the view . . .: ED to a friend, May 1871.
138   'I feel the time has come . . .': WMG to ED, Nov. 1871.
138   'the same unsatisfactory method . . .': WMG to ED, Nov. 1872.
138   'at some later hour . . .': ED to EHM, Nov. 1872.
139   'Rachel Cook's translation . . .': Stephen 273–6.

CHAPTER 15
'The way to kindle faith is to show it by taking risks'

Page
141   'Her excuses . . .': ED to BB, Aug. 1872.
141   'nothing but the impossibility . . .': ED to HT, July 1872.
141   'It has often occurred to me . . .': ED to HT, Mar. 1871.
142   'I always said I could not be . . .': ED to HT, Nov. 1872.
142   'respond with smiling faces . . .': ED to HT, Nov. 1872.
143   'Oh why did things . . .': ED to BB, Dec. 1872.
143   'bits and pieces . . .': ED to BB, Dec. 1872.
143   walkers . . . to 'take a look': B. Megson and J. Lindsay, *An Informal
       History of Girton College*, 1864–1959, pp.19–20.
144   'It is not possible . . .': ED to LlD, Nov. 1872.
146   'It is a red raw building . . .': ED Papers, Oct. 1873.
146   'the throng of visitors . . .': ED to BB, June 1873.
147   'Don't you think . . .': ED to BB, Oct. 1872.
147   Mrs Russell Gurney 'is going to give us . . .': ED to BB, Aug. 1873.
147   Emily's thoughts . . . finance: Stephen 300.
148   'I am quite of your opinion . . .': BB to FM, 1881.
148   'scanty and rough': Stephen 300.

CHAPTER 16
Endless Winter

Page
149   'When I see such a spirit . . .':ED to HT, Mar. 1874.
150   'nothing but the impossibility . . .': ED to HT, July 1872.
150   'I have only one brain . . .': ED to AM, Oct. 1873.
150   'all the cultivated thought . . .': ED Papers, 1873.
151   Emily could tell . . .: ED to BB, 1874.
152   Clark had written . . .: E.C. Clark to ED, Feb. 1874.
152   'This, Clark says . . .': ED to HT, Feb. 1874.
152   'It is all very vexing . . .': ED to HT, Feb. 1874.
152   'It is the fierceness of fear . . .': ED to HT, Feb. 1874.

153   'Tell me, by return of post . . .': ED to BB, Nov. 1879.

154   'she is so dear and firm . . .': ED to HT, April 1874.

154   Adelaide to be . . . 'official visitor': ED to HT, 1874.

CHAPTER 17
'Men like this have done much harm'

Page

155   'it is very sweet . . .': Manton 212.

156   'Girton suffers from the determined opposition . . .': FB to ED,
       April 1874.

157   'Why could he not have waited . . .': ED to BB, April 1874.

157   She and Lizzie together . . .: ED to EGA, June 1874.

157   'Is menstruation . . .': The *Saturday Review*, June 1874.

158   'direct moral teaching': BB to ED, June 1874.

159   Barbara hoped . . .: BB to ED, July 1874.

159   On her return . . .: ED to AM, May, 1875.

CHAPTER 18
A Family Composed of Women

Page

162   'to improve our status . . .': Speech to the Social Science Association,
       Oct. 1864.

163   'Would Dr Maudsley . . .': LL to BB, April 1874.

163   'When I talk things over . . .': ED to BB, Nov. 1874.

164   It rankled for years . . .: Megson and Lindsay 23.

164   'so selfish, so opinionated . . .': LL to CM, Nov. 1874.

164   'So far as I can see . . .': ED to BB, Jan. 1874.

164   'Sometimes I feel . . .': ED to BB, Mar. 1874.

165   Barbara's advice to Emily . . .: BB to ED, April 1874.

166   'It is hard enough to have delicate . . .': ED to BB, Feb. 1875.

166   '. . . I should like to tell you . . .': ED to BB, June 1875.

168   'authority might be the making . . .': ED to BB, Nov. 1874.

168   'larger staff, each using her own gifts . . .': ED to BB, Nov. 1874.

CHAPTER 19
A Traitor in the Camp

Page

169   'I think the people who just look in . . .' ED to BB, Jan. 1875.

170   'I told her quietly . . .': ED to AR, Mar. 1875.

170   'Louisa got hot and angry . . .': ED to BB, Mar. 1875.

170   'I have the strongest objection . . .': Stephen 295.

170   '. . . it is only a step . . .': JST to ED, Mar. 1875.

171   'poor Miss Lumsden . . .': CM to BB, Mar. 1875.

173   'As to their sometimes feeling . . .': ED to BB, Jan. 1875.
174   Girton 'was not for young girls . . .': ED to BB, Jan. 1875.
175   '. . . being on the Committee . . .': ED to FB, Mar. 1875.

CHAPTER 20

No Harm in a Little Fun

Page
176   Emily was certain that flaws . . .': ED to BB, Mar. 1875.
178   'She should be conversant . . .': ED to BB, July 1875.
179   'I am immensely interested . . . we march under a stout-hearted general.': FB to ED, Nov. 1875 and May 1876.
179   'These sisters will be found . . .': ED Papers, 1868.
181   She had been surprised . . .: ED to BB, Nov. 1876.
181   'Cannot Madame Bodichon . . .': Letters of A.F. Bernard, 1876, in ED Papers.
181   'I am much inclined . . .': ED to BB, May 1876.
182   '. . . I am glad to find . . .': ED to BB, Nov. 1876.
182   'Is it rather too much telling . . .': Stephen 301.

CHAPTER 21

Patience and Tact Bring Results

Page
183   'It was plain that we counted . . .': Stephen 232.
183   'heartless' and 'very kindly but . . .': CMay Manuscript Autobiography, bundle 21, 533, Westfield College Archives.
184   'I think Madame Bodichon . . .': ED to EGA, Mar. 1877.
185   'I went to Cambridge . . .': ED to BB, July 1877.
185   '. . . Professor Liveing has heard them . . .': ED to BB, Sept. 1877.
185   One had only to look . . .': ED Papers, undated.
186   'looking uncomfortable' and 'an eager and intelligent bunch . . .': ED Papers, 1877.
186   . . . one, more ridiculous than the rest . . .': Anonymous letter to ED, Jan. 1878.
186   'there is hardly anyone . . .': TH to ED, May 1875.
188   'One must show that this offer . . .': ED to AM, Oct. 1880.

CHAPTER 22

'No better than a slave'

Page
189   'Forty-five is a good age . . .': ED to BB, April 1875.
189   'You will wonder why . . .': ED to BB, Oct. 1875.
190   'any extra fatigue or weakness . . .': ED to AM, Mar. 1876.
190   'If I feel equal to more work . . .': ED to AM, Feb. 1876.

190 'a traitor': ED to BB, June 1876.

192 'The specific work of Secretary . . .': ED to AM, June 1877.

192 Adelaide thought this . . .': Stephen 305.

193 'such fun scrambling for breakfast . . .': E. Sharpe, *Hertha Ayrton 1854–1923*, p.143.

193 Emily . . . rather taken with the idea . . .: AM to BB, May 1877.

194 it flattered her . . . hoped it would not spoil her appetite . . .: ED Papers, 1877.

194 '. . . I hope that you may . . .': ED to BB, June 1878.

194 'the rest scatter themselves over German . . .': ED to BB, Oct. 1878.

195 'One must always behave . . .': ED to BB, Nov. 1877.

CHAPTER 23
'There is no going back'

Page

197 He had heard . . . two rooms all to herself.: *Cambridge Chronicle*, 1882.

198 'This great boon . . .': An address by ED to the annual meeting of the Birmingham Higher Education Association, 1878.

199 'in a state of stagnation . . .': ED to AM, Oct. 1880.

199 'there is no thought now . . .': From the inaugural address given by the Rev. Llewelyn Davies in Girton College Chapel, May 1902.

200 '. . . that we should take the major part . . .': ED to BB, May 1881.

201 'Since she is nothing . . .': CS to ED, May 1881.

202 '. . . some really good mathematicians . . .': ED to BB, June 1881.

202 'I do not think they have one candidate . . .': ED to BB, Aug. 1881.

203 'People at a distance . . .': ED to BB, Aug. 1881.

203 'Great ignorance . . .': ED to BB, Mar. 1882.

204 'harmful and merely harmful': HS to ED, reproduced in A.S. and M.S. Sidgwick, *A Memoir of Henry Sidgwick*.

205 'What we gain . . .': ED to BB, Feb. 1882.

205 'victory . . . I think it would be difficult . . .': Dr Stuart to ED, Feb. 1882.

CHAPTER 24
Not Rights but Justice

Page

206 It would be no use . . .: ED to BB, Dec. 1885.

207 'What has happened . . .': ED to AM, Jan. 1886.

207 'being on the committee . . .': ED to BB, April 1875.

207 'As the college grows . . .': ED to BB, 1869.

209 'Well, Vice-Chancellor . . .': ED to EP, June 1888.

209 'at the way some ladies . . .': Part of a speech given by Dr E. Perowne (EP), the master of Caius, then Vice-Chancellor, in the Arts School, Cambridge, May 1888.

210   'The old humbug . . .': Stephen 325.

210   '. . . since several students . . .': Letter to *The Times* by ED, May 1888.

211   'women are better off . . .': Prof. G. Gardener to *The Times*, May 1887.

211   'I heard only yesterday . . .': ED Papers, 1887.

211   'They cannot refuse us now': ED Papers, 1887.

212   'Agnata Ramsay's success . . .': ED to HS, June 1887.

212   'Girton students have been asking . . .': ED to Dr Henry Jackson, 27 July, 1887.

212   . . . he saw no connection . . .: EP to R. Potts, Feb. 1887, Cambridge University Reporter 61–9.

CHAPTER 25
'We'll take care the world shall know it'

Page

214   'limits the freedom . . .' and 'any serious increase . . .': Cambridge University Library, CUR 61 (1896/7) 748–51; 102 (iv, v, xvi, xxix).

215   '. . . a separate women's university is dead . . .': 'Report of a conference convened by the Governors of Royal Holloway College, 4 Dec. 1897' (1898) p.41.

CHAPTER 26
'A treasure not lightly to be thrown away'

Page

217   'a long period of slow decline': Sidgwick 511.

218   'At first you can't wake . . .': ED to NL-S, Feb. 1860.

CHAPTER 27
A Touch of Heartbreak

Page

220   'Her wisdom, courage and fidelity . . .': *The Times*, Feb. 1901.

222   honorary doctorates: Stephen 354.

223   'There will be no talk . . .': ED to AM, June 1904.

224   'to catch up with the news': ED to AM, June 1904.

225   Anne Lloyd, the intelligent Quaker . . .: Lloyd 68.

226   . . . an eastern-style garment . . .: ED Papers, undated.

226   . . . men had no idea . . .: Extracts from speeches by ED, ED Papers 1901, 1905.

227   What resentment she had caused: Stephen 155.

227   'After each lesson . . .': Lloyd 50.

227   Dressing for dinner . . .: ED Papers, 1905.

228   he never spoke to any woman . . .: The *Girton Review*, 1920.

CHAPTER 28
Fear as a Deterrent

Page

230 'extension of male suffrage . . .': E.J. Feuchtwanger, *Democracy and Empire: Britain 1865–1914*, p.330.

231 'Women's suffrage is the entertainment . . .': Part of an article by ED in the *Girton Review*, 1906.

231 The women had come to enjoy . . .: H. Blackburn, *Record of Women's Suffrage: A Short History of a Great Movement*, p.227.

231 Married women did not want . . .: M.G. Fawcet, *Women's Suffrage*, p.227.

231 'indifference to the movement . . .': From an article by ED in the *Girton Review*, 1905: 'The Women's Suffrage Movement: Why should we care for it and how can we help to further it?'

232 'the general public are alienated . . .': ED to AM, Dec. 1906.

232 'You are wrong . . .': ED Papers, 1907.

232 'It is alleged that of late . . .': ED Papers, Dec. 1906.

233 'What about too old now?': ED to AM ?

233 Millie Fawcett led the deputation: Stephen 349.

233 'they were the sort . . .': Fawcett 1912:15.

234 'Here is a group . . .': ED to AM, April 1908.

234 'Women will then play . . .': ED Papers, 1902.

234 . . . she looked on the question . . .: Fawcett Library Papers, 1902.

235 'I desire the removal . . .': From an article by ED in the *Girton Review*, 1910.

235 'It is clear . . .' and 'You are younger . . .': Manton 72.

236 'Good men are not conscious . . .': From ED's speech on 'Justice', first delivered in 1880, ED Papers.

237 'The old law-abiding school . . .': ED to Viscount Milner, 1911.

237 'Men will believe what they want . . .': ED to AM, June 1911.

237 devastation wrought . . .: ED to AM, 1911.

237 'not to desert a cause . . .': ED's paper 'A Plea for Discrimination', ED Papers 1906.

CHAPTER 29
'A novel and ambitious sound'

Page

238 'Miss Jones read a short . . .': ED to EGA, June 1912.

238 'I wish it to be applied . . .': EGA to ED, June 1912.

238 'as the most wonderful spot . . .': Constance Jones, *As I Remember*, p.77.

240 Manipulative skills . . .: *Girton Review*, 1920.

242 'So much brainwork . . .': ED Papers, 1917.

243 'Miss Davies was right . . .': *Girton Review*, 1919.

244 'In this connotation . . .': ED Papers, 1920.

CHAPTER 30
The spirit of her age

Page

247   the classics were important . . .: FC 1869.

248   'I should like it to be understood . . .': ED Papers, 1868.

248   'They enabled me to combine . . .': Jones 69.

249   'it is such a shame . . .': ED to AM, May 1898.

250   '. . . the absence of any definite occupation . . .': 'Letter to a Daily Paper', ED Papers, 1860.

250   recently published book . . .: Essay by Mrs Henry Sidgwick in J.A. Mangan and R.P. Park (eds), *From 'Fair Sex' to Feminism*, pp. 52–3, 1987.

Bibliography

Published Writings of Emily Davies

1860   'Letters to a Daily Paper, Newcastle-on-Tyne'*

1861   'Report of the Northumberland and Durham Branch of the Society for the Promotion of the Employment of Women.*

1862   'Medicine as a Profession for Women' (Social Science Association)*

'Female Physicians' (*English Woman's Journal*).*

1863   'The Influence of University Degrees on the Education of Women' (*Victoria Magazine*, June).*

'Needleworkers *v.* Society' (*Victoria Magazine*, August).

'The Social Science Association' (*Victoria Magazine*, November).

1864   'Secondary Instruction as Relating to Girls' (Social Science Association).*

'Reasons for the Extension of the University Local Examinations to Girls' (Social Science Association).

1865   'The Application of Funds to the Education of Girls' (Social Science Association).

1866   'The Higher Education of Women' (new edition, 1988, ed., Janet Howarth, Hambledon Press).

'Letters to the *Morning Post*' (Women's Suffrage leaflet).

1868   'On the Influence upon Girls' Schools of External Examinations' (The *London Student*).*

'Some Account of a Proposed New College for Women' (Social Science Association).*

'Special Systems of Education for Women' (The *London Student*, June).

1869   'The Training of the Imagination' (*Contemporary Review*, reprinted for the London Schoolmistresses' Association).

1871   'College Education for Women' (unpublished, read before the Nottingham Literary and Philosophical Society).

1878   'Home and the Higher Education' (Birmingham Higher Education Association).*

1896   'Women in the Universities of England and Scotland' (London: Macmillan).*

1897   Speech at the Conference on University Degrees for Women, convened by the Governors of the Royal Holloway College. (Report published by Eyre & Spottiswoode 1898).

1900   'Some Recollections of Work with Miss Buss' (*Frances Mary Buss Schools Jubilee Magazine*, April).

1905   'The Women's Suffrage Movement' (two articles in the *Girton Review*).*

1906   'A Plea for Discrimination' (Women's suffrage leaflet).
1907–8 Letters to *The Times* and the *Spectator* on Women's suffrage.*
1910   *Thoughts on Some Questions Relating to Women*, London.

Printed Sources

Allingham H. and Williams, E.B., *Letters of W. Allingham* (London 1911)
Amberley Papers, 2 vols., ed. Bertrand and Patricia Russell (London, 1937)
Bell, E.M., *Josephine Butler, Flame of Fire* (London 1962)
Blackburn, H., *Record of Women's Suffrage* (London 1906)
Blease, W. Lygon, *The Emancipation of English Women* (London 1913)
Bradbrook, M.C., *'That Infidel Place': A short history of Girton College 1869–1959* (London 1969)
Branca, P., *The Silent Sisterhood* (London 1975)
Brittain, V., *Lady into Woman* (London 1953)
   Women at Oxford: A Fragment of History (London 1960)
Burton, H., *Barbara Bodichon 1827–1891* (London 1949)
Cambridge University Reporter 1896/7, Cambridge University Library
Carpenter, J.E., *Life and Work of Mary Carpenter* (London 1879)
Castle, B., *Sylvia and Christabel Pankhurst* (London 1987)
Chapple, J.A.V. and Pollard, P., *Letters to Mrs Gaskell* (Manchester 1966)
Clough, B.A., *Memoirs of Anne Jemima Clough* (London 1897)
Cobbe, F. Power, *Duties of Women* (London 1881)
   Essays on the Pursuits of Women (London 1882)
   Her Life as Told by Herself (London 1884)
Crow, D., *A Man of Push and Go: Life of J.M. Booth* (London 1965)
   The Edwardian Woman (London 1978)
Dunbar, J., *Early Victorian Women* (London 1978)
Edwards, M. Betham, *Reminiscences* (London 1898)
Elton, G.R., (ed.), *Historical Problems: Studies and Documents* (London 1969)
Ellis, Mrs William, *The Women of England*
   The Wives of England
   The Sisters of England
   The Mothers of Great Britain (London 1833–1843)
Fawcett, M.G., *Women's Suffrage: a short history of a great movement* (London 1912)
   Women's Victory and After: Personal Reminiscences of Millicent Fawcett 1911–1918 (London 1920)
   What I Remember (London 1925)
Feuchtwanger, E.J., *Democracy and Empire: Britain 1865–1914* (London 1985)
Figes, E., *Patriarchal Attitudes: Women in Society* (London 1970)
Firth, C.B., *C.L. Maynard, Mistress of Westfield College: A Family Portrait* (London 1949)

Forster, M., *Significant Sisters: The grassroots of active Feminism* (London 1984)

Fulford, R., *Votes for Women: The story of a struggle* (London 1957)

Gurney, E.M. (ed.), *Letters of Amelia Russell Gurney* (London 1922)

Girton Review, The, issues 1905, 1906, 1907, 1910, 1919, 1920

Haight, G.S., *Letters of George Eliot* (Yale 1940)

Haldane, E., *From One Century to Another* (London 1960)

Hill, G., *Women in English Life* (London 1896)

Jenkins, J., *Frederick Denison Maurice and the New Generation*: the Maurice Lectures (London 1938)

Johnson, G.W., *The Evolution of Women* (London 1896)

Jones, Constance, *As I Remember* (London 1922)

Kamm, J., *Hope Deferred* (London 1960)

Lloyd, Anna, *A Memoir, with extracts from her letters* (London 1928)

Lumsden, L., *Yellow Leaves* (Edinburgh 1933)

Mangan, J.A., and Park, R.P. (eds)., *From 'Fair Sex' to Feminism: Sport and the Socialisation of Women* (London 1987)

McGuigan,D.G., *Women's Lives: New Theory, Research and Policy* (Michigan 1980)

McGuigan, D.G., *A Dangerous Experiment* (Ann Arbor 1970)

Manchester Guardian, 1868

Manton, J., *Elizabeth Garrett Anderson* (London 1965)

Marshall, M.P., *What I Remember* (Cambridge 1947)

Martineau, H., *Society in America* (reprinted London 1983)
  Autobiography, 2 vols (London 1877)

Maurice, F., *Life of Frederick Denison* Maurice (London 1884)

Maynard,C., *Between College Terms* (London 1910)

Megson, B. and Lindsay, J., *An Informal History of Girton College 1864–1959* (Cambridge 1950)

Mill, J.S., *The Subjection of Women* (London 1869, reprinted Oxford 1975)

Neff, W.F., *Victorian Working Women* (London 1929)

O'Neill, W.L., *The Women's Movement* (London 1969)

Parkes, B. R., *La Belle France* (London 1863)
  The Flowing Tide (London 1863)
  Essays on Women's Work (London 1865)

Percival, A., *The English Miss* (London 1939)

Pethick-Lawrence, E., *My Part in a Changing World* (London 1938)

Pratt, E.A., *Pioneering Women in Victoria's Reign* (London 1897)

Punch Magazine, 4 Jan. 1871.

Ramsey, M., *F.D. Maurice and the Conflicts of Modern Ideology* (London 1938)

Ridley, A.E., *Frances Mary Buss* (London 1895)

Roach J., *Public Examinations in England 1850–1900* (Cambridge 1971)
  Victoria County History: Cambridgeshire, vol. IV (Cambridge

Robson, J.S. and Stilleger, T. (eds), *Collected Works of John Stuart Mill* (London 1981)

Saturday Review, June 1874

Schneir, M. (ed.), *Feminism and the Essential Historical Writings* (New York 1972)

Sharpe, E., *Hertha Ayrton 1854–1923* (London 1926)

Sherreff, E., *The Intellectual Life of Women* (London 1865)

Sidgwick, A. S. and M. S., *A Memoir of Henry Sidgwick* (Cambridge 1906)

Sinclair, A., *The Better Half* (London 1966)

Speight, R., *Life of Hilaire Belloc* (London 1957)

Spender, D., *Women of Ideas, and What Men Have Done to Them* (London 1982)

Somerville, M., *Personal Recollections* (London 1873)

Stephen, B., *Emily Davies and Girton College* (London 1927)

Strachey, R., *The Cause* (London 1978)

Thistlethwaite, F., *The Anglo-American Connections in the Nineteenth Century* (University of Pennsylvania 1959)

Ticknes, L., *The Spectacle of Women: Imagery of the Suffrage Campaign 1909–1914*

Times, The, May 1887, May 1888, Feb. 1901

Todd, M., *Life of Sophia Jex-Blake* (London 1918)

Vicinus, M., *Independent Women's Work and Community for Single Women 1850–1920* (Chicago 1985)

Weeks, J., *Sex, Politics and Society: The Regulation of Sexuality since 1800* (London 1981)

White, F., *Life of W.T. Stead*, 2 vols (London 1925)

Wilson, A. N., *Hilair Belloc* (London 1984)

Winstanley, D. A., *Late Victorian Cambridge* (Cambridge 1947)

Wood, H.G., *Frederick Denison Maurice and the New Reformation* (Cambridge 1950)

Woodham-Smith, C., *Florence Nightingale 1820–1910* (London 1951)

Woodward, E. L., *The Age of Reform 1815–1870* (Oxford 1962)

Index

Aldis, Mr and Mrs Steadman 204, 212
Alford, Dr 58, 86-7, 91
Amberley, Lady 38, 80, 97-8, 136
Anderson, Elizabeth *see* Garrett
Anderson, Henry Skelton 129, 140, 144, 155, 241
Anti-Suffrage League 234
Arnold, Matthew 41, 54, 61
Asquith, Herbert Henry and Mrs 233-4, 236
Austin, Annie 11, 16-17, 23, 108, 122, 140
Austin, Thomas 108

Baker, Sir Samuel and Lady 38
Beale, Dorothea 48, 61, 69, 226
Beauvoir, Simone de: *The Second Sex* 2
Bedford College 36, 68, 89
Belloc, Louis 43-4
Benslow House, Hitchin (1869–73) 93-122, 131-40
Bernard, Frances 178-182, 184, 189, 194, 198, 206
Blackwell, Dr Elizabeth 26-7, 55, 156
Blanc, Louis 38
Bodichon, Barbara 20-3, 26-9, 44-5, 137, 153, 155, 193, 199, 216, 244, 252
    deception/duplicity 40, 75-6, 115
    and Emily Davies 21, 23, 28, 126, 153-4, 169, 173-4
    and *English Woman's Journal* 38-43
    and girls'/women's education 46, 73, 75
    and Girton College 84, 86, 89-90, 93, 96, 105, 131, 133, 148-9, 154, 157-60, 181, 184-5, 206
    and Louisa Lumsden 163, 165-6, 171, 173
    and women's suffrage 73-4, 76-7, 79-81
Bodichon, Eugène 22, 153-4
Bostock, Miss 47, 67, 87
Boucheret, Jessie 39

Bradley, Mrs 97, 131
Brittain, Vera: *Lady into Woman* 2
Brodie, Sir Benjamin and Lady, 49, 99-100, 202
Brougham, Lord 61, 64
Bryce, James 86, 88, 90, 93, 102, 121, 168
Buss, Frances 48, 59, 61, 67-9, 156, 175, 225-6
Butler, Josephine 2, 134-5

Cambridge University 101-2
    and admission of women to examinations 120, 138, 204-5
    and attitudes to women's education 1, 83, 99, 209-14
    and degrees for women 209-14, 229
    and Girton College 83, 87, 90, 143
    and Local Examinations for girls 47-8, 50-3, 56-60
    opens some lectures to women 184-6, 188, 214
    proposes special examination for women 101, 135-6
    see also male prejudice
Campbell-Bannerman, Henry 233
Cartmell, Dr 120
Chadwick, Edwin 124
Chapman, John 22, 27-8, 253
Churchill, Winston 236
Clark, Mr 110, 116, 151-2
Clough, Jemima 134-5, 152, 200-2, 218
Cobbe, Frances Power 45, 58, 80
Cobden-Sanderson, Mrs 232
Cook, Rachel 139, 163
Craig, Isa 35, 47, 51
Creighton, Mrs 234
Croom-Johnson, Alice 207
Crow, Annie *see* Austin
Crow family 11-12
Crow, Jane 16-20, 140, 189

Davies Emily
  and Barbara Bodichon 20-3, 73-6, 86,
    90, 96, 104-5, 152-4, 158, 160, 166,
    169, 173-4
  calling a spade a spade 157, 250
  and Elizabeth Garrett 17, 30-4, 126-8,
    155
  and *English Woman's Journal* 38-43,
    217
  'Family Chronicle' 10, 241
  fight for full University membership
    102-3, 144, 151-2, 186, 204-5, 208-
    14, 222, 229, 244
  fight for Local Examinations for girls
    1, 46-60
  frustrations of early years 1, 7-19, 23,
    82
  Gateshead experiences 11, 14-15, 23-
    4, 49, 125, 127-8, 159, 167, 174
  and George Eliot 252-4
  and Girton College
    ambitions for 144, 187-8, 208, 225
    Benslow House, Hitchin (1869–73)
      93-122, 131-40
    College opening (1873) 145-8
    conception of 1, 73-5, 82-5
    as Mistress (1872–5) 130, 141-75
    obsession with student sets 109,
      198-200, 218, 238-9, 248-9
    opposition to Mistress on Executive
      121-2, 170, 175, 181, 206-7, 221-
      2, 223-4
    opposition to research spending 208,
      218, 222, 243
    preliminary work 86-95, 104-6, 133-
      4, 143-4
    religious considerations 111, 144-5,
      249-50
    resigns from Governing Body 221-4
    visits to Girton after retirement 225-
      8, 238-9
    work for College after 1875 180-2,
      195, 197-8, 202-3, 219
  and Henry Tomkinson 50, 58, 65, 86,
    100-1, 113-14, 152, 174, 178
    break with 189-92
    differences of opinion 124-6, 141-2,
      152, 191
  The Higher Education of Women
    (1866) 111
  illness/nervous collapse 189-93
  lack of scholarly qualifications 186-7
  and Ladies' Lectures 134-7
  and Louisa Lumsden 111, 161-73
  on men's attitudes to women's
    education 37, 49, 210, 226, 234, 236
  and National Association for the
    Promotion of Social Science 35-6,
    54-6, 63-4, 82, 92-3, 179-80
  on need for women's education 3-4,
    7-8, 45-6, 49, 56-7, 67-8, 72, 247
  passion for higher education for
    women 32-3, 47, 68, 70-1, 82-3, 97,
    112, 114, 136-7, 174
  rational disciplined feminism of 2-3,
    54-5, 248, 251
  religious attitudes in later life 36, 87-8,
    111, 125-7, 144-5, 159, 249
  religious training in childhood 13, 15
  and Royal Commission on schools 1,
    61-9, 157
  School Board work 123-30, 141
  and 'separate and inferior
    qualifications for women' 27, 55, 72,
    100-1, 119, 135-8, 152, 243, 254
  on a separate university for women
    100, 214-15
  The Training of the Imagination
    (1869) 71
  unwillingness to accept praise 222-3,
    242, 244-5, 247-8
  views on marriage 3, 45, 49, 82, 192
  'Women in the Universities of England
    and Scotland' (1896) 213
  and women's suffrage 1-2, 73-82, 208,
    220-1, 229-37, 239, 243
Davies, Henry (brother, d. 1858) 8, 23
Davies, Jane (sister, d. 1858) 7, 15,
  17-18
Davies, Dr John (father, d. 1860) 8-13,
  15, 18, 29-30, 107
Davies, Llewelyn (brother, d. 1916) 8,
  19, 24-5, 30, 32, 65-6, 104-5, 196, 223,
  240-1
  and Social Science Association 35-6,
    64
  support for Emily 26, 90-1, 110, 119-
    20, 124, 177, 199, 241
Davies, Mary (mother, née Hopkinson,
  d. 1886) 8-13, 15, 18, 29-30, 65, 107-8,
  140-1, 169, 190, 195
  support for Emily 47, 124
Davies, Mary Llewelyn 24-5, 29, 37, 65,
  177, 190-2, 223

Davies, William (brother, d. 1858) 12-13, 18, 20, 23
Disraeli, Benjamin 230
Dove, Jane 176, 185
Drewy, Ellen 115
Dyke Acland, Dr Thomas 48-50, 61

education, girls'/women's
  conditions in girls' schools 15-16, 45, 51, 55-6, 61-70
  mothers and 17, 56, 71, 97-8, 105, 131, 225
  newspapers and 38, 59, 72, 98-9, 101, 155-7
  Royal Commission on 61-9
  schoolmistresses and 48, 51, 61-2, 68-9
  see also Cambridge/London/Oxford Universities; Davies, Emily; male prejudice
Eliot, George 44, 158, 216, 252-4
Ellis, Mrs 224

Fadden, Isabella 15
Faithfull, Emily 39, 59
Fawcett, Henry 235
Fawcett, Millicent 76, 80-1, 231-7
Fearon, Dr 69
feminism
  nineteenth-century movement 3, 20-1, 39, 217, 251
  twentieth-century 2, 251
  see also Women's Movement
Fisher, H.A.L. 247
Fitch, George 71

Gamble, Jane Catharine 198
Gardner, Professor G. 211
Garrett, Elizabeth 16-18, 36, 38, 41, 64, 80, 115, 155, 239-41
  rejection of euphemisms 157, 250
  School Board work 123-4, 126-9
  struggle to become a doctor 26-7, 28, 30-4, 123, 202
  support for Emily Davies 46, 54-5, 59, 84, 133, 155, 205, 238, 247-8
Gaskell, Elizabeth 21
Gibson, Emily 106, 111, 114-15, 117, 146
Girton College
  fiftieth jubilee 242
  first Tripos successes 138-9
  offered Trinity College Dublin

degrees 222
  opening (Michaelmas 1873) 145-8
  Prayer Meeting Society 226, 249
  preliminary work 86-95, 104-6, 131-4, 143-4
  student agitation for degrees 208-9, 212-13
  students accepted for some University lectures 184-6, 188
  students' attitude to Newnham College 200
  see also Benslow House; Bodichon, Barbara; Davies, Emily; Tomkinson, Henry
Gladstone, W.E. 230
Goldsmid, Lady 47, 51, 86, 94
Granville, Lord 32
Greer, Germaine: *The Female Eunuch* 2
Griffiths, John 47, 48
Grote, George 32-3, 61, 64
Gunson, Dr W.M. 138
Gurney, Amelia Russell 51, 59
  and Girton College 86, 94, 131, 133-4, 141-2, 146-7
Gurney, Russell 35, 47

Hardie, Keir 234
Hastings, George 47
Herschel, Constance 159-60, 180, 188
Heywood, George 47-8, 51
Hill, Octavia 54, 61
Hinde, Archer 248
Holloway College 186-7, 214-15
Holloway, Thomas 186-7
Howell, Thomas 86
Hughes, Thomas 128
Humphreys, Professor 185
Hutton, R.H. 38, 72
Huxley, Professor T.H. 67, 99, 124

Jackson, Dr 212
Jameson, Anna 21, 42
Jex-Blake, Sophia 2
Jones, Constance 207, 218, 221-2, 238, 248
Jowett, Dr Benjamin 38

Kensington, Frances 207, 211
Kensington Society 62-5, 76-7, 230
Keynes, Dr J.N. 221, 248

Ladies' Lectures, 134-7, 235

Lehmann, Rudolf 194
Leigh-Smith, Annie (Nannie) 20, 216
Leigh-Smith, Benjamin 20
Lewis, George 252
Lightfoot, Professor 92
Lister, Mr 12-13
Liveing, Dr John and Mrs 47, 50, 83,
    135, 185
Lloyd, Anna 98, 106, 225-6
Lloyd George, David 237
London University
    admits women (1878) 202
    attitudes to women's higher education
        32-3, 35, 70-3, 123
Lumsden, Louisa 111, 139, 161-73, 183-
    4, 188, 206, 226, 243, 249
    Yellow Leaves 113, 118-19
Lyttelton, Lord 46, 54, 64, 91, 94-5, 133
Lytton, Lord 247

Maitland, F.W. 214
male prejudice against women's
    education 31-7, 45, 48-50, 55-8, 71-2,
    83, 94, 98-9, 127, 156-7, 187, 209-14
    see also Cambridge/London/Oxford;
        newspapers/periodicals
Maltby, Dr Edward 10
Malton, Mr 96
Manning, Adelaide 108, 111-13, 117,
    153-4, 190, 192-4, 196, 223-4, 241
Manning, Charlotte 38, 58, 61, 77, 86,
    142, 152
    first Mistress of Girton 108, 111-12,
        117, 178
Manning, Dr H.E. 9, 40
Markby, Dr Thomas 57, 59
Marks, Hertha 158, 193, 225
Martineau, Harriet 3, 21, 54
Maudsley, Dr 155-7, 163
Maurice, Rev. Frederick Denison 35-6,
    46, 56, 97, 216-17, 244
Maynard, Constance 164, 167, 171, 183-
    4, 188, 226, 249
Metcalfe, Fanny 61, 86, 147-8, 239
Mill, John Stuart 38, 54, 67, 79-82,
    216-17, 229-30
Mohl, Madame 11
Morgan, E.H. 138
Morley, John 146
mothers and higher education for their
    daughters 17, 56, 71, 97-8, 105, 131,
    225

National Association for the Promotion
    of Social Science 35, 45, 54-6, 63-4,
    82, 92
National Society for Women's Suffrage
    220-1, 229-30
Newnham College 200-3, 250
newspapers/periodicals and women's
    education 38, 59, 72, 98-9, 101, 155-7
Nightingale, Florence 1, 2, 35, 143, 225
Norris, Canon 55-6

Oxford University
    admission of women 202, 213
    attitudes to women's education 47, 49

Pankhurst, Emmeline 232, 236
Parkes, Bessie Rayner 27, 39-44, 79
Pattison, Rev. Mark 67, 85
Perowne, Dr E. 209, 212
Pfeiffer, Madame 199
Pipe, Hannah 48, 61, 111
Plumtree, Dr 55, 70-1
Potts, John 50, 57-8
Proctor, Adelaide 39
Pusey, Dr Edward 25, 88

Queen's College, Harley Street 36, 68,
    244

Ramsay, Agnata 211-12
Rich, Julia 183
Richardson, Anna 13, 16, 23, 46-7, 151
    and Girton College 73, 83, 88
Robertson, Mrs Croom 192-3
Robey, Dr Henry 55, 61-2, 66, 68-9, 86,
    91, 128
Rossetti, Christina 74, 144
Rossetti, D.G. 27, 74
Royal Commission on conditions in
    schools (1865) 61-9

Salisbury, Lord 64
Scott, Charlotte 188, 201, 203-4, 212
Sedley Taylor, Rev. John 86, 91, 93-4,
    134, 136-7, 170
Seeley, Professor Henry 86, 89-91, 93-4,
    103-4, 114, 119-20, 168
Sherreff, Emily 117-18, 121-2
Sidgwick, Professor Henry and Mrs 52,
    91, 93, 134-7, 173, 200-1, 204, 211,
    217-18
slums in Victorian England 14

Smiles, Samuel 24
Smith, Julia 21, 62-3
Smith, Louisa 26
Social Science Association *see* National
  Association
Spender, Dale: *Women of Ideas* 2
Stanley, Dean 38
Stanley, Lady Augusta 38, 80, 97, 136,
  199, 248
  and Girton College 86, 94, 131, 140,
    178-9, 198
Stephen, Barbara: *Emily Davies and
Girton College* 67, 92, 147, 218, 249
Stephen, Sir Leslie 59, 227-8
Strasser, Dr 53
Stuart, Mr J 96, 116, 205

Taylor, Helen 38, 71, 75, 80-1, 88
Temple, Dr Frederick 46, 48
Thompson, Professor 58, 227
Tomkinson, Henry 49-50, 81-2, 107-8,
154, 194, 241
  and Emily Davies 65, 72, 77-8, 81,
    124-30, 141-2, 150, 152, 190-2
  and Girton College 86-92, 100, 106-9,
    113, 133-4, 138, 144, 174, 178, 181-3,
    192, 224
  and Local Examinations for girls 50-60

Trinity College, Dublin 222
Trollope, Anthony 38

Venn, Dr 227
Victoria, Queen and Prince Albert 101,
114, 220

Ward, Mrs Humphry 234
Waterhouse, Alfred 83, 133-4, 141, 143-
7, 150, 159
Wedgwood, Julia 87, 118
Welsh, Elizabeth 180, 195, 207, 219-21
Whewell, Dr 58, 94, 173, 176
Wollstonecraft, Mary 3, 21
Women's Movement 21, 36, 60, 62, 65,
82, 118, 128, 209
women's position in Victorian England 3,
7-8, 11, 14-15, 21, 23-4, 31, 36, 224-5,
230, 244
women's suffrage movement 2, 80-1,
229-37, 243-4

Yonge, Charlotte 105, 224